WOMEN WHO *Rise*

WOMEN WHO *Rise*

30 STORIES THAT INSPIRE YOUR SPIRIT TO RISE!

First Edition

www.katebutlerbooks.com

Design by Margaret Cogswell
margaretcogswell.com

This book is dedicated to you. We see you, we feel you, we relate to you, and we connect with you, because ... we are you. At the core we are more alike than we are different. We are beings of light and love who deeply desire to make a positive influence on the world with our unique type of brilliance. The pages of this book promise to fill you with the wisdom, insights, and inspiration that will align you further with your soul's path. Our hope is that the vulnerability and authenticity of these stories will remind you deeply of who you are and inspire you to rise up and shine your light in the world.

It is your time. It is our time. It is time.

enjoy the unfolding ...

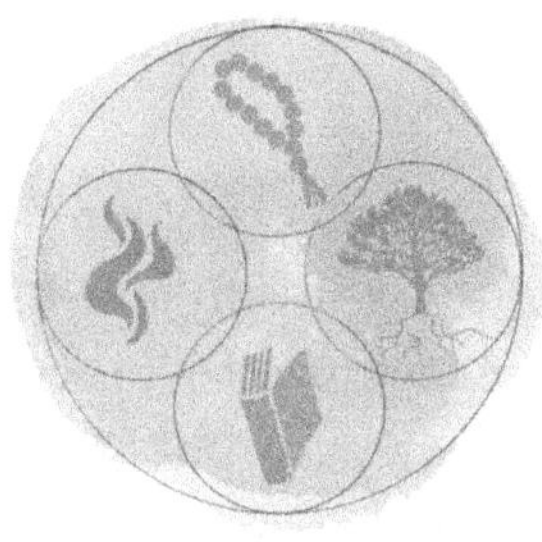

FOREWORD

Erin Saxton

When I was 19-years-old I faced a proverbial fork in the road. Of course it was not my first fork, but quite possibly it was the first time I had an awareness that my choices would propel my life in unique directions. I was majoring in Speech Communications with a concentration in Broadcasting at East Stroudsburg University. My advisor at ESU contacted me to let me know that two internships had been "approved" for me to participate in. They were both at local TV stations. The year was 1991 and obtaining an internship back then was not easy - not like it is today. Back in 1991, it wasn't the "in" thing to do. It was not unheard of, but there weren't social media postings with opportunities - think of the year - there was not even "social media". In a phone call my advisor announced the two locations. "Hello Erin, are you still there?" My advisor asked after a long pause on the phone. I thanked her for the news, and let her know I needed to think about my choices. You see, I had to go where the university "said" I could go because they had to approve the college credits for it. Upon hearing the internships that were "approved" I got a "gut feeling". And it was not a good one. These two internship opportunities were not me. They did not feel right and I knew in that moment that no matter which I chose it was not going to get me where I knew I needed to be.

I needed an internship as big as my aspirations, and so I threw all my energy into applying for my dream job. As I signed in for the *Good Morning America* interview I learned that there were 250 applicants, 25 spots available and the interview would be 6 hours long. I knew this is where I belonged, and so I dug my heels in and knew it was time to go for it. I had already turned down the opportunities my university was willing to give me, and now faced huge odds for landing this job. It was a long day, and waiting to learn if I was one of the 25 candidates chosen seemed like an eternity. A few weeks passed when the phone rang. It was the Head of the Research Department welcoming me to her team. I did it! I was elated.

After that internship, *Good Morning America* hired me full time. That position led to a role within Barbara Walters' production company BARWALL PRODUCTIONS. I spent many years working directly with Barbara. We were a small staff of 8 people. We traveled everywhere producing Barbara's primetime celebrity specials, *The Barbara Walters Specials*. Barbara Walters became my mentor and what I have learned from her is invaluable. I went on to work at *The Rosie O'Donnell Show*, WBIS+, a Dow Jones TV show, and was one of the original TV producers who launched Barbara Walters' talk show on ABC's TV, *THE VIEW*. While there I earned multiple Emmy nominations.

Fast forward many years later to when I was a TV producer at *The View*, I had an idea for a company that would bridge the gap between the media and authors, thought leaders and companies that wanted to garner more media attention. It was a risky idea. The thought of this company put me at another "fork in the road". Do I leave Barbara Walters and *The View*? Do I take a chance to become an entrepreneur? What if I fail? Scarier thought - what if I succeed?

As I write this to you today, I launched that company, named it The Idea Network, and have since sold it. I currently run my own consulting company called elevenCommunications. Under my direction, both public relations agencies have worked with powerhouse speakers and celebrities, created more best selling books than I can keep track of, spread positive messages of help, support and hope through our clients, and have helped to create many of the "household names" we all speak about daily. My decision to leave *The View* and Barbara Walters did not come easily. I knew I had to make a choice though. I knew I wanted to keep evolving. I knew I wanted to help make a positive impact on the world. For me my choice was and still is simple. I choose to help others spread the word about the positive things they are doing in the world. If I can help someone help another person through their work, then that is a mission accomplished for me. On a personal level, I choose through my own online TV show, *That Girl from Jersey* (YouTube), to talk about the choices and observations I come upon. *That Girl from Jersey* has allowed me to speak honestly, be vulnerable and share with my audience things that I know I cannot be the only one going through! I am the first to laugh at myself and if I can help anyone else realize that they are not so different, I am doing something right.

When publisher Kate Butler approached me to write this Foreword I was excited. Kate and I met when I spoke at one of her conferences. We had an instant connection. I was drawn to her positive outlook on life and the way she had built camaraderie and trust within a wonderful community of women. While I was attending the conference, she introduced me to the co-authors that would be writing this wonderful book you are about to read, *Women Who Rise*. Kate's ability to bring together authors to convey motivational messages that positively impact the world is a unique talent not many people possess. The authors in this book are no strangers to making CHOICES. Within each and every chapter in this book you will be moved, touched, and inspired. Many of these women found their voices, their bravery, and themselves in the choices they made. Although each story and each author is vastly different there is one thing all of these brilliant authors have in common.

ALL THESE AUTHORS MADE A CHOICE TO RISE.

So when you find yourself faced at your proverbial fork in the road, remember these stories you are about to read. Instead of choosing to go right or left at the fork - may you choose to RISE instead.

My Best Wishes for You All,

Erin Saxton

Erin Saxton
Award winning TV Producer
Host of *That Girl from Jersey* (YouTube)
President of elevenCommunications, Inc.
www.theErinNetwork.com

IG: @erinthatgirlfromjersey
FB: @erinthatgirlfromjersey

table of contents

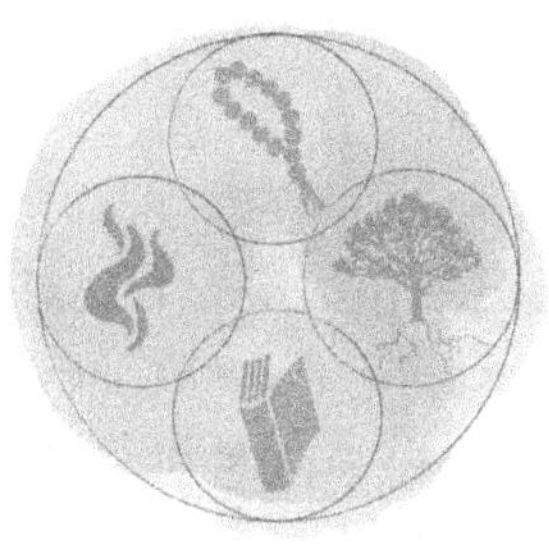

INTRODUCTION

Kate Butler

Did you know that there is a 4% chance that you will deliver your baby on your due date? 4%.

Both of my daughters are in that 4%.

We were on our way to the hospital, and although there was shooting pain throughout my body every five to six minutes, I felt elated because all of my dreams were about to come true. My first baby was coming. I was going to be a mom.

The day before I was sitting on my yoga ball, rolling around while rubbing my tummy. This was one of my favorite things to do while I connected with this little life growing inside me. But this day, our conversation was a little different. I was experiencing this unique feeling that was powerful and new, but it wasn't foreign. I had never felt it before, but yet, the moment I did, it was like it had been there all along. It was a hit of peace, joy, connection, grounding, and clarity all at once. I know now that this was God expanding my divine connection and deepening my intuitive abilities. I just knew it was time. Tomorrow would be the baby's due date and I was ready. I could feel the baby was too, but I also sensed the baby needed a little reassurance. So I gave it. "It's time," I said aloud. "It's time, " I repeated softer. "I am ready for you. I am ready to love you. I am ready to protect you. I am ready for you to grace this world. I am ready for your life to make our dreams come true, and I'm ready to help all your life dreams come true. It's time."

I never quite went to sleep that night. My water broke. I went into labor. And we were on our way to the hospital.

We did not know what we were having. I convinced myself it was a boy, because in the deepest part of my soul I longed for a girl more than I ever let anyone know. I told myself, and everyone else, I was definitely having a boy, because honestly, I just didn't think I could be lucky enough to have the baby girl I always dreamed of.

Labor was smooth-ish, until the doctor yelled to stop pushing. The baby was stuck on my pelvic bone. My doctor was an old school doctor and he knew I wanted to avoid a cesarean section, if possible. My thought process was that I was going to have enough to worry about with an infant, and I could not imagine having to heal from a surgery, too. So the doctor looked right at me and said, "The only way to avoid a C-section is for me to go in and get the baby with the forceps." My eyes widened and all I could think about were the horror stories I had heard about doctors scarring the faces of babies after using forceps. As if he could read my mind he then said, "I have been doing this for forty years. If anyone knows how to use forceps, it's me. I am the best." Our doctor had a lot of experience and he was not shy about sharing it. So, I looked at the nurse with a pleading look, as if to say, "Is he really the best? Or is this his ego talking again? Because this is my BABY we are talking about." She nodded and said, "I can attest to that. He is the best." So I closed my eyes, dialed inward, and there it was again: this strange but calming and powerful feeling that gave me the certainty that everything would be ok. I looked the doctor square in the eyes and said, "Ok, but if you leave one mark on my baby's face, I'll kill you." He looked at my husband and Mel said, half serious and half apologetically, "She might."

The doctor was true to his word and moments later I heard a cry. We all braced ourselves. "It's a GIRL!" I burst into tears. Not streaming tears, we are talking heavy sobbing, can't-catch-your-breath, loud-gaspsin-between-crying tears.

The doctor looked at my husband again and said, "Is she ok?"

He said, "She's good. She's just really, really happy."

The truth was, I was releasing everything that I had held in for so long. Fear, dreams, uncertainty, worry, elation … I was releasing all of it in this moment.

And then they handed her to me and my world stopped. Actually, my world ended. The world I knew up until then was completely over and this moment right here was the first moment of my new life. These beautiful deep blue eyes looked directly into mine, our eyes locked instantly, and we only released that connection when she would close her eyes to sleep … my beautiful Isabella Katherine.

The whole time we were in the hospital all the nurses would say, "We have never seen a baby stare so intently at her mom." Or, "We have never seen a baby be so alert and engaged, she won't take her eyes off you!" Or my personal favorite, "Look at her eyes, it's almost like she understands what we are saying."

My mother's intuition was now in full swing, and I knew she absolutely did understand. She was special. This soul was here to make an impact.

It did not take long for the novelty to wear off once I got home. Between the drastic changes in my body to the sleepless nights, I was coming down from my birthing high and quick. I loved this little girl. But I was beginning to hate myself.

I can pinpoint exactly where the self-loathing started. It was the first time she wouldn't latch. I was a new mom, trying to do everything perfectly, and quite frankly, constantly worrying about keeping this tiny human alive. Now, I could not even feed her.

I felt defeated. I felt worthless. I felt like a bad mom.

I was beating up myself constantly.

My mind chatter was on overdrive. It seemed this whole being a mom thing was natural, easy and effortless for everyone except for me. And that always seemed to be confirmed when others were around.

My oldest and dearest friend had a baby nine months before me and was a nursing machine. She was very vocal about her opinions of how and why nursing was the best. I agreed, I thought it was best, too, which is why it was even more devastating when I could not "produce". I actually hid my struggles from her, my best friend in the world, because I was embarrassed about my "shortcomings". Although I was doing everything humanly possible from eating special cookies to buying fancy machines that were supposed to help, I still came up short. I was ashamed and would always convince myself that there was something more I could be doing.

My dearest friend was only sharing her experiences with me. She was opening up and letting me into her world, meanwhile, I felt like mine was crumbling.

I remember going to the doctor for Bella's weekly weigh-in and she had actually lost weight. The doctor said something to the effect of, whatever I was doing was not cutting it, and if she didn't gain by the following week they were giving her formula before she left the doctor's office. That one stung. I felt like they were implying I would intentionally harm my baby, when here I was pumping and feeding every three hours around the clock, literally, to do what I believed was best for her.

One night, as I was rocking Bella to bed, I was reading her a bedtime story. This story was centered around a fear-based mentality, counting on someone else to save the day and the language seemed very restrictive and limiting to me. The books would say things like, "He was sent to his room to think about what he did." *My* perspective was to send kids to their room to think about what they could do differently and how they could make a better choice next time. I believe in encouraging the good versus reinforcing the bad. I would also find stories that focused on kids lacking something until someone else came along and helped or saved them. Help from our friends is always great, but I still believe it's important to teach our children that you have everything you will ever need right inside of you. It's important we teach them that whenever they are lost all they need to do is come back home to themselves and they will find their way again.

The more I read, the more I found the same things in stories. Every night as I would rock her, I would dream wildly elaborate dreams for my little girl. I would plant these seeds of greatness and kindness and grace and compassion. My dreams for her were endless. The more I read these bedtime stories, the more conscious I became of the language I was imprinting on this tiny but growing mind. I fundamentally disagreed with the messages I was reading in these traditional books.

One night, I got this crazy idea that I should start to write down the way I wanted my child to see the world. If she was not going to read it in these books, then it was up to me to teach her. "Maybe I should write a book?" I thought. And then dismissed the thought as quickly as it came. Who was I to write a book? Who was I to share the way I saw the world? Who was I to teach children a new way of thinking? Who was I to think this could be done? I did not know anyone in real life that was a published author. Did I really have the audacity to think I could pull this off? I was floundering in my life and I couldn't even do this mom thing right. Who did I think I was?

So I buried it.

I buried that dream for three long years.

Two years later I gave birth to our second daughter, Livie. Our piercingly gorgeous Olivia May. Her birth experience was completely different. But it began the same. The day before her due date I sat on my yoga ball, rubbed my tummy, connected to my daughter, and told her it was time. The next day would be her due date; I was ready, and I knew she was, too. This time we had a huge gender reveal party and knew we were having another precious little girl. We were elated. I went to sleep that night and woke up knowing it was time to go. We went to the hospital and our precious Livie was born a few hours later. I was wrapped in a handmade birthing blanket given to me by my dear cousin, who is a doula. She said it was mine to borrow as so many warrior mothers had done before during their child birthing experiences. Just having this red tapestry wrapped around my shoulders shifted something in me. The blanket was soft, thick, warm and comforting. It was a deep red with beautiful designs woven throughout in deep purple, gold and yellow. I felt powerful, in control, like I knew what I was doing … I felt like a warrior. I insisted they play meditation music in the background and save my placenta. My old school doctor who was still in the picture had said, "I didn't peg you for 'the type'." Well, surprise! It was a surprise to him, and quite frankly, a surprise to me, too. I was becoming "the type". The type who was connected, grounded, certain, and clear. This new me was not quite here, but I could tell she was coming through.

And with the birth of Livie, there was new birth given to my life, as well. I often say, "Who gave birth to whom?"

The postpartum period after Livie was night and day compared to my first experience. I was not in a deep depression. I loved my body and the miracle that it had just gone through. And I was not beating myself up with my internal dialogue at every turn. In fact, I was becoming gentle with myself. I had grace with myself. I was loving myself again.

Once again I found myself in the nursery reading boring bedtime stories, but this time, something felt different. As I dreamed my dreams for Bella and Livie, I could actually begin to see them make their mark on the world. And it blew me away.

I also downloaded a vision that all of that started with me. I needed to stand up for my dreams, show them the way and begin to pave the path for their greatness to unfold in the way it was truly meant to.

And then it came, "Are you following your dream?"

I answered in my head quickly, "I don't even know what my dream is anymore."

And then I heard, "If you did have a dream, what would it be?"

And it came, "I would write a children's book teaching my children the way I see the world, so they always knew the power they had in their thoughts."

Just like that, the idea crystalized. The dream I had buried away three years before was now back with a vengeance. How could I expect them to believe in their dreams if I did not believe in mine? I had to chase my dreams and show my girls that it was okay for them to chase theirs.

My first children's book was published less than a year later. It hit the charts as a #1 best seller and stayed on the best-seller charts for over 100 weeks straight. That book paved the way for more children's books, a planner and journal series, and this incredible movement, the Inspired Impact Book Series.

It was time for me to RISE up to my dreams to show my children how to RISE up to theirs. This has now opened the space for thousands of women to step into their divine dreams, because this is the ripple effect when one person decides to RISE.

We may not always feel worthy, we may not always have it in us, and we may be combatting some serious villains inside our heads. If you have experienced any of this, I can assure you, you are not alone. We all experience these pockets of time in our life, and the most profound thing for me was realizing just that: that it was a pocket of time, a season of my life, but that didn't mean it had to define all my moments moving forward. I began to give myself grace through my depression, through my darkest places, and that was not always easy. But with that grace came hope. I began to realize I could experience these feelings, but I did not have to live in that place forever. I could have a pocket of time, but I could also make choices to step out of it and begin to RISE up. The emotions that did not serve me still knocked on my door, but eventually I realized that I did not have to let them in. I definitely did not need to offer them something to eat. And I sure as heck was not going to invite them to stay and hang out! No, they could knock, I could acknowledge they were there, but I could also close the door and move on. They did not have to stay.

You see, what I came to realize is, my children could not be my *excuse* of why I was not following my dreams, because they were my *reason.*

We all have that *reason*, that *pull*, or that *why* that drives us. There are times when we cannot do it for ourselves, and during those times, do it for those for whom you are paving the path. When you choose to RISE above, you choose to pave the path … the path of greatness for generations to come.

It's our time to RISE,

Kate Butler

Kate Butler
#1 International Best-Selling Author
Award winning Author
International Keynote Speaker
President of Kate Butler Books + Coaching
Creator of the Inspired Impact Book Series
www.katebutlerbooks.com

FB: @katebutlerbooks
IG: @katebutlerbooks

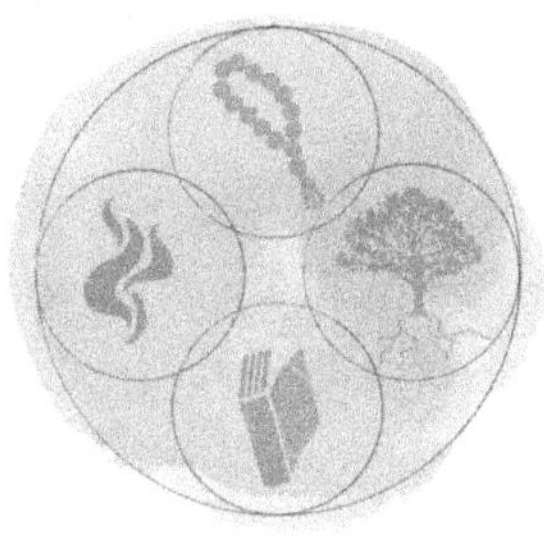

IT'S A HEALING JOURNEY

Cathleen Elle

Most people in society would have said I was a successful and powerful woman. I had owned and operated businesses, was an elected Legislator, served for the governor of Vermont, and was CEO of the largest commercial construction association in Vermont. I had raised two children as a single parent and gone to college as an adult. I was dedicated to making the lives of others better. To most, on the outside I was polished, confident, determined, and living the dream.

On the inside I was living a nightmare.

When my son, Logan, was a senior, my daughter, Ashley, was in her first year of college. Throughout high school, Logan struggled to find his way. His mood would swing from high to low, and he would challenge me often. Isn't this the way all parents feel with teenagers? He started to make choices that were unhealthy for him and I attempted to guide him in a direction that I felt was best for him. We became disconnected and distant. I tried guiding him the best way I could, but I wasn't succeeding. For about eighteen months we attempted to work through the challenges, but eventually he chose to leave Vermont and move to South Carolina to his Dad's. He left angry and would not speak with me.

On March 31, 2010, two weeks later, I was preparing for a board meeting, determining if I was staying or leaving the construction association I led. Deb, my employee, knew the struggles Logan was having and asked if I had heard from him. I was shocked because that morning I had the feeling I needed to call him. I had ignored that feeling and focused on what I needed to do to finish preparing for the meeting. When she spoke, I paused from prepping and answered, "No, he's a little lost right now, but he'll find his way. I know he will. He'll be okay."

I thought, as I returned to prepping, *I just need to get through the meeting today, then I'll find a way to reach out to Logan.*

I was presenting to the board members several hours later, when I spotted two figures walking to the front doors of the office; colleagues from the State House, Betsy and Shawn. Shortly thereafter, one of my employees opened the door and announced, "I'm so sorry for interrupting, but Betsy and Shawn are here to see you. They're in your office waiting and they say it's an emergency." When I entered my office, I saw Betsy's face and knew it was Logan.

"Oh, no, no, no, no! Please, no. Not Logan!" I pleaded.

She just looked at me with tears in her eyes. "I'm so sorry, Cathy. Logan committed suicide this morning."

My world shattered at that very moment never to be the same again.

My memories of events that followed this devastating news are nothing but fractured moments that fade to black. The mental anguish, the physical pain and heaviness, the denial, and the soul-wrenching inability to believe my son had taken his life just doesn't allow me to remember the details of the day he died, nor many that followed.

I had such a deep desire to connect with Logan. There were signs his spirit was near, but I needed more. I reached out to a Medium in New York, so I could communicate with Logan directly. I have always believed in Mediums. Something about the spiritual world spoke to me. Since I was a child, I have believed there is more to life than what we can see and touch. In my twenties, I bought my first tarot card deck, and I've continued my practice and study into the Divine and spiritual side of life ever since. Now, I needed it more than ever.

When I spoke with the Medium, one of the things she said was there was something I didn't know and that I needed to get the records of Logan's death. She gave me other messages about how much he loved me and that he was sorry for the pain he caused. I followed her guidance and called the law enforcement office to get his records. The detective confirmed that what the Medium had said was accurate. He informed me that Logan left a short note which included his wish that I not attend his services.

I was devastated. I started shaking, but somehow I was able to ask the detective to send me a copy. I needed to see that it was Logan's handwriting. It was.

I had been holding onto one last sliver of hope that maybe this had all been a terrible mistake. But no, there was no mistake. I collapsed onto the floor, screaming and crying, "Oh my god. Oh my god. Oh my god." I repeated this over and over for who knows how long?

I thought the worst day of my life was when I learned Logan had died by suicide. I was wrong. The days were dark, full of emotional and physical pain. Every part of my body hurt. It felt like a vice grip that was getting tighter and tighter around my heart. My shoulders were weighed down with what felt like the remnants of a blown-up building. The emotional pain wasn't any better. I questioned what if? If only? To self-blame, guilt, shame, resentment, hatred toward myself, and anger toward everyone but Logan. I just wanted to hold my boy again.

Really, the only person I longed to connect with, to talk to, to hear from, was the one person I couldn't reach—Logan. I talked out loud to him regularly, telling him how much I loved him and how sorry I was. I would write to him and ask him to give me a sign. I would even beg him to let me know he was still around me. And he *DID* let me know by sending me signs I couldn't ignore.

I began to recognize his presence everywhere. I remember shortly after Logan's funeral, I was standing in the kitchen talking with a friend, Bianca, when I heard a strange yowling. I turned and spotted Logan's cat, Hilton, who had jumped on top of a table near the wall. He was standing on his hind legs with one front paw against the wall for balance and the other tapping at a picture hanging on the wall. The picture was of Logan.

Then there was the time I was laying on Logan's bed playing cribbage, our game, on my phone, when I heard Hilton start yowling from the doorway. Since Logan's death Hilton was always in his bedroom, but that night he wouldn't step across the threshold. As I was coaxing him in, he suddenly vaulted across the threshold and jumped high into the air, swiping his paws as if he was trying to catch a fly, yowling like he was talking to someone.

I just knew it: Logan's spirit was with us.

I turned and was sobbing on his bed, feeling as though my heart was going to stop beating. Suddenly, I felt this long, lanky body laying behind me as an arm draped over my waist. It was Logan's spirit. I felt him close to me.

Then, there was the time my friend, Beth, had brought me to stay at her home in Massachusetts. We were at a gas station and a car pulled up next to us. I looked at the license plate and couldn't believe what I saw: LV 33.

Logan's full name was Logan Voyer (LV) and his number in basketball was always 33. In fact, the baseball team from his high school put his initials and the number 33 on their hats that spring. These were just little moments interspersed throughout the darkness, but they were enough to keep me alive. I believe his spirit is close by always.

One day I found myself lying on Logan's grave. It was late July, just four months after he transitioned. Weeping. *Why? I'm so sorry, Logan! I love you! Please forgive me, I'm so sorry!* I called out to the Divine. *What had I done so badly that I deserved this punishment? Had I been that horrible of a person?* I believed what goes around comes around—what had I done to cause this? I loved my children with all my heart and gave all I could; to my children, to the community, to everyone. Why did this happen to my boy?

I didn't see how I could go on. Despite seeing a grief specialist every week, all I felt was despair. *How was I supposed to go on living? Why should I?*

After Logan's transition, it was Ashley who gave me any will to survive and to keep living. I couldn't imagine leaving her alone when she was already in tremendous agony.

Still, I didn't see how I could live with this enormous, unending pain, with the torment caused from the belief that my actions had killed my son.

"Please," I begged the Divine, "Please take me too. I can't live like this anymore. I don't *want* to live like this. How am I supposed to go on?"

I have no idea how long I laid on Logan's grave like this, or how long I pleaded and begged the Divine to strike me down. I felt such suffocating guilt and shame that I didn't see a path forward for me; there was no light at the end of this tunnel.

Suddenly, while lying there, I received a Divine message. I heard the words, "If this happened in your life, then you're meant to do something with it. Now *do* it."

I knew in my soul this was a sign from Logan.

Nothing had been clear prior to hearing this message, but this was clear. I was meant to bring more awareness to the public about suicide prevention—to assist others in their pain. I had to help others to recognize the signs of suicide—signs that I had missed. I needed to help them to learn the language. To squash the myths, so they could prevent another suicide.

I had the contacts throughout Vermont to actually make a difference. I had the connections to the media, and knew I was a public enough person that this would be a story.

I had the voice and the platform to do this.

For the first time since Logan's transition, I took a deep breath. It was up to me to make a difference for him.

I started to speak publicly. I educated people about how language around suicide matters. I informed people that the word "committed" is offensive to those who have lost their loved ones to suicide. Speaking out also helped me realize that I needed additional assistance to move through the extreme pain I was living and feeling. I reached out to a Cognitive Thought Therapist.

It was important for me to understand that I had to move through the pain that was stuck deep within my heart, body, and soul. I first needed to express all of the guilt, shame, and self-blame I felt. Then, I started to create some practices that included writing out my anger, without editing it, and then burning the letter. It felt healing to release some of those emotions without worrying about who saw it or what I said. Each time I moved through a layer of pain, I found a glimmer of hope and it allowed me to see things slightly differently. Moving through the pain changed as I continued along the journey. The more I healed, the settings changed. I realized there were layers of pain not only from my son's transition, but from my life prior to that. My therapist and I worked through a twelve-to-fifteen-week program for post-traumatic stress. I learned to breathe again. I worked with Mediums and energy healers. I read inspirational books, meditated, walked in nature, and began a daily gratitude list. I tried everything including a grief support group. I delved into personal development work which led me to one of the most amazing healing modalities I've ever experienced: Regenerating Images in Memory (RIM). I made so much progress with it that I became a Certified RIM Facilitator.

I didn't "get over it" or "move on," because that's impossible. What I did do was start to forgive others, and through that forgiveness, I realized I needed to forgive myself. Each time I stepped into the pain it allowed me to see things slightly differently. I became aware that life didn't need to be painful, and, while peeling back the layers of darkness, the light came shining through. The more I forgave myself, the more I was able to trust my intuition and embrace what I was hearing, seeing, and feeling. I started to trust my inner self instead of seeking outside of me for answers. Through this I realized that I was an intuitive, and, when I listened to my inner guidance, life worked better and was so much easier.

I started to release old patterns through this new awareness. The fear of feeling the emotions and getting stuck in them no longer had a hold over me. I was freed. Avoiding pain wasn't an option. As I released stuck emotions, I became lighter, happier, thinner, and more present in my own life. I started new patterns, creating the life I live now. I am fulfilled and have never been happier! I know that Logan's energy is always with me, guiding me along this amazing life I live.

Although I do identify with living a life of love, abundance, joy, and fulfillment, healing is absolutely a lifelong journey. I put time into keeping my life fulfilled by continuously moving through forgiveness, pain, and living in gratitude. When something comes up that doesn't feel good to me, I do a RIM session or write it out; I work through it. I also have a daily practice. This has been one of the most important grounding processes I have maintained throughout the past ten years. It has changed as my life has changed, but I maintain a practice today.

My daily practice includes connecting with gratitude and meditation. Every morning I list ten things I'm grateful for. I center myself by meditating. It is up to me how I experience life and I choose to feel joy. I also move through emotions, happy and not so happy, by exercising and connecting to nature. I love to hike, walk in parks, lift weights, and run. I choose a daily Oracle card. I get daily guidance from multiple spiritual tools.

Logan's transition was not my choice. His physical body is no longer here, but his energy is always present. Healing through the layers of darkness I was carrying has granted me a gift of connecting my light with his. He has gifted me the knowledge that we all have a story we can cling to. He gave me a choice—to live my journey in light or in darkness? I choose light. I am forever grateful for Logan's presence here on earth and constant guidance in the energetic realm.

ABOUT CATHLEEN ELLE

Cathleen Elle is a transformational speaker, intuitive coach, certified healer, and author of *Shattered Together.* Cathleen revolutionizes lives by assisting people with moving through layers of pain, healing through trauma, and breaking cycles and patterns.

For more than twenty-five years she served alongside the Vermont Governor, was an elected legislator, and was the CEO and lobbyist for The Associated General Contractors of VT. As a legislator, she addressed the Brazilian Parliament on women and minorities serving in Government and Israeli Government for the Young Political Leaders. She has also served by speaking with high schools, colleges, CEOs, businesses, individuals, and many different organizations.

Her life's work became refocused in March 2010 after her son took his life by suicide. Cathleen educates and assists with emotional, spiritual, and energetic processing, clearing everything from deep trauma to habits of behavior. Cathleen has worked with large corporations, school systems, individuals, and in small, intimate group settings to bring swift and permanent change.

To connect with Cathleen:

Website: www.cathleenl.com
email: cathleen@cathleenl.com
Instagram: @cathleeninspires
https://www.instagram.com/cathleeninspires/
Facebook: @inspirationatcathleenl
https://www.facebook.com/inspirationatcathleenl/
Twitter: @cathleenelle
https://twitter.com/cathleenelle
LinkedIn: Cathleen Elle
https://www.linkedin.com/in/cathleenl/

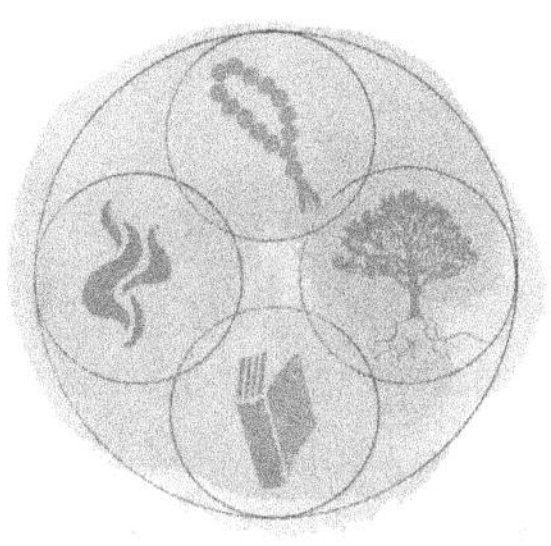

BRAVE CHOICES

Ann Marie Smith

I was blessed to be raised by two incredible parents who taught me and my siblings to make brave choices and always reach for the stars. Putting into practice these words of wisdom ensured we could be, do, and have anything we put our mind to. My mom was a living example of that. At the age of twelve, her parents died. She was brought to the US from Mexico. Despite the tragic circumstances, she chose to look at this new adventure as an opportunity to live the American dream. Her new life would open up the opportunity to make some brave choices. And her dream was that these brave choices would open the door to amazing things for the future of her unborn children.

My mom, Connie, dreamt of learning English, becoming a US citizen, marrying an amazing man, and having children—her American dream. By the age of twenty-six she was fluent in English, a US citizen, married to her prince charming, my dad, and pregnant with me. While I make it seem easy that in fourteen years she accomplished her dreams, those dreams came with some horrible circumstance which forced her to make some brave choices. From the young age of twelve she had been molested by her sister's husband. She was bounced from her brothers' homes back to her sister's home. That alone would have made a young person give up on their dreams. But Connie's dreams and future were so much more important to her that she chose to forge ahead and not let her tragedies define her or stop her.

In December of 1965, her greatest dream was realized (although my brother and sister might disagree), I was born! I say I was her greatest gift because I was born on her birthday. My mom and dad subsequently had three more children.

As we were growing up, being of service to others was more important than anything else in our home. The choices we made always took into consideration the impact it would have on our family, friends, and community. When you grow up in a home that has a fundamental practice of being of service to others, it becomes who you are. That practice shaped the kind of person I became, the kind of profession I chose, and the life I created.

While I had tragedies of my own, none compared to my mom's journey and the brave choices she had to make. I also realized that there was nothing I could do to change her past. But I could live my life as a thank you to her. To live such an amazing life, a miraculous life, a life with purpose and passion that would, without any doubt, let her know that her journey was worth it and that it impacted me.

In my late twenties I found myself in an unhealthy marriage and faced with some life-changing decisions. Would I stay in an unfulfilling relationship? Was I willing to face the consequences of leaving? Was I willing to live a life that was not fulfilling? Who was I? Who was I meant to be? Was my life a reflection of the life my parents wanted for me? So many questions.

As a little girl, I had a very strong spiritual connection to God. So, as I contemplated my future, I drew on my relationship with God to help me navigate my life. I was in constant prayer. I knew that I was about to embark on some very difficult choices. With God in my heart, I made the decision to divorce my husband. That decision rushed me into uncharted waters.

I no longer had a home, a car, or money. That choice to leave put me at the lowest point in my life. It also put me in a place to re-analyze my life. Where was I going? What did I want? Could I rebuild my life? As I was praying for guidance and direction and asking myself these questions, I realized that I needed to find my purpose. I have always believed that each and every one of us was born to answer a question. Each of us are uniquely created and we each have a question to answer. Finding that answer brings us to our life purpose. I started asking myself, "What do I love to do? What do my habits show me? What excites me? What do I find exhilarating? What could I spend all day doing? Who do I want to be of service to? How can I make a difference?" After answering those questions, meditating and prayer, I asked, "Who am I and what question was I born to answer?" That's when it hit me. The question I was born to answer was, "How do I make things better?"

Knowing my question brought so much clarity to why I do what I do. That's why my cars and home are meticulously clean. That's why I can take a run-down real estate property and make it better. That's why when I meet someone who needs help, I make it better. "How can I make things better?" drives every part of who I am and what I do.

Now that I knew my question, it was time to get to work. I realized that although leaving my marriage resulted in the darkest days of my life, they soon turned into the best days of my life. I started to figure out what I wanted my future to look like. What did I really want? I began to dream of a crazy amazing® life. I wanted to make a huge impact in this world, I wanted to change lives, to be a billionaire, have several multi-million dollar homes that I would share with my friends and family, a husband to die for, and the crazy amazing® kids. I wanted to travel to the most beautiful places in the world in my private jet. It was like ordering from a restaurant menu.

I could hear my parents' words, "You can be, do, and have anything you want in this life if you put your mind to it." But then my belief system would scream, "You don't deserve that! You are crazy! You have no money, no education, no semblance of any of what you dream of!"

I once heard Joel Osteen say, "God would not have put a dream in your heart if he hadn't already given you everything you need to fulfill it." I realized that the only one stopping my dreams from happening was me. I was putting limits on myself. I had been walking with God as his favored daughter all these years; why was I putting limits on myself when He wasn't?

I had everything I needed to fulfill my dreams. My daily mantra was, "I am so grateful to have everything I need to fulfill my dreams." I became very clear on the impact I wanted to make in this world, the difference I wanted to make, and the legacy I wanted to leave. I also was very clear that I wanted to show my parents how thankful I was for the brave choices they made by creating my crazy amazing® life.

My state of mind and belief system began to change. I went from scared, from, "How is this going to happen?" to "It's as good as done, my order is in." I began saying yes to opportunities that opened up. I wrote a list of what I wanted and followed up with pictures that matched my dreams. Yes, the husband, kids, homes, money, and cars all followed the world impact I wanted to make. My vision board had me as a best-selling author, an educator who had a huge impact on people's lives, a generous soul, and a job-creator.

I believe that there were some specific things that have led to me manifesting this life. First, have a spiritual connection with something: God, the Universe, whatever you believe in. Second, surrender and allow that spiritual connection fulfill your desires. Don't get stuck on how it's going to happen. Your job is to make the choices and be clear about what you want. Third, it's my belief that if I give others my best—the best house, car, job, dinner, money—that God would give me his best.

It's been twenty-two years since I started making some brave choices. I have a Crazy Amazing® life! My brave choices allow me to financially thank my parents for their brave choices. We enjoy spending lots of time together as a family, we all travel to some of the most exotic places in the world, they live in a million-dollar home, and they never have to ask, "How much?"

Oprah once said, "What material success does is provide you with the ability to concentrate on other things that really matter. And that is being able to make a difference, not only in your own life but in other people's lives." Living a life that allows me to make an impact required that I do the work. I had to figure out what question I was born to answer. Once I did the work to find that out, I had to figure out what I wanted and be very clear about that. I used a vision board as a visual reminder of what I wanted. I read about people who had a life and legacy that I wanted to replicate. Once I received the knowledge, I acted on it. You see, once you receive the "how-to", you have to do something with it. You have a new awareness, new tools. Maybe meditation, quiet time, and prayer are new to you. I encourage you to be open to trying something different.

It may be that you don't think you deserve what you dream of. What about the future of your unborn children? What about the future of your family? Figure out who or what would motivate you to stretch out of your comfort zone. Make that so big that when you want to give up, you are motivated to stick with it. There were many times that my mom wanted to give up, but her future unborn children were counting on her to stick with it and forge ahead. And boy, I am so glad she didn't give up! There were many times that I couldn't see my dreams coming to fruition, but I kept repeating Joel Osteen's words, "God would not have put a dream in your heart if he hadn't already given you everything you need to fulfill it."

Figure out what you need to tell yourself and say it over and over again until you feel your dream, feel what it would be like to acquire it, feel the emotions. Really feel the emotions, laugh or cry as you would when it happens. I would imagine what it would feel like to help a homeless family out by giving them a place to live, a car to drive, job training and a job. When that happened, I felt the same emotions I had been practicing. Things always happen twice, once in your mind and once in reality. Get in the habit of seeing it in your mind first, feel the emotions, and believe that you deserve whatever you dream of.

I have some big dreams left, and there is no doubt they are on their way. What I have learned is that my brave choices opened up the door to a life that I was meant to live. A life that allows me choices. A life that allows me to impact this world. I thank God for my life and for his guidance in navigating every step in this journey. I believe every person has the ability to create the life of their dreams ... when the opportunity opens up to make brave choices, take it.

ABOUT ANN MARIE SMITH

Passionate about creating a life of her dreams, Ann Marie Smith has spent years researching the blueprints of success. She knew there was more to life than just existing. She knew that with the right tools she could learn to intentionally create a life that would matter and make a difference in the world, and with an abundance of financial resources, she could serve the needs of others as well as her own.

Ann Marie Smith is a thirty-five-year veteran educator and entrepreneur. In 2009, she resigned her position as a school administrator to pursue her dream of becoming an entrepreneur. She is the CEO of several companies with over 600 employees. After spending over two decades working as a teacher and administrator, developing educational programs for her community, she learned what truly drives people and how to bring out the best in her teams. She has mastered how to connect with people in a way that brings out the best in them and teaches them how to become servant leaders that bring out the best in their teams.

Ann Marie is an award-wining professional and entrepreneur. In 2019 she became a Best-Selling Author. She has landed coverage in print and broadcast outlets around the world, including Univision, Telemundo, CBS, NBC, ABC, iHeart Radio, Success Today, and most recently, Fortune magazine. In addition to her extensive background in education and business, she recently earned her California Contractors License, to pursue her goal of building custom homes for at-risk members of her community. Ann Marie holds a master's degree in human development/ educational leadership and social change.

Ann Marie leverages positive psychology to help people focus on their best qualities and talents and then uses that to help them develop into amazing leaders. She is passionate about creating jobs for people and growing them to become leaders in her companies.

Ann Marie lives in Southern California with her husband and two children. In her spare time, she loves investing in real estate, reading, going to the movies, watching her dogs and micro pig play, listening to music, and just laughing and having fun with her friends and family. When asked what she believes is the key to her success: meditation, prayer, gratitude, giving to others, and making everything she does fun… if it isn't fun, she's not doing it!

Visit annmariesmith.TV to learn more.

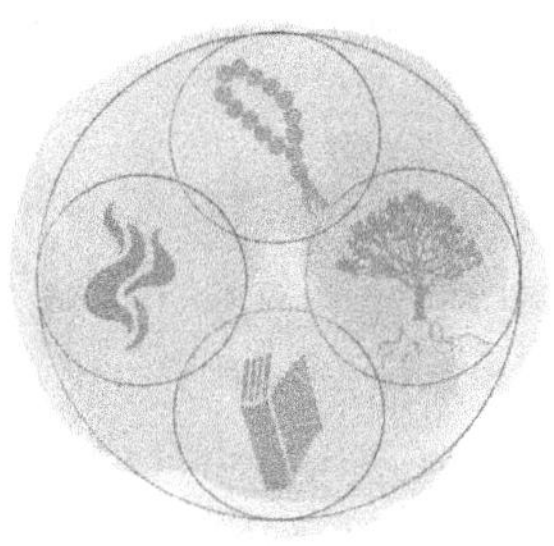

LIGHT AFTER DEATH

Jennifer Amabile

My mom was my best friend. In another life I swear we were friends or sisters because we were always close. As a toddler I would cry hysterically if she ever left me to go somewhere. I hated to be away from her. I know lots of women say this about their mom, but she was truly the best mom in the world. We rarely had conflicts and she made being a mother look so easy. She made growing up easy. Whatever I was going through, I knew my mom would support me through it. She was my rock and always seemed to make an impossible situation a breeze to walk through. She was also a lot of fun to be around. I was incredibly blessed to have her as a mother. I would always say to her, "I don't know what I would do without you."

It was May of 1991 when my worst nightmare came into reality. My mother was diagnosed with stage 4 ovarian cancer at the age of forty-seven. I was crushed. My mom, the woman who I looked up to. My mom, the woman who was always there for me. My mom, the woman who always made everything better in seemingly the worst situations. The woman who seemed invincible was suddenly facing the most terrifying time in her life. Back then, stage 4 ovarian cancer was a death sentence. I didn't know this at the time and it wasn't until years later that I found out the doctors only gave her six months to live. She lived nine years after her initial diagnosis. It was a miracle. The same woman who I described earlier, who seemed to make an impossible situation a breeze to walk through, stayed true to form. She walked through this nine year journey with cancer with such grace and herculean strength. She wasn't ready to go. She still needed to raise my brother and me. She had some miracles to perform. She had to teach me some lessons that would then carry me through the darkest years of my life after her death.

Living with a family member who has cancer on and off for nine years can chip away at so much of your birth right to happiness. I didn't have the tools back then that I do now to cope with such devastation. The emotional roller coaster becomes a habit. It becomes ingrained in you so deeply that it's your normal. With remissions that turned into reoccurrences, chemotherapy, radiation, and all of the side effects of these treatments, it becomes so very difficult to allow yourself to be truly happy. You are always waiting for the other shoe to drop. And it did many times. But she would always bounce back. My mother chose a combination of traditional Western medicine cancer treatments and vitamins, diet, and alternative therapies proven to fight cancer in Eastern medicine. And I believe this is what prolonged her life.

Then on September 1, 2000, the inevitable happened. My mother could no longer fight. Her body did all it could to fight the cancer and it was done. She was done. I was in such denial in the weeks and days leading up to her death. She had miraculously bounced back so many times before, I didn't want to believe this time would be any different. My rock, my best friend, my mother, was gone. The previous nine years in some way prepped me for this moment. In a way, it was almost a relief. No more suffering, no more sickness, no more false hopes and scary doctor visits. She was not suffering anymore, but in the years that would follow, I would experience some of the worst suffering of my life. My mother's death was a gateway to deep depression and anxiety. The years she lived with cancer chipped away at what I thought my life was supposed to look like. In the years that followed, I wore the extreme grief

I was experiencing like a cloak. I carried it around on my shoulders. I would experience more death. In the span of six years, I lost my mom, my aunt, my paternal grandparents, and my cousins' father which we were all close to. Grief became a way of life.

Several months after my mom died, I went into fix-it mode and swore to myself that if I just got married and started a family it would fill the horrible void I was feeling. The void my mother left when she died would be gone. I could follow in her footsteps and be the mother she was and have a wonderful life. I clung to the relationship I was in at the time so very tightly in desperation to make this happen. All would be well.

But that plan did not work out. The relationship ended. I still clung to the idea that getting married would be the answer. After all, I was in my twenties and that is what you are supposed to do. Get married and have kids. That was what I wanted. Or so I thought. But my grief clouded any other solution for my sadness and depression. The only viable solution I saw was the next logical step in life. It made others look so happy and content. That was where I needed to be.

So I dated. But never quite found the right match in a relationship. When dating became unfulfilling, I started to focus on myself. From the outside, no one would think I was suffering because the whole time, I still strived. I am my mother's daughter and tried so very hard to make the right choices for myself, even in grief. I reached for external things that I thought would help heal me and move me closer to my goal of finding a wonderful partner to share my life with.

In the ten years following my mother's death, I got my master's in counseling (I started classes the week after my mother died), moved out on my own, was hired in an administration job at a university and went to culinary school. I ran marathons, traveled, dated some more, drank too much, and still managed to socialize. All the while though, there was an underlying sadness. It wouldn't go away. I was just getting by on an emotional level. At one point I thought about what it would be like if I didn't exist anymore. It was that bad. I was single and miserable, and

I just wasn't living the life that I wanted for myself.

I was just existing.

It would continue to get worse. In September of 2006, my father went in for a routine hip replacement surgery. The surgery was not successful and my father ended up disabled as a result. This was another hard road to recovery for my dad who had just lost his wife six years earlier. My brother and I needed to be his caretakers while he healed. It was December of 2006, and I remember laying on my couch feeling sorry for myself. It was frustrating because I still had such big aspirations but was so deep in despair I didn't see a way out. The more time that went by that I didn't find "the one", the more I made it mean something about myself. I thought there was something wrong with me. I thought I wasn't meant to be in the kind of relationship I wanted. I turned those feelings in on myself, and let's just say there was a lot of self-loathing and victimhood. But I carried on.

After culinary school, I felt I could start to see a light at the end of the tunnel. I had met some new friends and my dating life was sparked back to life. I started to feel better theoretically, but I was still suffering physically and emotionally. I was tired all the time, I wasn't sleeping well, and I would wake up with a sense of dread. There were days I couldn't get out of bed. At one point, I remember looking out my bedroom window at a concrete parking lot, feeling so stuck and wishing for a better view literally and figuratively. I was drinking too much and was still so emotional about my mom passing. I still managed to have a lot of fun though. In between the fun times, I had so much doubt about where I was headed. It didn't seem like getting married or starting a family was in the cards for me. After a particularly difficult breakup around this time, I yet again threw myself into various things to make myself feel better. I decided to get in shape and started to train for a biathlon.

One day as I was running with the friend I was training with, I mentioned to her that I was considering going on antidepressants. I told her that I just couldn't seem to shake the depression. It seemed that even though I was doing all the "right" healthy things, nothing was really shifting from the inside out. I really thought something was wrong. I didn't actually want to take any medications. I had been on them briefly right after my mom passed and I felt worse taking them. But I was desperate and didn't know what else to do. I also believed in holistic alternative medicine but wasn't aware of anything to help with what I was going through.

What I am about to say next is what makes me believe and know for sure there is a God and prayers are always answered. You are always being led to your healing.

During this time period my dad had suffered some setbacks with his surgery. Still unable to walk and really struggling, I said to him that he needs to try a different approach. Nothing he was doing was working. I remembered a few years prior speaking to a woman who had multiple sclerosis. My dad has that as well. She was seeing this holistic chiropractor that helped her so much. Not knowing what else to do, I reached out to this chiropractor and made an appointment. Little did I know this appointment would be life changing for me and an integral part of my healing.

As my brother, my dad, and I sat in the chiropractor's office, he said that he prefers to treat the whole family. So the next thing I knew I was having my spine scanned for possible subluxations, which are misalignments that can affect nerve and organ functions in the body. He looked at my scan and said, "I can tell you are suffering from anxiety and depression." I thought chiropractic care was only for bad backs! I immediately was put on a plan to get adjustments three times a week. The morning after my third visit, I woke up and something miraculous had happened. The depression lifted! It was as if the years of grief and fog and darkness that I had been carrying around in my body dissipated. I could breathe again! I felt awake! The light returned to my body.

This was the beginning of my new life. I was finally able to look inside and reclaim all of the things that I had been putting on the back burner for years. I had been living on the sidelines waiting for a relationship to save me. I learned that the only thing that was going to save me was me.

This miraculous healing set off a massive chain of events that has led me to this moment. A passion had been sparked in me to set off on another journey of personal growth. I felt like I had been asleep for so long and I had so much catching up to do. In 2014, I went to the Institute for Integrative Nutrition to become a certified health coach. Attending this school opened up so many doors for me and introduced me to so many mentors/teachers/spiritual coaches that continued to help me heal on my path.

In 2015, I attended a retreat in Costa Rica that even further clarified what I wanted to do. I wanted to become a life coach. It also pushed me to make major changes in my life. Changes that I had thought about for so long but wasn't healthy enough to pursue. I decided to give up my apartment of eight years, sell all my things, and downsize to living with a roommate while I looked for a place to move out of state. Within one year of doing so, I quit my job and moved to Asheville, NC. I started my business as a life coach.

The journey I had been on sparked a passion and mission in me to help single women move past fears, blocks, limiting beliefs, and heal from the things that are preventing them from living a life that is calling to them. My mission is to help them listen and trust their intuition, follow their purpose, and let their bliss lead them. My mission is to support them in getting beyond the loneliness, get unstuck, and take action to remember their worth and move through the sadness and emptiness.

The one thing that I learned from my move to Asheville is that following your heart never steers you wrong, no matter how scary taking that first step may seem. On the other side of that fear are so many blessings and bliss that it makes you wonder what you were even afraid of to begin with. I see so many women who hang on to this fear and are so afraid of what others will say if they pursue their dreams. They themselves are their biggest block. So they stay stuck and stop participating in life which eventually leads to depression, sickness, and other health problems. We are living in a time where we are being called more than ever to pursue our passions and our hearts' desires. Those are the very things that when fully expressed can help heal the planet. The world needs you and your light!

It's been almost four years since I moved to my new home and as I look outside my window now, I am no longer looking out at a concrete parking lot where I felt stifled and stuck. I am looking at the trees on a mountain side. This was the life I was always supposed to be living and I'm doing the work I was always supposed to be doing. It was like I had to be stripped completely of everything I thought I knew to be true, only to be rebuilt to the version of myself that I am today. My mother's death was not in vain. God had a greater plan. I know my mom was my teacher in so many ways and her death allowed me to be on a path towards my purpose. It brought me to a place where I can help other women come through their own beautiful journey. So that I can help them come back to themselves, so they can look out their own window and see the light they always dreamed of being reflected back to them.

ABOUT JENNIFER AMABILE

Jennifer Amabile is a transformational life coach who supports and empowers single women in healing from heartbreak, cultivating more self-love, and amplifying their self-worth through meditation and spiritual practice. She has been leading guided meditations for five years and uses them in her practice with her clients to facilitate healing. She believes a consistent meditation practice is essential for remaining grounded in the craziness of life.

Jen is a Reiki practitioner, has a master's degree in counseling from Montclair State University, and a Health Coach certificate from the Institute for Integrative Nutrition. When she isn't seeing clients, you can find her in the kitchen fulfilling her passion for cooking and baking. She received a culinary diploma from the Institute of Culinary Education in New York City in 2008. Jen is also an admirer of chocolate and believes having a bit each day is one of the keys to happiness. She was born and raised in Montville, New Jersey and moved to the Blue Ridge Mountains in Asheville, NC in 2016 to start a new life.

You can find out more about Jen by visiting:

https://www.facebook.com/myhabitualhappiness/ on Facebook.

https://www.instagram.com/jenamabile/ on Instagram.

Join her Facebook group Breakup to Breakthrough, where she addresses all issues single women face and creates a safe, healing environment for women to feel supported on their journey: https://www.facebook.com/groups/breakuptobreakthroughwithjen/

If you want information on her coaching services, send her a note at Jennifer@JenniferAmabile.com.

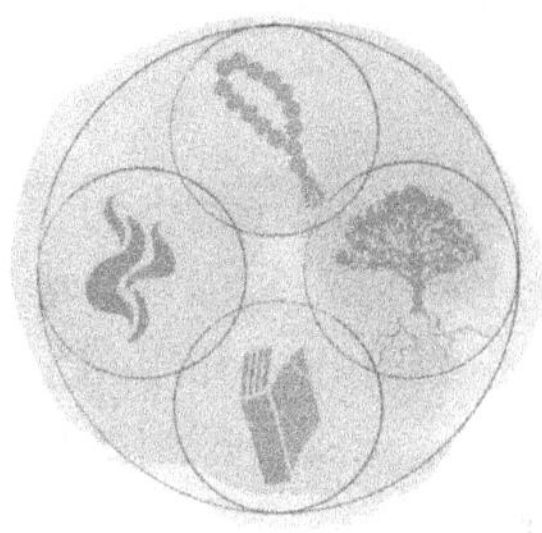

TRUST YOUR INTUITION: YOUR FEELINGS ARE SMARTER THAN YOU THINK

Eva Alberts

It was March 2015 in Reykjavik, Iceland. I was working as a midwife at the high-risk pregnancy ward at the National University Hospital, helping women through difficult times during pregnancy and doing home visits after birth, helping with breastfeeding, and providing guidance. I was also working in direct sales, training my sales team and helping people improve their health. My business was blooming and growing fast. Very exciting times! Every day was a new adventure. I loved watching my twenty-year-old son, who is a horse trainer and pro athlete, participate in equestrian sports and play handball with his team in the Icelandic Premier League. He was also playing with the national under 21 handball team and his future was bright.

Then it happened: March 9th, 2015, our lives turned into a nightmare! I was in bed when my son texted me from the next room. It had never happened before, so I immediately sensed that something was off and rushed into his room. He was in so much pain, trembling and sweating, the pain increasing every minute. Six months earlier he had pericarditis and my first thought was that this had escalated. But this was so much worse. Unbearable chest pain, racing, irregular heartbeat, sweating, shortness of breath, radiating pain in the left arm and two fingers, and very high blood pressure. I rushed him to the ER and his blood pressure was 199/120 (normally 120/80) and honestly, that night I thought I would lose him. In terror, I watched his condition get worse. My strong and healthy son was lying in a hospital bed in terrible pain, screaming for help. No pain killers worked, even a high dose of IV morphine did not ease the pain. He was drugged but the pain was still unbearable. I had never seen anything like this.

This was the beginning of a six-week hospitalization, three weeks in the ICU. During my time there, even in the first twenty-four hours, I was given every indication that I was going to have to be the advocate for my son's wellness. Not because I was a health care professional but because I felt like the care that he needed was not going to be provided.

At the ER the doctors suspected aortic dissection, a life-threatening condition. He had blood tests and imaging of the heart, but the doctors said that he had probably been moving during the imaging, so it was probably not an aortic dissection. "Probably not" was not acceptable, his condition was worsening and still no diagnosis in sight. So, I asked for another imaging to rule this out. This set the tone for the medical treatment during the time he was there. I realized that I would have to ask, push, and make demands on his behalf. He was admitted to the cardiac ward and there we experienced prejudice and unacceptable behaviour, to a point where I broke down crying. He had severe pain attacks that lasted up to five hours. I insisted they called an anaesthesiologist and he was transferred to the ICU. Nothing worked to ease the pain, so they ended up using Propofol to put him to sleep during the episodes. He was on a respirator for three days. It became clear I had to be by his bedside all the time, so I slept in the ICU for three weeks.

Later I found out that serious medication errors were made that could have killed him. The doctors did all the testing they could think of but after six weeks, there was still no diagnosis. Then a doctor at the ICU decided he should be admitted to the psychiatric ward. We refused. He has never been mentally ill. Then everything exploded. He was transferred to the cardiac ward where a cardiologist told him he was taking up space from others and should be in the psychiatric ward. The situation had become unbearable—so bad that the day he left the ICU was the day he went home. That's not protocol, people never do that. He wasn't ready to come home, and he shouldn't have but he didn't feel welcome and felt that his care would be better at home.

At this point it was clear that my job was not only to be the advocate of his wellness but also the facilitator of his healing. His life was in my hands. Here the fight began for real. The day after he came home, he went to the ER, the doctor told him that the only thing he would do for him was to call a psychiatrist. We were facing the fact that he would not get the help he needed. His condition worsened as new symptoms started showing up. In the fall he had high fever, was throwing up and had terrible back pain. I´ll never forget my frustration, knowing that he wouldn't get help at the ER. "Where can we go?" I said to him with tears in my eyes. I decided to take him to the GP who immediately sent him back to the ER. He had a serious kidney infection. The ER visits continued. I had to fight harder every time.

A year after he became ill, in March 2016, he was admitted for a week, two days in the ICU. The doctor told him that this was psychosomatic pain. We didn't agree and had an argument. My son went home, no plan, no follow up, no support. In August he got Bell's Palsy, half of his face was paralyzed, he had constant terrible headaches and the next months he fainted, got severe swelling and pain in the right cheek and throat, and his blood pressure was dangerously high at 165/135.

Countless visits to the ER, fighting the doctors, demanding they treat him and sending him abroad. It got to a point where I refused to leave the ER until I got a meeting with the Chief Medical Executive. I sent an email to the CEO and spoke with the Health Minister. When his blood pressure was life-threatening, I asked for help. No answer. Then I got a lawyer to force the hospital to respond and send him to Sweden for a PET scan. It took three months. Still no diagnosis, no one from the hospital contacted my son regarding the PET scan results. I asked the

GP to refer my son to an endocrinologist who was not working at the hospital. He did, still no diagnosis, and during 2017 my son's condition got worse. One terrifying moment was in the summer of 2017 when his blood pressure dropped to 77/56. He was at home and I thought I would lose him. The next months he had posterior nosebleeds, severe headaches, dizziness, nausea, and vomiting—on top of everything else. Never could I have imagined that this would last three years! That I would wake up every morning with anxiety, not knowing if he was still alive. Why did the doctors give up?

After his hospitalisation in 2016, I crashed. "I can't believe you're still standing," my doctor said. I was diagnosed with PTSD and put on sick leave. To top it all off, I lost my job. Three of my sons were also diagnosed with PTSD, one of them seventeen-years-old, quit school. He locked himself in his room playing computer games and gained fifty pounds. During this battle we had been in survival mode, we had no wellness advocate. When one family member is sick, the whole family is sick.

I knew I needed help to stay mentally strong. I could have gone into the dark space of negative thinking and subscribed to the fact that this was the way my life was going to be, or I could look towards possibility, which is what I did and always do. The key is to manage your emotions and remain in control of your mind—your thoughts and visualizations. I know, from my experience, that it is crucial to be positive and forward thinking, seeking solutions and ways to get help. There is always a way. This mindset was my wellness lifeline, a lifeline of possibilities that helped me identify what changes I needed in my life to start a ripple effect towards a new direction.

During this time, I found and studied neuroscience and personal growth online. It gave me focus, strength, and helped me cope. But for all of this to happen I had to open the gate and accept these changes. I came across Jack Canfield and immediately sensed that with his tools I could use my experience to help others. In October 2017 I graduated as a certified Canfield Trainer in the Success Principles. In November

I got an email that encouraged me to apply for the TTT live program 2018. My instinct told me to apply but my thoughts were, "I can't, he's so sick, I don't have the money ..." But I was drawn back to the email again and again, my intuition telling me that I should apply. It was scary, it didn't make a lot of sense and on paper it certainly didn't add up, but I still followed my intuition. Even if I didn't have the money or the time, or didn't know how any of this was going to be facilitated, I still filled in that application. In the application I was asked what my biggest obstacle would be. "My son's illness," I wrote.

I got a phone call from the Canfield office but what was supposed to be an initial screening conversation for the training quickly turned into something completely different. The woman said, "Eva, before I came to work for Canfield, I used to work for a doctor who everybody turns to when nobody knows what's wrong. And I´m going to connect you to him. His name is Dr. Darren Clair." I stared at my phone, speechless, tears in my eyes and thought, "This is a miracle! Wow, this is why I was meant to be in this moment!"

We got an online appointment with the doctor who recommended stem cell treatment in California. He couldn't promise that my son would be cured but based on his experience it would be worth trying. He had nothing to lose and everything to gain. My son and I agreed and this was the beginning of his healing journey—and mine too. But I had to fight one more battle to get on that journey. He needed virus tests before the treatment. I had to fight to get these tests done—to get to the place where I knew, in my heart, the healing was waiting. My mindset, believing in myself and following my intuition, made all the difference. I had no guarantee. I had to be brave. I followed my gut feeling, what I knew in my heart to be true. This was the turning point. In December 2017 he had a stem cell treatment in California and two weeks later his symptoms had decreased by 70-80%. He had another stem cell treatment four weeks later and January 31st, 2018 he was cured! The diagnosis was a derangement of the autonomic nervous system of indeterminate cause.

The opening of that miracle was also the opening of my new life. This experience gave me a deeper understanding of how important it is to heal on every level and pay attention to wellness on every level. Everybody has a healing journey. Being a healthcare professional, a Certified Canfield trainer and a RIM facilitator gives me the tools to guide people towards their healing and help the facilitation of that healing on every level, whether it be something that needs to heal within the soul or physical body, mind or the heart. All of this is a result of what I´ve been through, my experience and education.

What led my son to this miracle was my mindset—my courage, taking full responsibility, following my intuition, not giving up, and allowing myself to seek help. I hope my story inspires and empowers you to take control of your life—RISE—and create a life you love.

Today my son is healthy and happy, training horses and playing handball. And I am grateful.

ABOUT EVA ALBERTS

Eva Asrun Albertsdottir lives in Reykjavik, Iceland. She has a successful career as a midwife, singer, radio and TV host, entrepreneur, direct sales representative and is the CEO of EvaAlberts ehf. In 2009 she founded a charity organization for the Women's Ward in the National University Hospital of Iceland. Her life took a u-turn in 2015 when one of her five sons became seriously ill. He was sick for three years and she was diagnosed with PTSD. This traumatic experience led to a healing journey and certification as a trainer in Jack Canfield's Success Principles and Methodology and a RIM facilitator. She is a Master RIM student and her education is ongoing. As a midwife Eva has been helping women for decades. Combining her certifications and life experience she is pursuing her passion for helping women on their healing journey to cope, recover and RISE—turn their lives around quickly and achieve success, inner peace and happiness—creating a life they love and deserve.

WAYS TO WORK WITH EVA:

Coaching, training, speaking and online courses: Master your mindset and get from where you are to where you want to be.

RIM: Online Breakthrough sessions: Healing on a cellular level. Transformational technique that frees you of negative thoughts, feelings and memories. Say goodbye to hurt and pain.

Wellness journey: Health tips to help you cope, recover, and RISE. How to turn off the inflammation in the body, heal the gut, and boost the immune system.

TO CONNECT WITH EVA:

Website: www.evaalberts.com
Fb: https://www.facebook.com/SuccessWithEva/
Email: eva@evaalberts.com

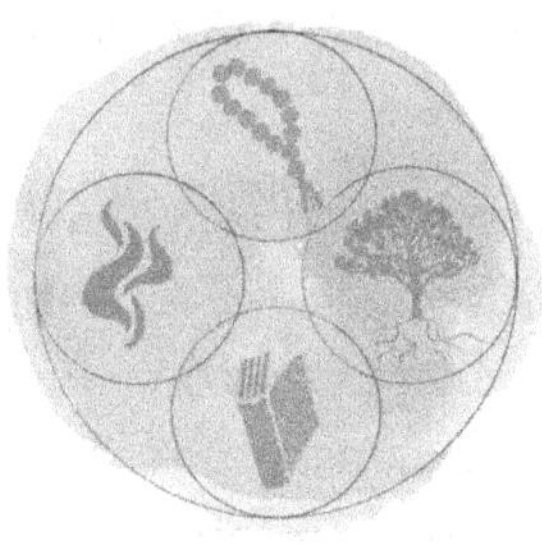

I AM TOTALLY WORTH IT

Donna Nudel Brown

Have you ever felt like there has to be something more? That you are here for a reason more impactful than how you are currently living your life? As though there is something more significant you are here to accomplish and you have no idea what that looks like? And does the mere thought of exploring that or making changes elicit indescribable feelings of uncertainty and perhaps panic? My answer to all of those questions was a huge "YES"! That was exactly how I felt for a very long time until I couldn't sit in those feelings anymore. The moment I actually faced and conquered a huge fear of jumping off a cliff from not wanting one more regret in my life, everything shifted! That jump has led me to a life I never could have dreamed of! It has led me to a place where I pinch myself most days because it is so amazing to be here fully in it. HERE is being able to support others, to inspire others, and to guide others for them to live *their* best life through my coaching, my energy work as a Reiki Master, and my passion for crystals and the support they provide. Honestly, I was not even aware of the possibility of my life looking differently from where it was. Leading up to that day, it often felt like I had been going through the motions without a clear direction other than my role of being a mom.

When I attended my first self-development workshop in 2006, I was so shocked and surprised to learn that we have so much power over our thoughts and our responses to all that occurred in the past and present. I learned that we can actually reframe our thoughts around events, that there is a way to let go of the constant barrage of negative self-talk, and with grace and compassion we can forgive ourselves and others. It was truly a revelation and it would take years before I fully embraced and was ready to commit to working on myself.

A few weeks after that jump, I was again introduced to a new way of being and began to see new possibilities that I had not known were an option. I was shown new techniques, new rituals, and a new mindset. I was filled with hope of how my life could become by seeing it through a new lens and soon after developed a daily routine that would allow me to feel centered and grounded. That routine now includes meditation, visualization, journaling, gratitude, and protecting my energy to keep it at a high vibrational level. I truly believe we must protect our energy fields and I now share tools and techniques on how to do that. I also share how to release any negative energy that does not serve us.

Meditation became a necessity for me to help quiet the constant flow of thoughts. Honestly, the thoughts never stop. What I actually learned to do was to notice the thoughts and thank them for showing up (yes, I actually say 'thank you'). I started small, sometimes as little as three minutes at a time because that was all I could manage. It was more about being present and focusing on those moments instead of the often-loud noise in my head. My mind never stops! I was sure there was something wrong with me when I knew that others meditated, and I couldn't understand HOW on earth they could sit quietly for SO long seated in the lotus position on the floor!! I eventually discovered what worked best for me and spent time practicing it every day without judgement. There is a reason they call it a practice, and it truly is transformative! When I realized that my struggles with meditation would allow me to offer varying methods for my clients, I became grateful for my journey.

Wherever we are in our journey is the exact place we are supposed to be no matter what aspect we are evaluating. When it seems like the path is slower than expected, I believe there is a lesson we are supposed to learn before moving forward. When you face challenges, pause and ask yourself, "What lesson am I meant to learn from this?" Sit quietly and listen for the answer.

Another shift occurred once I learned of the abundance versus lack mentality — focus on what we have, what is working, and what we have accomplished as opposed to what we do not have, where we fall short, and how far we still need to go to reach our goals or find contentment. I began to focus on gratitude and created a daily gratitude list. There were times that were challenging especially in the beginning of this journey, so I would list basic things such as my reliable car, my daily hot shower, or selling one crystal. The journey of gratitude was definitely not a straight line, but I forged ahead because I was committed to the practice and I was focused on the outcome.

The other benefit to meditation and gratitude is they both instantly raise our vibration. When we raise our vibration, we can more easily manifest and attract abundance to us. I also learned that as our vibration rises, so does our self-worth.

"Confident", "accomplished", and "worthiness" were definitely not words that I would have used to describe myself in the years leading up to my journey into self-development. I had always believed that we are a compilation of the decisions we make — good or bad — and we are to keep moving forward and deal with the ramifications. I believed that there was no way to feel better about my choices, so it was just best to ignore them, bury them deeply, and pretend they didn't happen.

Once I realized I could no longer sit in that space of regret and discontent, I faced the discomfort of stepping out of my comfort zone and said yes to every opportunity that was presented to me. I learned long ago if it wasn't 'hell yes' then it was a 'no'. No more tiptoeing around, no more playing small, if I was going to do this, it was going to be big! Now mind you, I am not THERE yet, we are never THERE. We can always grow; we can always learn because another lesson will appear just as we are ready to stretch a little (or a lot) more! And when you are open to the possibility of *amazing* showing up and taking over your life, what you are about to embrace *will change your life.* It did mine and I am so grateful!

Since sharing my story "Finding Fabulous at 52" in *Women Who Ignite*, there are some days I don't even recognize myself. In fact, others don't either. I am showing up in a way that barely resembles the old me. Thank goodness! I was hiding behind what I thought were my truths, which in reality were merely insecurities.

I want to be known as the person who broke through her limiting beliefs and now encourages others to live an inspired life. I am proud of who I am now, even though it wasn't always that way. Honestly, there are still times I wonder how I am able to help others when I felt lost for so long! At this writing it was five-and-a-half years ago that I took my leap and I am grateful for every second of my journey, which looked more like an EKG than the trajectory of an airplane taking off. There were many lessons I needed to learn along the way and frankly, I am still learning. What I did know is that I could no longer stay where I was, so I was committed to the process and the outcome no matter how uncomfortable or fear-filled it seemed. Failure was not an option.

Whatever you do, do not give up on your dreams. It may not look the way you thought it would, and it may not bring you what you were seeking. But what if it is SO MUCH BETTER? I didn't always believe that when I first started on this journey, but I knew without a doubt I could no longer stay where I was. I needed to make a difference even though I didn't understand what I was seeking, and I deeply desired to find *my* purpose. What finally emerged was my desire to support women by helping and guiding them to find *their* purpose. It often involved pulling back many, many layers of feelings — mostly of self-doubt, lack of confidence, low self-worth, and low self-esteem. *For them and for me.*

We are not in charge of the 'how' in any of this. We are in charge of our dreams and what that looks like down to the tiniest detail. The Universe handles the rest. I know that sounds absurd. I felt the same way in hearing these terms, but once I began to see shifts, began to see my business grow, began to see opportunities, *everything* changed for me. To be clear, it wasn't overnight and there were plenty of ups and downs, but I knew I was meant for greatness. It may be different for you, it may be a calling to help animals or a certain population, or to set up a retreat center in a beautiful location, or to create a product that will change people's lives. Each of us has unique dreams and is called to something.

Perhaps you are reading this and are thinking, "Maybe she can do it, but there is no way I can." I completely understand because that is what I used to think. Frankly, sometimes I still do when I see others who have achieved more than I have or when meeting someone who has grown a successful business larger than mine. My thoughts may be "Oh, my business will never generate that level of income," and I realize if I change it to, "Wow, I would love to sit down with her and learn how she grew her business so fast!" I could actually benefit from the encounter and interaction instead of feeling badly by comparing myself to others. I learned long ago that comparison doesn't serve anyone, collaboration is the key!

I am here to say: YES YOU CAN! Visualize that outcome already in place in all aspects of your life, focusing on every detail as though they have already happened. Breathe it, see it, feel it, and be in it. What does that look like for you? My visualizations included speaking to large groups, sharing my love and knowledge of crystals, traveling to beautiful locations for events, meeting incredible people who want to collaborate with me, and having deep, meaningful relationships with those closest to me. I began to see part or all of these visions become reality, so my dreams continue to grow as well! Our minds cannot differentiate from what is currently happening or what we envision our lives to be, so dream big!

I have definitely made huge strides but realize that disappointments can happen. Regardless of various events and interactions not yielding the results I was expecting, I was still on the right path with the confirmation that I have the ability to impact someone's life and it is my calling to continue. What I observed is that with each small win, my confidence began to build. There were many times I would take a step forward and two steps back. The way I move forward is to focus on each of my small wins, including hearing that a man who bought crystals from me a few years ago clutched them whenever he was in pain, they brought him relief and continue to do so years later. Or when my client who lives in California feels the energy from the Reiki I am sending her from Maryland and instantly feels relief.

No matter how far I have come, I still have those voices in my head that want to remind me of where I was and that I am not worthy of success, of abundance, or of recognition. I am grateful beyond words that I did not listen to the voice in my head questioning my worthiness of being an author! Becoming an author has literally changed my life! There are many times we just have to push through the fear, and if someone is encouraging you to take steps that you do not see for yourself, believe they see something in you far greater than you can imagine. And the signs from the Universe? Confirmation appeared when I received the amazing, uplifting feedback from someone who read my chapter and they shared how it changed their life! That message literally brought me to tears.

Please hear me when I say we are all deserving of worthiness, happiness, and fulfillment. Do you have a dream that you never thought was possible to achieve? Do you have a deep desire to take your own leap to create what you have always envisioned? Do you ever lie awake at night and wish you could have an amazing life but you have no idea how or where to start? And are you completely enveloped in fear of making a change? If so, I encourage you to dig deep and uncover your dream or vision because I am here to support you on your journey and to tell you that we can *all* have everything we want because each one of us is totally worth it!

ABOUT DONNA NUDEL BROWN

My passion is supporting women in living a purpose-filled life of joy using my Lightworker gifts as a Reiki Master, Crystal Healer, Coach, Trainer, Speaker and your personal Cheerleader. I will guide you step-by-step in uncovering your true passions and desires including sharing techniques for you to confidently make decisions in all areas of your life. These techniques rely on energetic responses whether using a tool such as a pendulum or simply your body's response through muscle testing. Energetically our bodies know what we need before we know intellectually. Protecting yourself energetically is crucial and I provide practical tools and techniques and offer solutions to raise your vibration and clear negative energy that does not serve you. I am passionate about crystals and as an Energy Intuitive I work with clients to determine which crystals would best support them. I am an expert at selecting the exact right crystal that is meant for you.

My three-part video series 'Finding Joy" is a great way to learn many of these techniques and can be accessed via link below or on my website: www.DonnaBrownDesigns.com. I am so grateful to have found my joy, allow me to help you find *your* joy!

Video Series link:

https://www.donnabrowndesigns.com/finding-joy-video-series

I am here to support you! One of my core values is providing a sense of belonging, and I want you to feel that you belong and are welcome in my community; I am always available to connect.

Donna@DonnaBrownDesigns.com
www.DonnaBrownDesigns.com
FB: @AccessoriesByDonnaBrownDesigns
Instagram: @crystals_to_clarity

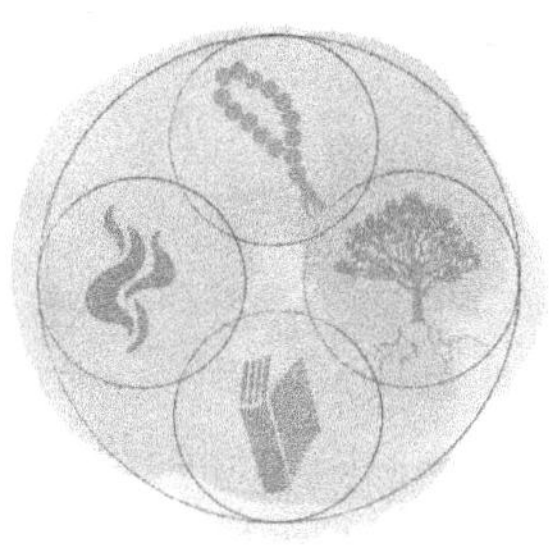

JUST SAY YES

Sally Dunbar

> *"You don't inspire people by revealing your own super power. You inspire people by helping them reveal their own super power."*
> *Nothing You Don't Already Know,* by Alexander den Heijer

I am holding the hand of a young twenty-something stranger. She is fresh-faced with white blond eyelashes. I look her in the eyes and say "You are too young to be here." "Tell me about it," she responds. It is 2013. We are walking into a football stadium, in the survivors' procession at the end of the Susan G. Komen 3-Day walk through San Francisco's streets and parks. In order to walk the event's course of twenty miles a day, three days in a row, we each raised $2,300 toward the Komen goal of ending death from breast cancer. Yes, like me, my baby-faced companion is a breast cancer survivor. In her early twenties. I am shocked. She is too young to have faced that. As we enter the stadium, I hear thunderous applause from the 800 other walkers who just finished their sixty-mile walk, directed at us survivors. There are tears. Smiles. Sobs from some. Then the most amazing thing happens. Each walker removes one shoe and respectfully raises it high in the air — the Komen One-Shoe salute to the survivors. To me. I am stunned. My tears flow.

When my friend, Becky, had asked, I said yes to walking in my first

Komen 3-Day event as a challenge to see if I could really walk twenty miles a day, then get up and do it the next day — and hey, maybe I would lose some weight. But on that day — that walk into the stadium — my life shifted. My role on this Earth as a survivor changed. I understood that they were not saluting me personally. They did not even know me. Rather, they were saluting my aliveness. My presence. My symbol in their life that a breast cancer diagnosis is not necessarily a death sentence. I got that I was the face of hope for when their mom, or their daughter, or they themselves get a breast cancer diagnosis. I got it. Profoundly.

Later that year, I walked in the Seattle 3-Day event with my mom, on her ninetieth birthday! We honored her sister Margaret — her only sister — who died of breast cancer in Seattle at fifty-five. Mom walked five miles on the first day. I returned the next year with two friends, Becky and Barbara, to walk the 3-Day again. The fresh-faced girl from San Francisco was always on my mind.

AN IDEA IS BORN

In 2015, I sat at my computer to register for my fourth Komen 3-Day walk, scheduled for San Diego in November. I was stuck on my entry declaring my financial goal. I had easily raised $7,000 my first year, and $3,000 my second. But I wanted to do more. The fresh-faced girl had inspired me. The women yet to be diagnosed inspired me. I typed in $25,000 as my fundraising goal. *Hmmm … can I raise that much?* I thought about what it would take and decided that was doable, but too small. I typed in $50,000. *Whew. How would I do THAT? Well, what if I recruited some friends and built a team?* I ran some numbers. *Huh... I think I can do that.* Then my inner voice threw down a challenge: *No giant achievement has ever been reached without an even bigger goal. Step into it! Just say YES.* I typed in $100,000 then hit SEND before I could change my mind.

Hands Up for Hooters, my new team, was born! Game on.

Doing calculations, I set a goal of recruiting forty-five walkers, figuring ten of them would not complete the training. Thirty-five walkers would raise $100,000. I begin recruiting my friends. "Wanna train all year, walk twenty miles a day three days in a row, AND raise $2,300 for breast cancer? We'll do it in sunny San Diego! You will be a Hooter!" Karene signs up. Then Patty. Then Patty gets her sister Judy. Becky joins. And Pat. We start walking in January from Fair Oaks Village near Sacramento every Sunday, rain or shine — our "Sunday Fun Days". Just for one hour — three miles. We have coffee afterwards and chat. On our first Sunday, there are seven of us. *Click — post photo to Facebook. Tag everyone.* "Come walk with us. Join our team." I tell my Marketing Group. Jeff signs up. His wife Jill joins. Twelve show up the next Sunday. *Click — Post photo to Facebook. Tag everyone.* Our team begins to grow.

TRAINING BEGINS - DISCOVERING THEIR SUPER POWER

April is our first formal training walk, as we begin walking every Saturday and Sunday morning, at 8 a.m. from Fair Oaks Coffee and Deli. To be able to walk twenty miles in a day, you start slow, then build up each weekend. Three miles a day at the beginning, adding one mile at a time. Easy peasy. We keep recruiting. Nicole hesitantly joins. "I'm worried I won't have the time to train. And for sure I can't walk that far. But I'll try." Kathy thinks about joining. "I don't think I can do it. I have lung disease. I can barely breathe sometimes." "Kath, how long can you walk now?", I ask. "Maybe forty minutes," she responds. "Talk to your doctor, then just start. Go slow and see what happens." She does. I run into Joan. Her daughter Erika has stage 4 breast cancer. "I want to, but I don't think I physically can. I have a torn meniscus in my knee, and don't want surgery." "How long can you walk currently?" I ask. "I walk three miles a day now," she responds. "Try. And see what happens — as long as your doctor agrees," I say. She signs up. Cathy considers joining, but has a pacemaker and diabetes. "Talk to your doctor, and just take it slow," I say. "Just say yes." She does.

One by one, our friends, family, co-workers and friends of friends sign up. We, shockingly, recruit sixty-nine walkers — fifty-seven of whom have never walked in the Komen 3-Day. After each Sunday training walk we talk. About walking shoes. Socks. Blister control. Hydration. Attitude. Diet. Fundraising. Breast cancer. We discover each walker shares one of 3 fears. 1) I can't walk that far. That's impossible. 2) I can't raise that much money. That's impossible. 3) I flat out don't have time. That's impossible! I have a life, after all!

As we walk, we talk. "Tell me something special about yourself that I might not know," I ask Jean Marie. "Well, I was the personal chef for Rod Stewart". "What??? How did THAT happen?" I exclaim as my eyebrows shoot up. Marty casually mentions "I travelled to Russia in support of the Refuseniks in the 1970's." "You did what??? You actually flew to Russia? Behind the Iron Curtain?" Teresa volunteers "I slept in a brothel one night, with my husband, after being stranded in a foreign country." It turns out this team has some surprises. But after all — these are YES people!

In June, we begin to increase our miles. First four miles, then five. By October, we are up to twelve and fourteen miles at a time. The week of October 15th, we all share the same experience as we ratchet down our miles one rest weekend. I tell them a friend will ask "How far ya walking this weekend?" I tell them to notice as their mouth forms the words "Not far. It's a short one this weekend. We are only walking ten miles." *WHAT???!!?! Did I really say that???* But yes. We have become walkers. We have turned into THOSE people who think ten miles is a short walk. We ARE those people now.

Along the way, we begin noticing surprising changes with our walkers. I am walking with Kathy, who initially was concerned about her lung disease, at the end of a five-mile walk. As we climb the hill to our starting point, Kathy stops and looks at me. "Sally, this is the first time I have climbed this hill that I didn't need to stop to gasp for air." I tear up. This is helping her! Cathy with the pacemaker reports that her last appointment registered no pacemaker episodes since she began our training. Unbelievable. She will eventually go off her diabetes meds. Walking is what does it. She is stunned. Joan's torn meniscus is doing OK.

In November, our San Diego event finally arrives. Fifty-seven of us fly from Sacramento to San Diego — an explosion of pink at the airport. The walk is long — twenty miles each day. But we are trained. We are ready. It is hard, but not as hard as chemo.

Finally, three days and 59.9 miles later, the finish line is in sight. Most of our team waits thirty yards before the end for the whole team to gather. We march across the finish arm in arm. A huge team. We are jubilant. Exhilarated. Exhausted. Nicole is blubbering with tears streaming down her face. "I can't believe I did this! I am so proud of myself!" Joan is in tears as well, but for a different reason. "I felt Erika with me the whole way. I walked for her, and with her." Kathy averaged fifteen miles each day! Unbelievable.

That night, I open the cards and letters my team has written me. Kathy with the lung disease wrote: "This will be a year to remember, and a year of gratitude for me. No more 'I can't do this'. This is a year of I CAN."

From others, "There are lessons I learned about myself that I will keep with me for the rest of my life. I learned I am pretty powerful when I set my mind to it."

"Being a Hooter has awakened things in me. Enthusiasm, happiness, energy, a purpose, inspiration to think beyond myself. But so much more than just the words."

"This experience has been the highlight of my year. My why is ME. I want/need to be here for my kids and my husband and live a healthy meaningful and productive life. Contributing physically emotionally and financially to the 3-Day and Hooters has been deeply meaningful."

But my best comment was from my husband, Dave. "Sally, more than the money you were able to raise is the fact you have encouraged sixty-nine men and women to start walking, which has lowered each of their own risk for developing breast cancer. That's phenomenal."

And the goal? Did we reach our $100,000? Yes. And more. When the final check cleared, we had raised $147,598! We marched right past our $100,000 goal.

HANDS UP FOR HOOTERS - THE FUTURE

In the five years since, we have gone on to recruit over 300 walkers, and our team has raised $790,000. As we approach the lifetime milestone of raising $1,000,000 towards ending death from breast cancer, I am amazed, humbled and proud of what that little decision to set a higher goal has turned into. I am proud we have raised so much for breast cancer. I am proud that I didn't give up, thinking the goal was unreachable. But mostly I am proud that my choice has impacted so many women and men who have joined our team, by empowering them to learn they are way bigger and more capable than they ever thought. I'm proud that their choice to say yes unveiled their own super powers.

Recently, I ran into Nicole — the one who couldn't walk that far and didn't have time. She told me how profound the experience of being on our team and walking the event was for her, even five years later. "This experience of being a Hooter changed me. I discovered that if I can walk sixty miles, I CAN be a Mom. I CAN work full time. I CAN fundraise even though it is uncomfortable. If I can do THIS, I can do ANYTHING."

For me, that says it all. And now I want to ask YOU a question. Are you willing to take the challenge? Willing to find out you are bigger than you ever thought? That you CAN walk twenty miles a day? That you CAN raise $2,300? And you CAN do something to change the world by helping to end death from breast cancer? You CAN be a Hooter. Join us. Just say YES.

ABOUT SALLY DUNBAR

Sally Dunbar is a forty-year Real Estate Broker with Lyon Real Estate from Fair Oaks, CA, — near Sacramento. Since 2005, she has been a breast cancer survivor and thriver. She has built what has become one of the largest teams in the US walking and fundraising for Susan G. Komen, whose goal is to create a world where women and men are no longer dying of breast cancer. During her first five years as a team captain, she has recruited over 300 women and men to her team, Hands Up For Hooters, and is approaching a team milestone of $1,000,000 raised. They train all year long, walking each Saturday and Sunday morning beginning in May, to be able to walk sixty miles in three days in the San Diego 3-Day Event — held each November.

Sally welcomes new walkers from around the world to join her team, Hands Up for Hooters, as they prepare each year for the San Diego 3-Day event. Those near Sacramento will experience a varied and robust weekend training schedule of walks in and around Sacramento, including special training walks in San Francisco and Lake Tahoe. Those from afar will receive weekly encouraging emails detailing walking form, shoe selection, blister control, walking wear, hydration, fundraising ideas, encouragement, and much much more.

To register for the team, or to donate to Sally's efforts for Susan G. Komen go to www.HandsUpForHooters.com. Simply click on Sally Dunbar to donate.

Email Sally: Sally@SallyDunbar.com

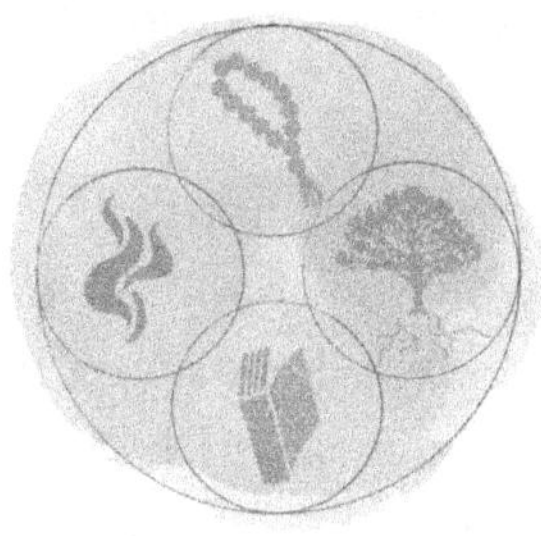

COMING HOME TO MYSELF

Claudia Fernandez-Niedzielski

"What is the dose of abandonment that will equate to obesity?" A question full of power and a message full of meaning. These words reached one of the deepest parts of my being. They were part of a long Facebook post that spoke about the fact that 90% of all illnesses are caused by the emotions and feelings we push down and avoid facing, the ones we choose to hide; the ones we force ourselves to not show or decide not to express for fear of how others will respond or the opinions they may form of who we are.

For a moment I felt completely overtaken by pain and disappointment as I realized this was exactly where I had been for a very long time with the outcome staring right back at me (for just as long) every time I looked in the mirror. "I am the heaviest I have ever been in my life," was what I would think and say, and this had been a reoccurring theme. Every single time I found myself in this familiar yet undesired place again and again, I would acknowledge that I was here and would, once again, look for the latest and greatest "diet secret" to lose the weight. I would begin to exercise and move more, accomplish the goal, feel great about it, and then go back to my old habits and gain all the weight back plus more.

The next moment was full of understanding, love and compassion for myself as I had finally come to the realization of why I was carrying all that extra weight and why my approach was never going to work long term, for no "diet" would ever address the roots and causes of the real issue and the reasons why I kept going back to my old habits: It was extremely difficult to realize that I had fully and completely abandoned myself; I had been using food to cope with all my emotions and feelings. This time I knew and felt it deeply in my bones and soul, for abandonment of myself was something I had never considered.

It was true that I had left so much of this behind on my journey of healing and self-care that started in 2012. That year I had discovered Jack Canfield and his audio series called "Maximum Confidence - 10 Steps to Extreme Self Esteem". He had soon become a daily companion in my car who shared concepts that provided awareness, direction, peace, meaning and understanding of everything I was feeling and going through and granted me with the amazing gift of beginning my self-discovery, self-love, and acceptance.

Looking back, I can remember how desperately I needed to hold on to all of these things as I had finally hit the wall and realized how completely drained and defeated I felt. The weight of the pain, anger, and guilt I had been carrying for so long as a result of the events life had dealt our family was finally crushing me alive. We had moved to California in 2005 and the expectations I had of how our life would be were immediately demolished by the reality I faced. My immediate family was still very far away from me and I longed so much for them to be close. My husband had been diagnosed with Muscular Dystrophy in early 2006, a chronic illness that would continue to progress and one that has no cure. My daughter had been diagnosed with the same illness in 2009. My son had been dealing with the guilt of being the only one who was not ill and trying to do the best he could to cope, and I was holding so tightly to any glimpse of happiness, joy, and hope I could. I had no idea how to deal with all the pain, despair, anger, and loneliness I was experiencing and feeling.

What I did know how to do was pour myself into my outside world in the same way I had done for as long as I can remember. I kept trying to keep it all together. I kept working very hard to make it all work and I kept pushing forward relentlessly to fulfill my personal and financial obligations for our family. I always managed to show up with a sunny, happy, and positive attitude for the world to see while being an absolute controlling, demanding, fearful, and angry bear at home. This cycle only brought more pain, disappointment, and guilt.

From afar, you would have said that I had a very happy, joyful, and successful life. Those close to me, including my dear friends, my dear parents, and myself, knew something totally different. My internal engine was done and the race was over. The five months off I had taken back then to process the effects of all these events and work on my personal healing had taught me that when we keep moving at more than 100 miles an hour on this race we call life, without making the critical pit stops along the way to check on our physical, emotional, mental, and spiritual well-being, we will always, always eventually crash. Many of us are fortunate enough and are granted another opportunity to start all over again. I also know that many others are not as fortunate.

I had taken my opportunity full of gratitude and had finally granted myself permission to engage in therapy, personal and in groups; I engaged in any recreational activity that would nourish my soul and spirit. I was spending hours at our local knitting store, taking regular trips to the ocean and to any lake or body of water I could find, reflecting and writing what I was feeling. Taking a long pause to take care of myself had become my daily routine.

It was now 2013 and I would soon realize the tremendous impact this prolonged "pit stop" had had on my life. I felt lighter, happier, and more confident. Joy had returned once again to my heart. I was showing up more fully. I was willing to be vulnerable in my personal relationships and ask for forgiveness. I was willing to work on my need to control all aspects of my relationships and began to embrace a healthier way to connect with my husband and children. I was willing to work on my need to always have the right approach for what my children were experiencing. I was willing to take more risks and ask for things and opportunities I wanted. I was willing to work on myself and my growth at any level on a daily basis, and I was willing to shed the many layers of protection I was carrying. That year, there were significant improvements in many areas of my personal and professional life, and the results were showing up in how I felt about myself, about my family, and about life. I know that quantifying all of this is extremely difficult, if not impossible, for it all has to do with how each one of us feels about ourselves. The perspective others have of our growth may not match how we truly see ourselves.

Looking back at my professional life, the actions I had taken and what I had accomplished since then, I was also full of amusement and internal pride. I had built a healthy real estate business; I had become a mentor and trusted advisor for new real estate agents who entered the business; I had become a leadership-mentor-liaison within the same company; and the one area we can all quantify, which is money, had also dramatically improved. By the end of 2013 my income was almost four times what I had earned in 2012. It was the first year I had earned more than I had ever earned in any other year in my entire life. Being held back by our state of well-being had now gained a totally different and amplified meaning.

Looking back at my personal development journey, I realized I had accomplished so much with the assistance, support, and guidance of so many. I had become a fearless public speaker advocating for the empowerment of women and the end to the stigma on mental illness; I had become one in a million of Jack Canfield Success Principles certified trainers around the world; I had become a small business consultant and a trusted advisor for women in my community; I had become a #1 Best Selling Author by sharing my own story of mental illness and I had become someone people respected, admired, and looked up to.

I had become more than I ever thought I would in so many areas of my life, and yet, as the words on that long post echoed inside my mind, the painful truth was now crystal clear, demanding my full attention. This time I was completely aware that I needed to grant it absolutely all of my attention, all of me.

The painful truth was that I had become the woman I wanted everyone to see. I had become someone who faithfully followed and pleased others; I had become someone who was afraid to say exactly what I felt; I had become someone who was beginning to question myself as I was confronted with the fact that I knew I was not following my own heart in all areas of my life.

I have no doubt in my mind that spending seven days by the beach with my lifetime friends back in my own country served as the perfect stage for me to truly look into my own eyes and soul. Their message was as clear as the sound of the waves. The level of "abandonment" was evident by the extra weight I was carrying, by the fact that it had been a long time since I had truly taken care of my body, and by knowing deep inside that I had lost the clear idea of what I truly stood for. I had abandoned myself in so many ways. I had abandoned my fun and intimate presence with my children and in my marriage; I had abandoned my own convictions; I had abandoned my own beliefs as a strong woman; I had abandoned my own needs for deep connection, creativity, fun and collaboration within all my environments; I had abandoned my own direction, my own ideas, my own desires; I had abandoned the woman who was seeking so much more meaning out of life as a human being in everything I did. In short, I had abandoned who I was. I had lost myself in the ideas, opinions, way of thinking and dreams of others and it was time to come home. It was time to come home to myself.

There is a great sense of peace, joy, and relief to finally have realized that the most important task I have in my life is to get to know myself again. To acknowledge that I am choosing to appreciate all parts of me and to have the courage to recognize and understand that I am imperfect in many ways, for I am human and so is everybody else. To realize that

I am the one who needs to lead my own life, my own dreams. my own desires. To know that every place I go will be surrounded by others who are on their own journey and that I hold the freedom to keep moving in my own direction. I have recognized that I am not proud of some things I have done, some things I have said, some ways I have acted and behaved. There is so much more internal work to be done as I continue to shed the person I had created and re-discover the Claudia I was born to be and have always been deep inside. Free to fly, free to dream, free to express myself with no fear and free to become absolutely and authentically all of me.

Coming home to my self is not action I took; it is a journey I just began and one that will continue as the discoveries, lessons, challenges and gifts from doing so are still unfolding. I feel unbalanced in many ways and alone in many others. I also feel lighter as the extra weight has begun to disappear. There is a great sense of internal peace as I embrace the huge desire I have to be the most authentic human being I can be for myself, for my family and for the rest of the world to experience, full of love, understanding, and compassion - completely free of judgement of myself and others.

Are you ready to be free? I believe you owe it to yourself to explore your freedom and if you are ready, I will be here to support you every step of the way!

ABOUT CLAUDIA FERNANDEZ-NIEDZIELSKI

From an early age, Claudia became obsessed with positive information and positive quotes after her father introduced her and her brothers to books that would inspire them to always strive to be the best they could be.

Claudia is a survivor and a woman who has learned to thrive despite the many challenges she has faced. She loves her parents, brothers, children, husband and extended family with all her heart and continues to learn how to live a life full of passion and in full harmony with herself. Claudia is currently on a quest to be the best version of herself and fully master that. She has a genuine and profound impact on others as she mentors and leads them to live life to the fullest and shares the tools she has utilized on her own personal search for meaning, self-discovery, understanding and compassion for herself and others and her deep self-worth.

She is a Jack Canfield Success Principles® Certified Trainer and a Barret Value Center® Certified Practitioner and Consultant. She is an entrepreneur, an accomplished speaker and #1 international best-selling author.

To learn more about Claudia Fernandez-Niedzielski, you can visit her website at:

www.ClaudiaImpactsLives.com

To book Claudia as a speaker or work with her, please contact her directly at:

ClaudiaImpactsLives@gmail.com

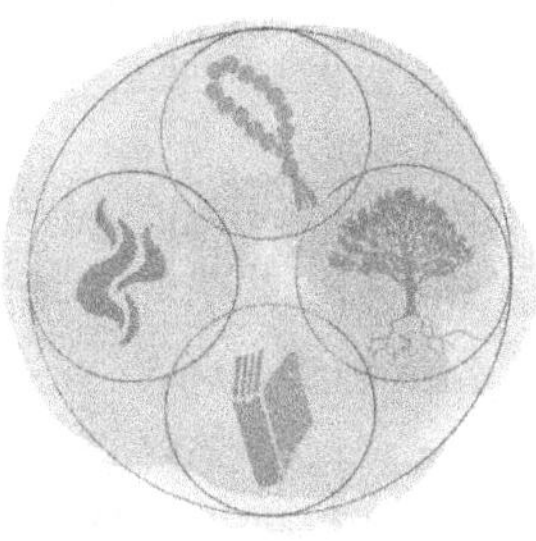

CRESTING THE HILL

Holly Fitch Stevens

It was mid-January 1966, and it was moving day. It feels like it was yesterday. Mom, Dad, my brother, Glenn, and I were moving into our "forever home" in the small town of Weirton, West Virginia! I was eight. Excited to know the constant moving was finally over, I entered our house and dashed up the staircase to my beautiful bedroom. I ran downstairs and stood on the front porch and gazed up and down our street at all the neighbors' houses. Visions of a huge circle of "forever and best friends" filled my brain! I was excited! The years of being constantly uprooted made it very difficult to establish friendships. Working his way up the corporate ladder as an executive, every promotion my dad got required him to move an average of every 1.5 years, making this home my fifth since I was born. But this was going to be it! He was now second in line for promotion to President and CEO. What a glorious day!

Our family was very loving and close, because *we* were all we had. You could describe us as a "Norman Rockwell" type of family. My mom was that perfect executive's wife and mother, my dad a perfect husband and father. I never heard my parents argue. They loved to dance, often right in our living room. Love just embraced our family.

Mom was beautiful and had the biggest heart. She was always upbeat and positive. Before marriage, she sang professionally for big bands, acted on Broadway, taught dancing for Arthur Murray, and was a professional model. My mom's background caused her to remind me to dress right and have perfect posture. She was always gentle and nurturing in her constructive criticism and I always took it that way.

My father was an Army Colonel in World War II where he was awarded the Bronze Star. He planned to make a career out of it, but the year he was to ship out he was home on leave and met my mom. He would always say, "I am not letting this beauty get away, I must have her in my life forever." After a short courtship, they were married. The day after the wedding he left for Germany. He served in Europe for four years. He rejected re-enlistment after counting the days until he had Mom in his arms.

My dad, being aware of the sacrifices all of us made, made every effort to be totally present when he was at home. I got a lot of his attention. He was my hero and rock! I always came first. He would ask me about my day, tell me about his, and do magic tricks for me, even teaching me a few. Then it was time for "Daddy and Mommy talk time" before dinner. This was the time for Dad and Mom to iron out any challenges and talk adult issues in order to make dinnertime conversation pleasant and fun. Dad was my world … he was all of our worlds.

Years went by. I was still struggling to be accepted as I was growing into my teen years. I was now twelve-years-old. I was still very attached to my father. One afternoon, I was taken from class, driven home by a strange man and told by my Mom, "Sweetie, Daddy's gone." I was in shock! Then it sunk in, my Dad was dead. He was only forty-nine, getting ready to turn fifty in a couple of days. How could this be?

When the dust settled, my mother explained to me that my dad went to work that day. He said he wasn't feeling very well but couldn't spare taking time off to rest. He had been working feverishly to get this promotion and it was finally in his sights. So, he went off to work as he normally did. Around 10:00 am that morning his secretary walked into his office and found him slumped over his desk. When the ambulance arrived, he was already gone. He had a massive heart attack. This life as we knew it and planned would never be the same.

My father's wake/funeral took four days. There were so many well-wishers supporting my mom during this time. Then, suddenly, it stopped! Mom was alone now. I started to isolate myself. Mom knew about running the household, but not all the financial responsibilities. My brother quit school to be home with the family. The dream of the "forever home" was gone.

Mom sold everything and moved us all to Pittsburgh.

In order to be accepted by the crowd, I became the class clown, aka the "problem" student. However, the following school years I became the brunt of practical jokes and bullying. I yearned to be accepted. When trying to be myself, I was laughed at and ridiculed so I learned to not be myself--just to fit in. I took on a new persona. Anything not to show my true self. The combination of all the years of being the "new kid" had set the path.

I survived the high school years, just barely. I was so sick of school that I walked out within six months of graduation. My mother was furious. But my mind was made up.

The yearning to find my identity and true self was burning inside me. Seeing all my friends graduating first upset me, but then it seemed to set a fire in me. I decided that if everyone could celebrate their graduation, I would celebrate my "un-graduation". I rented out our apartment complex party room and had the biggest party of all, complete with a popular local band, food, drinks, and even a $5.00 cover charge. (Come on! I had to recoup the money somehow—Mom sure as hell wasn't going to pay for it!)

Now I was that "lone wolf" doing things my way. After summer, I decided I wanted to be in college. Having never taken the first college entrance exam (not to mention I had no high school diploma), how was I going to do this? Let's just say the times were prime for my situation. Vocational schools were grabbing up students from colleges because they were paid higher than those who graduated college. Perfect timing for me to execute my plan. I went into a local theatre college with a wad of cash and slapped it down on the desk and proceeded to "negotiate" my way into school. The offer was this: I pay them for allowing me to audit a history class I needed for my high school diploma while taking my other college classes. To my surprise they agreed. I was now a college student with a theatre major.

However, I still lacked a key element to be a success in theatre—confidence. I watched the upper classmen work their magic on the stage. I thought, "I am never going to be worthy or good enough to do that."

After my first year in theatre and deciding I wasn't ever going to measure up, my mother informed me that I had inherited money to attend any school I wished to attend. So, I decided to attend a fashion marketing school in, guess where? Switzerland! I stayed until the money ran out, about eighteen months later. At home, I went to work as a waitress and attended a local college just because "everyone else was" but never got a degree.

So here I was, unknowingly armed with skills I never knew existed—determination and a "never quit" attitude. I saw myself as a quitter without determination. I was now twenty-two and I knew I didn't want to wait tables or bartend the rest of my life. I had heard from a friend of mine that the largest corporate travel agency in Pittsburgh was hiring. I had no experience, but I also had nothing to lose. I marched myself into the interview, with no resumé, just an application. I interviewed with Bonnie, the founder and CEO. The interview went well; however, Eastern Airlines had just gone out of business and Bonnie had to hire those people first.

I left disappointed but not defeated. She didn't say "never," just "not now." I wanted that position more than ever. For almost an entire year, every weekday, before I clocked in at my waitress job, I called Bonnie and asked, "Are you ready for me yet?" She never said no, just "not yet". I figured, what the hell, if she really wanted me to stop calling, she'd tell me, right? Then one day as I came into work, my boss said I had someone named Bonnie on the phone. "OK, are you ready to come to work?" Two weeks later I was a travel agent!

After a few years, the urge to move on was seeping in. I loved the job. But I still felt I needed something more. Once again, I seized a so-called opportunity--the Pittsburgh weather. Yep, one morning the snow was a foot deep and still coming down. I dressed and jumped on the trolley and headed to work. I was wearing a beautiful winter white outfit. As I entered work and hung up my beautiful coat, to my horror, the back of it was covered in mud and slush from me kicking it up as I walked. I'd had it with this weather. I marched into Bonnie's office and said, "I appreciate everything you have done for me, but I need to move on. So, however long it takes you to replace me, I am giving you my notice." She was gracious about it. A month later, I was packing up my things and heading, well, somewhere warmer.

I had no clue where I was going to end up. It was scary. I had limited funds and time was running out for my "declared" departure date. Without a job or place to live, a friend and I packed my things and headed to Myrtle Beach, SC. I knew it had seasons, without the snow. After a twenty-eight-hour drive with a neurotic cat and pulling a U-Haul, we arrived in Myrtle Beach. I checked into a motel and my friend, JT, dropped off the trailer and hauled ass. He didn't look back either! The next day I got a job in a popular night club where I met my future first husband during my first night on the job.

Still searching for what I really wanted, I got married despite the obvious red flags while we were dating. Our first date ended with me bailing him out of jail because he beat up a guy for asking me to dance. Years later our marriage ended abruptly when he gave me a gash across my brow that required a large amount of stitches. I had him arrested and never looked back.

Again, I was broke and alone, but this ignited that fire in me like never before. I started to reclaim my life! I realized that it actually took courage to do everything I had done in the past. I was ready to turn it around. I started by volunteering for a domestic violence center. I landed a senior director position at a local hospital. I started to really take care of *me*—body and mind. I became super-fit and healthy. I had taken a course in Dale Carnegie years before, so I started applying those lessons I learned. I grabbed every book on personal development that I could.

I decided to re-evaluate where I was in my life. I embraced the fact that I was worthy of anything I wanted. One day I started to write everything I wanted in my life—not the materialistic things, but the "feeling" type things that were going to feed into my joy. I also made this a list of values. Ones that spoke to the person I truly wanted to be. As a start, I wanted to finally be my true self. Next is what I wanted in relationships with others and how I wanted to *be* with others. My list included things such as, "I am happy enjoying being healthy and fit. I love my nights that I stay home and enjoy a good book and a glass of wine." And many others. However, my values were powerful and really switched the course of my life.

I want and deserve to be treated with respect as I desire to be with someone whom I respect. I want and deserve relationships with others that are as interested in my desires and dreams as I am in theirs'. I am worth more than a dinner and a few drinks. I am worthy and deserve to be heard as I wish to hear about others. And I let the men in my life know of my "ground rules" anytime anyone would ask me for a date. A typical conversation with a new potential date went as follows: "I appreciate your invitation. However, before we go any further, I feel it only fair to be up front with you to give you an opportunity to decide what you want to do. I love myself and my life just as it is. I don't need someone in my life to make me happy, I am already happy. However, that's not all. If you are ok with that, understand that I am not looking for an intimate relationship and I am happy in my own skin. I am certainly worth more than a night out. My worth comes from within, meaning it takes time to build a connection that may go further. Oh, and another thing, since we are just dating, you too can see whoever you want. We have no commitment to each other. However, if you think that taking me out for a night gives you the right to come up for that "proverbial" nightcap, save your money. It's not going to happen. Oh, and make sure you call ahead to make a date, because last minute doesn't work for me." Now you may say that that was arrogant, but, on the contrary, it was just standing on my values and looking for mutual respect. Not only did it get me some amazing dates, it opened the door for me to find the love of my life, my husband, Jim.

Jim and I had a beautiful courtship and wedding. Jim's two children, Jamey and Natalie, were in our wedding. Life was grand. Two years later Jim and I had our son, Zac. It was wonderful. Then, as in many marriages, life began to get in the way. Jim's law practice was thriving but also becoming more and more demanding. Early in our relationship I was struck down by an illness that took me out of the normal workplace, so I started to build a business from home. I was also busy raising our son. I still stayed busy all day.

Then, life got in the way of our relationship with each other. Jim became distant and I was left alone at home with our son. Though we had a live-in, I was so very lonely. When Jim was home it was usually late, and he would retreat to his study. We really had no clue what went wrong, but we knew it wasn't right.

With some coercing, I got Jim to agree to some time off for a family vacation. After a wonderful family vacation with Zac, I woke up in the middle of the night in excruciating pain. I was rushed to the hospital and was told I was having a heart attack. Though they wanted to operate immediately to give me a quintuple by-pass, an abscess from a previous injury prevented immediate surgery.

I was hospitalized to treat the infection pending surgery. That gave me an entire week to reflect on my life. I thought of the list many years ago before I met my husband. That list that included my values and purpose. Though I didn't have it with me, I started to tap into those things that meant so much to me, my deep-rooted core values. Was I still living a life that was feeding into *my* JOY? I knew that if I wanted change, I had to change. So, I renegotiated with *me*. I made a promise to live my purpose and let others know how important it is to live joyfully and authentically. I needed to let go of any resentment or self-pity or doubt and leave the rest to faith, hoping that by me making a switch, that Jim would eventually come around.

I woke up the next day, knowing the past was a gift given to me. I woke up to my life! When I arrived home, I continued with my journaling and working toward—not chasing love—but just "being" love. They say that heart patients have even stronger heart to brain connection. Even though we all have intuition, it seems to truly intensify after such trauma. As time went on, I continued to embrace how precious our life is truly. Slowly, day by day, week by week, Jim and I rebuilt our love. We learned to let go of the past issues and looked forward to what we could have in the future. The only part of our past we tapped into was the part that served us. The reasons we fell in love in the first place. Getting rid of grudges and resentment is powerful. It truly can rebuild a foundation twice as strong as the original. And that is what we have created. By looking to ourselves, taking full responsibility, not blame (ourselves or the other) we are stronger than ever.

I am now truly living a happy, healthy life of true joy. My core values? I refuse to allow anything try to steal my joy! I listen to my heart and because of this, it is my mission in my life to show and share with others how to live a life that is truly joyful and authentic.

ABOUT HOLLY FITCH STEVENS

J Holly Fitch Stevens is an Author, Board certified NLP Practitioner and Hypnotherapist, Human Potential Coach, and a Certified Trainer for Jack Canfield Success Principles. She is an inspirational speaker and trainer. She also is a certified Usui Reiki Master. She has spent the last ten years studying the principles of emotional intelligence (EQ) and has been coaching in that market for several years. She works with individuals and small groups, as well as organizing small retreats. She is on a mission to teach people how to live their lives with true joy and purpose. Holly loves to travel and is an advocate in supporting local charities wherever she goes. She is a supporter of Operation Underground Railroad (O.U.R.) that aids in the rescue of victims of human trafficking. She is also a mother of three and grandmother of five. For more info go to www.HollyFitchStevens.com

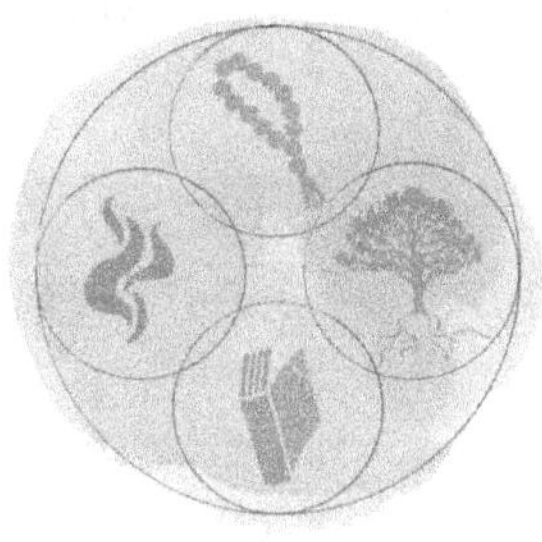

CATAPULT OR CONTAIN? THE CHOICE IS YOURS

Angela Germano

I wouldn't call it a fear, I just didn't think I'd live past thirty. My mom barely made it. I was nine when my mom started fighting cancer and its side-effects for five agonizing years. Her mom had breast cancer and believe it or not, her grandfather had cancer too. So we are at a high risk of battling cancer on my maternal side—who knew if I'd make it? My mom lost, and so did I. During that time, I was exposed to a lot a child shouldn't be—which now, as an adult, it seems that such dysfunction, abandonment, abuse, and manipulation have become our societal norm these days. And that is NOT an excuse ... it is what this story, my story of overcoming fear, is about.

I left my family trauma behind. I know what you are thinking: What? How? People struggle their whole lives to escape toxic family ties. At fourteen I realized that blood doesn't make you family, and you can't rely on someone just because you are related. Actions count. So, I made a conscious choice and continuously, to this day and forward, still work arduously to rise above any ties that try to pull me down. It's not easy because my heart is so big, but I keep my mind strong and focus on what my love can nurture, and what it can't. The power is in my choice.

For example, I made the choice to put myself through private college—earning scholarships, grants, taking out loans and working multiple jobs throughout my collegiate career to earn my Master's in Public and Corporate Communication from Monmouth University Magna Cum Laude.

I loved working in the ever-changing industry, offering instrumental value to all my colleagues and clients. I was in Public Relations, Advertising, Marketing, Event Planning, Education and Consulting in the Technology, Environment and Ad Specialty industries. Thoroughly enjoying life and every healthy opportunity that came my way. I enjoyed exercising, exploring, yoga, meditation, reflecting, crafting, photography, and loved meeting people—and I still do! I was making the most of my precious time here on this beautiful Earth.

I was a positive force to be reckoned with—no one seemed to be able to keep up with my friendly, ambitious nature, living life to its fullest. You would think that would be good, right? Interestingly enough, it wasn't.

I made it past thirty and I remember thinking, "Like, whoa. This has to be a matter of time or this is for a real *amazing* reason."

My husband and I revisited the having children conversation. I had no interest at first. Heck, I never even wanted to get married, let alone have a child. I didn't want to have a child just to die on them, leaving them to figure out the harsh realities of life on their own, not being there for them. From what I saw, even adults that didn't have life threatening illnesses couldn't handle being an adult, like keeping a job, or staying sober—- let alone keeping up with marital or family obligations. I had people in my family that just left their children, left their jobs, left their homes with seemingly not a care. I always thought, if anything, I would adopt and be completely independent. I could be that saving grace for a child that lost a parent, like I lost mine. I didn't want a child to have a parent who could let them down in any way, like I had seen countless times in my childhood. I took the idea of being a parent extremely seriously.

After a while though, I realized I was afraid and I shouldn't let that get in the way of living life to the fullest. I don't know how I got to this revelation. Maybe it was more about an appreciation for my soul, since I made it past thirty, I could risk losing a bit of control. Maybe I believed that the universe would take care of me. Maybe, it was so I could make more little loves like myself. However I got to this point, it was a compilation of empowering, deep, *amazing* thoughts for sure.

Luckily, I had some time to prepare for what may be. At this point, I was a full-time Advertising Executive in the city and taught three college courses in the evenings and two in the morning (before work) to high school students. I often travelled up and down the coast and/or across country monthly running events for my company. And as I thought about becoming a mom, as I thought about my strengths, as I thought about my weaknesses—I knew I couldn't do it in my current profession. Even if I cut back on the travel, or teaching college, I'd be cutting back on me, who I was, on what I was most proud of in this world. I always give my 110% to every life venture, and so I knew I had to come up with something else.

I continued to reflect, digging deep and analyzing myself as if a product in a marketplace that had changed. I needed to find a new use for me, a way to stay true to who I was and had worked so arduously to be. I kept extending my lens to seek opportunities for my strengths that complemented the potential new role of a mom. Months passed, a myriad of conversations occurred both inside my head and out with students, colleagues, and mentors. I remember chatting with my college students and them sharing what a difference I was making in their lives. Some said they wished they had met me sooner in life, a few said they needed a teacher like me when they were in middle school—they wouldn't have wasted so much time going down the wrong paths. This made me feel so good and I started remembering how my teachers were my saving grace through my horrific childhood, how they pretty much raised me and, through sharing and relating to my college students, I then realized my new career path.

I could be a middle school teacher. I could help children get through some of the most challenging times. I could be their saving grace, I could be their lifeline.

I know what you may be thinking, "Um, hello, you are an advertising, marketing guru. What do you know about teaching kids?" Well, perhaps at that point, nothing. But my strengths are analyzing an audience, seeking out opportunities, developing and bringing products and services to market and incentivizing buy-in from multiple stakeholders. I'm a fast learner, people-loving, growth-oriented, optimistic powerhouse that clients love and seek out to learn from for the long-term. And I am always up for helping people believe in the best versions of themselves. Who else needs that more than our coming- of- age middle schoolers?

I called on one of my most brilliant, best college girlfriends, who knows me inside and out, and is a hiring administrator in her huge inner city New Jersey district. I pitched the idea to her. She explained how it would be a huge pay cut, but mostly an ideal career path for moms with the hours, healthcare perks, tuition reimbursement and formalized pay scales. "It is hard to get into a school, but if anyone can do it, you can. Kids would be lucky to have your positivity around them. You are a natural teacher."

So, I decided I would go back to school to become a teacher. On top of my dual careers of advertising and teaching college in the Philadelphia area, (even though I lived in central New Jersey,), I now was taking education classes and applying for teacher positions in middle and southern New Jersey, from Newark to Little Egg Harbor. After months of soul searching for a career I could handle while potentially navigating motherhood, I stayed focused to open a new path.

My days went from 4am to 10pm nonstop, filling every nook and cranny with one of my passions. My commitment paid off when I landed my first long term substitute position. I was celebrating, but there was a flipside—I had to leave my advertising company and the paycheck that came along with it. I took the risk, adjusted my lens once again to look out in a different way. People matter the most and I was sad to leave my clients behind, but why did I have to? Because that was the norm? I am nothing like the norm, why start now? I opened my own marketing consulting company so I could still help my clients. I continued being there for them, supplemented my substitute teaching pay, and forged ahead toward earning that teacher certification so I could be the best mom ever, if it was meant to be!

By the middle of the school year, a new school scooped me up into a full-time teaching position, and within months I officially had my Teacher Certification K-8 with Language Arts Content Specialization. I had proven and secured myself a new career path that would allow me the time to take on motherhood.

I treated this new career with the same passion and commitment as I did my marketing one. I will never forget, the next year at Panera Bread with my husband, I received a call from an American Legion representative who wanted me to accept a nomination for Educator of the Year. At first I thought it was some kind of mistake, I was a non-tenured teacher and I didn't even have my own classroom. But he assured me that I was being nominated., "Word spread of this new teacher, who was teaching in an 'out of the box' fashion in the classroom, involved in a slew of school activities from leading the National Junior Honor Society to directing the school play, but also making a huge impact in our community building gardens, being in awareness parades, getting young kids involved in sending letters and care packages to soldiers abroad, helping out at the Ronald McDonald House, fundraising to save animals, helping to find cures to illnesses like American Cancer Society, and the list goes on. The kids and their parents really like you." I accepted and went on to win this prestigious award at the town level, advanced to the district and county level. That June I was in their parade, waving at children, delivering a speech on Wildwood's Convention Hall stage as I was awarded the title of American Legion New Jersey Educator of the Year. I solidified my value in this new career path.

My stage was set for the next act, and who knew?! This ambitious survivor was meant to be a mom! Our families welcomed the addition, however it was greeted with a lot of judgement too.

Now, up to this point, I had never been in such a vulnerable state as an adult. My college had prepared me to seek out confidence and paths. But now, I had another life depending on me. Surprised I made it through the whole child birth process (secretly thinking that giving of life was meant to be my end) and the people who were supposed to know the most about being a parent, second guessed my every move and put me down before I could even make a move. For a long while, I let it get to me.

"A stay at home mom?"

"Someone else raise my child?"

"You never know what daycares do."

"You can't trust people."

Snowballing into,

"You shouldn't do that."

"You need to hit your kids."

"You don't yell enough."

"They need more discipline."

"Can't you control them?"

These "experienced" voices were flooding my headspace and I was drowning.

I needed a lifeline, I thought I was doing a really good job being a mom. I was being the mom I remembered my mom being. Patient, kind, understanding, compassionate, fun, cuddly, always smiling, energetic and comforting. Yes, they were in daycare—*with women whom I talked to, admired and often asked for advice*. Yes, I worked during the day—*with seasoned educational professionals who have the latest research on childhood development at their fingertips*. Yes, I had another job—*bringing in money for my family*.

As my college students were my lifeline before, my middle schoolers and their parents are now. When I sit in guidance meetings with parents,

I listen as a human that has so much to learn and want to make the world better for everyone. I listen for where a parent's frustration is coming from. I ask questions and I learn from them. As students enter school, I see the worry on their faces. I see the smile my interaction brings. I see the comfort they feel with me. I have 100+ students that feel fortunate to have me as their teacher every day, during the good, the bad and the ugly—they know I sincerely care and want the best for them. I share my heart with them, tell them when I think I messed up in my motherhood and they perk me back up with their honest thoughts. These kids are preparing me for what is to come, giving me practice—they are my motherhood teachers.

And then I realized this new composition. I readjusted my lens.

I am an independent mom, self-reliant, resourceful and self-aware enough to reinvent myself to become this mom who leads the pack with my optimistic well-roundedness and evidence-based parenting methodologies. Am I perfect to the world? Yes, because my world is my children.

I know it is not the same for everyone.

I didn't think I'd live past thirty.

Maybe it was a fear.

Fear of not living, like my mom.

Fear of not knowing how to be a mom.

Fear is just a perception.

Not a reality.

We have the power to give it value, or not.

How will you value it? Catapult you or contain you?

I chose to rise above it, and I know you can too.

ABOUT ANGELA GERMANO

#1 Best-selling International Author, Angela Germano, was recently featured in The Jersey Storytellers Project, part of The USA Today Network, featuring a live night of storytelling. She is also a guest on podcasts such as Aggressive Optimism with Jenna Edwards.

Angela is a middle school teacher by day, college professor at night, and raising her two children the best she can with her supportive husband. She's been an award-winning debater, writer, actress, constitutional law student, world traveler, drive-time radio personality, but always a teacher and a coach devoted to positively impacting people's lives so they can achieve their dreams.

Angela has served on the Monmouth University Board of Directors and Chair of the Nominating Committee. She is involved with multiple charities such as Ronald McDonald House, American Cancer Society, and UNICEF. She is noted as having a true teaching talent; putting students at ease, increasing their confidence and allowing them to learn for the long term. She focuses on embracing teaching as an opportunity to inspire leadership, giving voice and choice to students through knowledge, exemplars, and opportunity.

Angela is also an Inspirational Speaker highlighting the specific topics of overcoming adversity, building confidence and leadership as well as organizes Selfie Celebrations where children practice positive self-worth activities such as yoga, meditation, positive affirmations, goal setting, and vision boards. To learn more, you can reach Angela Germano at angelagermanopositivity@gmail.com

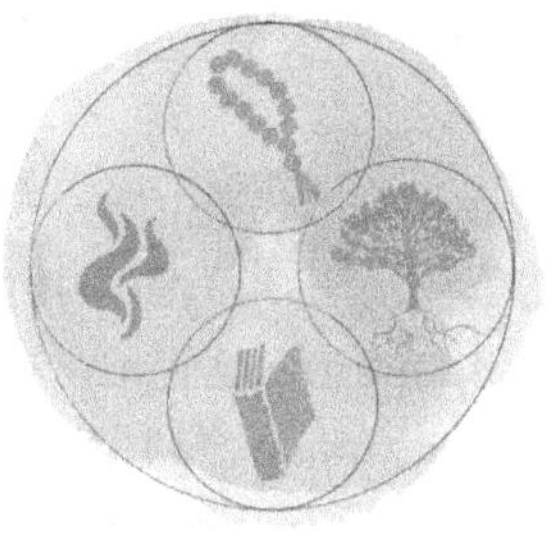

FRESH OUTTA PLANS™: WHEN NOTHING IN YOUR BAG OF TRICKS WORKS

Jeanie Griffin

No one escapes. Somewhere between birth and death, everyone comes up against something they can do absolutely nothing about. So it was with me. Nothing in my "bag of tricks" worked. My plans did not work anymore. I was weary. I was defeated, on my knees, unable to control an outcome, overwhelmed, and empty. Finally, I arrived at a place every human does just before surrender. I was FRESH OUTTA PLANS™.

As a kid, I knew my power was limited by the dictates of my parents, but I had no real concept of the powerlessness of being FRESH OUTTA PLANS™ until, at the age of fifteen, I stood over my father's dead body.

I was in Spanish class my sophomore year of high school when the school secretary called me to bring my books and go to the office. She was visibly upset as we walked toward the office. "Did anything happen to Mary?" I asked. My sister, Mary, had just left for her first year at the University of Texas. "No," Maxine said softly. "Well, then my father is dead," I whispered. She looked at me startled and softly said, "Yes."

I always knew I would be called out of class and told my father was dead, and here it was. Don't know how I knew. I just knew.

Two church members then took me to the school where my mother taught second grade so we could tell her. *We* did not tell her. *I* told her.

I was led to the teacher's lounge. My mother came in and looked at me with a questioning stare. "Momma, Daddy is dead," I announced. She then looked at the two adults standing in the back of the room and they confirmed it. It took thirty years and a lot of therapy for me to realize it was not the job of a fifteen-year-old girl to tell her mother that her husband was dead. It was the mother's job to tell the fifteen-year-old girl that her father was dead. But from the age of five I had told myself I needed to help lighten my mother's depression and my father's alcoholic sadness, so this event was no different.

Three days later we had a funeral. I stood looking at my dead father's body lying peacefully in the casket and realized I had never before seen a dead person. Where did he go? He looked like was going to wake up. Did the life I witnessed in him just stop? What is a personality? Do we simply die when our organs stop working? Is there a heaven? Did he go there? Do people wear clothes in heaven? Is he with God? Is there a real God? Why did he have to leave our family when I was thirteen? Why did he now die two years later? Why is God so unfair? Is his alcoholic life finally peaceful? I listened to the adults say he was in a better place and I accepted that idea, but the pain of his death would last thirty more years.

I had no idea that my father's death, freeze-framed into my memory, would be my first deep spiritual experience … the beginning of a long period of questions, wrestling and "figuring out" God, Higher Power, Spirit, Creator, or whatever IT is called. My father was one of my first spirit guides or angels. He is still with me.

I wish I could tell you that was the only time in my life my plans no longer worked but that has not been my experience. My life of powerlessness and surrender has resembled that Whack-a-Mole game found in pizza places. Just when I whack the mallet to push down one unexpected event, another one pops up!

The summer before I was twenty-one, my maternal grandmother died at age eighty-nine. During the funeral I noticed how tired and weary my Mom looked. Quietly, my mother said to me, "You know, you're never old enough to lose your mother." Another freeze-framed moment for me. I thought, "Oh my gosh! We are burying HER mother, not MY grandmother." Then immediately on the heels of that thought came, "What on earth would I do if my mother died?" Nine months later my mother was dead from kidney cancer. I was powerless to stop it. Again, I faced a situation I could do nothing about. With my father's death I rode on the coattails of my mother's faith. This time I was alone, and her death brought on my second spiritual crisis. I railed at the heavens and at God. At twenty-one I was now an orphan.

During the last time I was with my mother I watched as her faith never wavered. I heard her speak about the white light, a tunnel, and how beautiful things were. She spoke to her mother who had come to get her. I knew it was true and she seemed so at peace, but I selfishly wanted her to stay. When the end came, I agreed with her. You are NEVER old enough to lose your mother.

At my mother's memorial service our minister told me my mother's death was God's will. Fury welled up in me. I told him he could take his God and shove it. I did not speak to this Czar of the Heavens for ten years. Spontaneously, at the birth of my daughter I said a prayer of gratitude for a healthy baby girl. On the heels of that prayer my resentment flared. "I forgot. I am not speaking to you, God. Where is my mother to see this baby girl?"

These two deaths (or initiations) I refer to as spiritual sandpaper. They rubbed me and irritated me until I was smooth enough to see the spiritual gift each parent gave me. My father disliked organized religion, so he introduced me to the alluring and mysterious ways of Mother Nature, The Mystery. My mother introduced me to a Community within a church. Years later I would realize the spiritual gift my father gave me was the gift of Mystery and the spiritual gift my mother gave me was the gift of Community. Both gifts have become the foundation of my work with others.

I had been raised in a church community and loved the fellowship.

I never felt a spiritual connection there so when confronted with why bad things happen to good people, I became angry. I hated God and all the entire religious community. I became self-reliant and made the decision I would never need anyone else again and I would leave "him or her" before they left me. Out of my experiences, I held beliefs and made decisions that would later put me in a position to be hurt. Such beliefs went something like this: Everyone I love leaves me. I can't trust anyone. Rely only on yourself. Don't let anyone close. Religion is useless. I am invisible. God doesn't listen.

I have been FRESH OUTTA PLANS™ with two divorces, job changes, financial crises, alcoholism, single parenting, a near death experience in a car wreck, metastatic breast cancer, the murder of a friend's child, and Covid 19—to name a few. Out of deep pain I was led to the scary gift of surrender where I was finally willing to admit my way was not working. Powerlessness scared me until I realized it was in the surrendering of self-reliance that I gained power. I had to admit I did not have all the answers, especially as to why bad things happen to good people. What a paradox: I had to surrender to win.

I set aside everything I thought I knew and became willing to do something differently. In doing so, I realized my entire life was built on self-reliance. What a double-edged sword. Forced solutions left me lonely and weary. I begrudgingly began carving out a path to a Higher Power/God of my understanding that I call The Mystery. I took every question and every hate-filled thought directly to this thing called God. I wanted the faith I saw in others but could not quite get there. In time I got answers. A connection began to grow into the POWER I depend on today. At the same time, I found a fellowship that allowed me to explore spirituality and supported me during the process.

In retrospect, I see that when something "good" happened in my life, I relished the feelings and memories, but when something "bad" happened I allowed negative emotions to sweep me around like a tumbleweed in the wind. One day I was too weary to fight anymore. A thought crossed my mind. What if when the wind hit me, I allowed it to blow through me as I observed it? What if I learned from it and watched myself grow and change instead of resisting the wind or having to wade through the event in hindsight? I knew I could not control externals, but what if I let the wind go through me? That opportunity came for me when I took my daughter to college 3000 miles away from home.

As I drove away from her dorm, I was sobbing so hard I could hardly see to drive. This child was my heart. We were a team. The pain was so great I could hardly breathe. I finally surrendered to the pain and fear. I pulled over and sobbed to the bottom of my pain. It was then I had an epiphany. I was having an appropriate feeling at the time of the event! I did not need to drink over it, eat over it, shop over it or anything. I did not act out over it, so I did not have to make amends to anyone for my behavior and I did not need to go into therapy for thirty years to discover how I was feeling the day I took my daughter to college! I had stayed in the present. I allowed the pain, the sights and sounds and other details of the event, to move through me all the while using tools of spiritual presence and a community of others until I could breathe again. I had felt the depths of fear and faced it. More of me had awakened. More of me had changed. Funny how I felt more relaxed in my body. I had not died of pain; I just thought I would. I was still standing. I had gone from FRESH OUTTA PLANS™ to FREEDOM. This was a new experience for me, and the exhilaration was empowering. I had not allowed my emotions or negative thinking to blow me around like a tumbleweed. I stood grounded in the Truth that I was. Life passed through me, changed me, and I witnessed the whole thing. I saw a strong woman emerge and I liked her. I was the sky. The feelings were merely clouds.

Do you feel overly self-reliant, discontent, discouraged, struggling, powerless, unfulfilled? Don't do life like I did. My self-reliance and self-sufficiency almost killed me. The turmoil inside me showed outwardly as anger, impatience, and discontentment. I was an expert at running into walls and forcing MY PLANS to work! It took me a long time to finally stop forcing solutions, but it doesn't have to take you as long as it did me. I spent much of my life trying to avoid pain and trying to figure out life and who I was. I wasted precious time. The truth is there is no one true self. We are not static. Life is not static. We change. We grow. We become more awake if we live in the present. If we live in the past, we live in regret. If we live in the future, we live in fear. But if we live in the present, we can see how dynamic, how strong, and how vibrant we are. Our timeless self is forever.

I can show you a different path. I work with people who feel powerless, discontented, and unfulfilled. I call that Fresh Outta Plans™. With joy and playfulness, I connect clients to their own Timeless Self within, their own Higher Power (The Mystery) and a Supportive Community (Mystery with Skin On) so they are empowered to live a life of joy, peace, and authenticity no matter what is happening around them. Humor becomes the vehicle to lighten the fear. I can help so that your journey is not such a struggle. You will find the Universe becomes a friendlier place and during the process a community will rise to support you.

If you are facing a challenge and feel like you still have a plan that will work, then use it. Good luck.

But, if you are feeling powerless, facing into the wind, climbing a high mountain, forcing solutions, on your knees, feel out of control and weary or have no solid footing, I call you to surrender and admit your way is not working. STOP, FACE THE FEAR, GO WITHIN. TAKE ACTION, but do not do it alone. Join my program, FRESH OUTTA PLANS™. Your life will change when you discover your essence, a spiritual path and a community that can support you on your journey. On this path you will awaken to the authentic Light you are. You will shine that light to others and finally live in peace. Come rise with me. It is possible.

ABOUT JEANIE GRIFFIN

Jeanie Griffin is trained in both traditional psychotherapy and in ancient healing practices as a shamanic practitioner. She is a therapist, coach, speaker, retreat leader, best-selling author, funny lady, grandmother of three, slave to two cats, resident of Los Angeles, and formerly, a superwoman who could leap tall buildings in a single bound while keeping Saturn on its axis. Today, she lives a happy, authentic life.

Ms. Griffin holds a Doctor of Divinity, and a MA in Mental Health and Addiction Counseling in California and Texas. She is a trained shamanic practitioner, intuitive healer, and spiritual guide.

She has worked with over 3,000 clients, families, and businesses. For over thirty years, individuals, celebrity clients and their families, convention goers, and businesses have applauded her as a powerful healer.

Ms. Griffin works with clients live and online in the following ways: speaking engagements, individual or group coaching, multi-family workshops, intuitive readings and healings, spiritual and transformational online courses, and in-person VIP retreats.

You Can Reach Jeanie Griffin at:

Websites: https://jeaniegriffin.com or freshouttaplans.com
Email: info@jeaniegriffin.com or info@freshouttaplans.com

Social Media:
https://www.facebook.com/jeaniegriffin
https://www.instagram.com/jeaniegriffinla/
https://www.instagram.com/freshouttaplans/

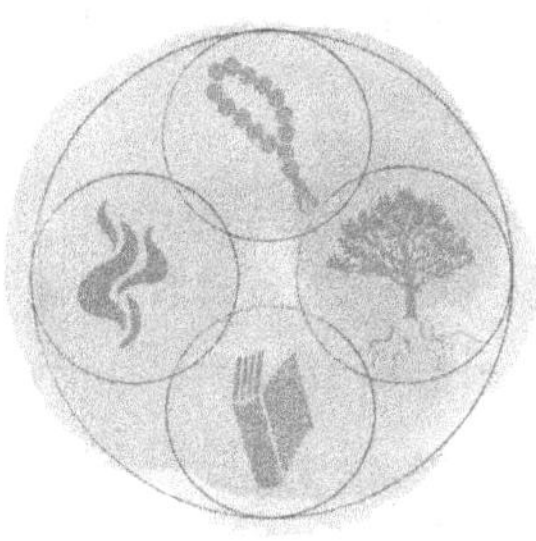

REPAIRER OF THE BREACH

Dr. Donna Marie Hunter

The release of dreams not realized, although slow and painful, has come over time. As a young woman I vowed not to have children, having grown up with six siblings, a mother on welfare, and a home with no food. My desire was to never be without, nor have children that may have to go without. "Without" meant more than just food and basic necessity. It meant a mother who was wounded emotionally and unable to be all that seven hungry, rambunctious, strong-willed children needed. I was the middle-born of seven and especially wanted to make my presence known.

I was twelve when my dad physically left us, and thirteen when my mom seemed to emotionally leave us. She was managing life the best way she knew how. At the time, I perceived that I was fine without either. I became the parentified child who would take up the responsibilities in the absence of parents. Becoming a parent was not in the forefront of my mind as I had worked to take care of three younger siblings and helped an older sibling pay for college, as well as paid the rent on our apartment/townhome we all shared when mom left.

Getting married was never a consideration as I thought about life. Nonetheless, I married Jeff and was content to not have children for almost four years. When we found ourselves pregnant, we were excited and Jeremey was a perfect child. Jeff's parents thought the sun and moon rose with Jeremey. He was a wonderful baby and fit nicely without very much effort. I found myself wanting to be home and be his momma, feelings I didn't know I'd have but welcomed freely.

Alexanda (Allie), our daughter, was not a surprise but an intentional blessing and would complete my new master plan. My motto became, "Hunter, party of four and no more." We would be the perfect family that I never knew I wanted. Grateful for this new-found happiness in motherhood, I was planning my children's future with no thought of my own. Around twelve months I began to notice something was wrong with Allie. She was no longer engaging, playing, and there was very little eye contact. I returned to the doctor with more questions and grave concerns about my baby. Finally, we learned the diagnosis was Autism. I did not have a reaction at the time, I continued caring for my children and hoping that all that lay dormant in Allie would eventually surface. I was unaware of all the therapies and early interventions that were available, and those that I knew of that might help were financially out of reach.

We were struggling in every area of life: financially, emotionally, and socially , all while doing everything we could for Allie, and she actually seemed to be getting worse. The tantrums were lasting for upwards of two hours, toilet training was nonexistent, and there was no verbal communication.

My love for my family called for an ALL IN mentality. There was no regret, I didn't have time to think about going back my original plan, my non-family plan. I chose to be an at-home mom because I was so in love with my children, I could not bear the thought of not being there when they had any of their "firsts". I wanted to be there for every moment and when the season was over, no regrets. The cry of my heart was to be with them, to be present and give them every ounce of love that I could possibly give. It was not clear to me at the time why I so desperately needed to be with my children. Why couldn't I leave them with grandpa and go to work? Did it have something to do with my parents? Was I loving my children the way I wanted to be loved? Perhaps I'd equated my staying home with them to heal my feelings of abandonment? Although not fully conscious of the breach in my soul, it was slowly loving myself to wholeness.

That old adage that we have children to fulfill our deep-seated desires, dreams, and unmet needs could not be true for me if I never wanted to be a parent, right? The reality we faced at every doctor's appointment was enough to dash anyone's dreams. In my case, each developmental milestone that went unmet was the gradual tearing away of a dream, my new master plan. I held my breath year after year, doctor after doctor, appointment after appointment, and each time the report was gravely dismal. At age five, the doctor told us that it was highly unlikely Allie would develop expressive language, or she would have been talking by then. Age eight, still nothing. She turned twelve, and I was hoping against hope that a miracle cure would zap her out of her autistic state, but nothing. I began to loathe birthdays. Sweet sixteen did not have a good taste. Age eighteen was the height of my low; there would be no prom dress, dance or party, no celebration, no graduation. All of the dreams that I did not know I had for my daughter went unfulfilled, and I sealed the breach with a busy life and career. Allie's godmother and my girlfriends made sure we celebrated Allie's birthday. For years I could not entertain the phrase "Happy Birthday!" I was not happy and did not welcome the solemn reality. I believed and perceived I'd made peace with the fact that she was nonverbal and continued to have highly involved social emotional deficits and physical challenges, including toilet training.

I received a beautiful box filled with a dozen white lilies. My family all stood by curiously as I read the card. It was from Ryan Nicole, my girlfriend LaDonna's eldest, whose nickname is Lilly. Ryan's note read, "Dear Auntie DonDon, I would be honored if you would accompany me shopping for my wedding dress." My head began to spin, I felt my heart beating, a flood of warm tears rolled down face, and I could feel a deep groaning in my gut. I could hardly talk. My family was wondering what was wrong? Who are the flowers from? And what did the card say? I showed them the card and each one of them knew what it meant. They knew about my wedding dress. I'd never shopped for a wedding gown; it was one of the dreams that I didn't know I had. My sweet daughter-in-law, Janessa, who learned later about my wedding dress, held me in her arms and let me cry. She finished cooking dinner because I was of no use to anyone–I went upstairs and completely fell apart while facetiming Ryan Nicole.

The breach in my soul was so deep, I could not contain the repair that was present in the invitation to experience a mother/daughter moment. I hadn't asked for this blessing, it was not on my wish-list. My resolve was clear, and I believed I'd made peace with the child of my womb, my AllieCat was enough. And yet, Ryan Nicole saw the breach in my soul and would not allow to me remain unrepaired. Ryan's invitation was more than a shopping date. It was a call towards healing and wholeness. Her love called me out of the past and into the present. I could no longer massage the wounds of "feeling without," the abandonment and disappointment of dreams dashed. Ryan repaired the breach in my heart. Her decision to make her wedding more than just a family occasion brought healing to my soul.

Repair and rising may come in stages. For me, the invitation to shop for a wedding gown touch my heart so deeply, I felt the beautiful blessing of the moment that had not occurred. I remember feeling nervous and immediately called my friend, LaDonna. What about her mother/daughter dream? I dare not intrude or create a breach between us. Through my tears I communicated that the invitation was enough, and my heart would relish Ryan's thoughtfulness forever. Ryan was insistent, so the three of us had the most beautiful lunch at The Ivy in Beverly Hills. Ryan spoke the most beautiful words to her mother, so honoring and affirming of LaDonna as her mother and best friend. It was an unimaginable moment. We gave toast to the day, shopped, and found the most beautiful wedding gown.

My initial master plan detailed Allie wearing my wedding dress on her wedding day. Clearly, I am that mother trying to love herself through her child, admittedly and emotionally unaware of the grave need in my soul to mother myself. The reality of Allie's diagnosis came after one of her doctor's visits. The psychologist looked at my tired swollen eyes from eight years of sleep deprivation. Allie would leave the house at night, so it was rare for me to get a full night's sleep. The doctor said, "The progress and functioning Allie has will not likely change." She then turned and said to me, "You, get to work, go do something with your degree." It was time for a new plan, a dual reality in which I would hold fast to faith and live with the facts. I was devastated, depressed, and disappointed. I released my wedding gown after that doctor's visit. I simply left my gown in our home. We were moving. I couldn't give it away; I couldn't keep it. I just left it in the closet and drove away.

Repairers are more commonly people who have experienced the healing of heart and soul. They are those sensitive, intuitive individuals that have experienced repair and allow themselves to be fully present in life. I believed this is true of Ryan Nicole. Although the origin of this repair dates back more than twenty years, I'm convinced repairers have graced my path in the form of friends, family members, pastors, and the like. The layering of love and godly counsel has attributed to the ground swell that opened my heart to healing that occurred. Ryan was the conduit I visibly attribute as the hand that touched my heart, although I am confident God was the power ultimately at work.

Perhaps you have been disappointed or feel disillusioned. You don't foresee rising from the brokenness that has occurred in your life. As far as you can see, there is not a repairer in your path, and the master plan you have has been truly dashed. I have found repair alone in my car, sitting at my desk, as well as in a prayer meeting. Recognizing that everyone and every situation is different and requires varying levels of support, the ability to rise is more dependent on our individual surrender than the presence of a particular person.

My invitation to you is that you give God room and space to show up because you don't know how your dream (conscious or subconscious) will manifest. You ask how. Start with the first disappointment that comes to mind. If you're at work, you can follow these instructions during your break. The main thing is that you're able to get to a quiet undistracted space and allow yourself to get completely quiet.

- Release - Close your eyes and allow the disappointment to surface. If you feel tears, let them come. Do not hold back. It may be part of the release needed emotionally and physiologically.
- Entreat - tell God the what, the how, and the who – even if God Himself is the source of your disappointment. He already knows and has made provision for your healing.
- Petition – Ask God to help you release the portion that has you stuck, cause rumination. Specifically ask Him to repair the breach.
- Action – Decidedly let it go of any anger, ill feelings, negative emotions associated with the disappointment. Mark the moment in your journal as a reminder of the release.
- Invite – Call in peace, intentionally replace the hurt with love, forgiveness and a healthy perspective for your heart, soul, and body.
- Restore – Restore the dream as He would see it best. Sow a seed in someone's heart that encourages healing of their breach. Become a Repairer.

Feel free to write me with your Repair story.

Isaiah 58:12

"And your ancient ruins shall be rebuilt; you shall raise up the foundations of many generations; you shall be called the repairer of the breach, the restorer of streets to dwell in."

ABOUT DR. DONNA MARIE HUNTER

Dr. Donna Marie is an inspirational keynote speaker, author, and counselor. She believes that dreams, both large and small, do not have expiration dates, even in the face of a harsh reality, like her daughter Allie's diagnosis of Autism. The emotional devastation and looming disappointment became the catalyst for the repair of the breach of brokenness.

Dr. Donna Marie is the founder of Allie's Allys www.AlliesAllys.org, a nonprofit serving families in underserved communities affected by Intellectual and Developmental Disabilities. With over twenty years of excellent leadership as a high school principal, counselor, and administrator, Donna is a well-respected expert in public education. Dr. Hunter's mission is to educate, enlighten, and empower individuals with knowledge that transforms thinking and leads to actionable steps toward positive change.

An advocate for children with special needs, Dr. Donna co-produced and starred in the award-winning short film, **"Colored My Mind: Diagnosis"** with friends Tisha Campbell-Martin, LaDonna Hughley, Tammy McCrary, and Shannon Nash. The film has aired on **CentricTV, PBS, CNN's Raising America**, with screenings for staff diversity trainings at **Viacom, Delta Airlines** and **Wells Fargo Bank**. Donna and the CMM Moms share their personal stories and heart wrenching realities of receiving a diagnosis. Their mission is shedding light on the disparity in timely and accurate diagnosis of African American and Latino children with Developmental Disabilities, particularly **Autism** and the hope that rising is inevitable, regardless of broken dreams.

She is an intuitive **Coach** for personal and professional growth; a knowledgeable **Consultant** in education and business leadership; and an inspiring **Champion** for equity, access and inclusion for individuals with Special Needs. She received a Bachelor of Science in Business Management from Pepperdine University, Malibu, California. Dr. Donna holds a Master's in Educational Leadership, Counseling Credential, as well as a Doctorate in Educational Leadership from Azusa Pacific University, California. She is the proud mother of Jeremey (wife, Janessa) and daughter Allie. Donna and her husband, Jeff, recently celebrated thirty-five years of marriage. They reside in California.

Dr. Donna Marie Hunter
www.DrDonnaMarieHunter.com
FaceBook @drdonnamariehunter
Instagram/Twitter @drdmhunter

To watch the "Colored My Mind: Diagnosis" movie trailer, visit:
https://www.youtube.com/watch?v=tNgbEHy03tg

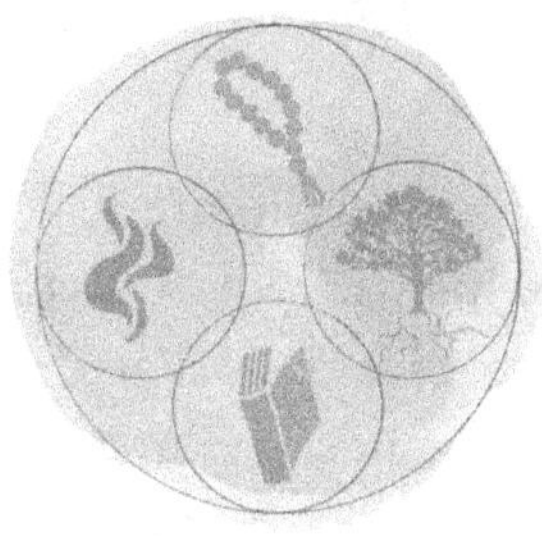

SELF LOVE AND SUCCESS

Tara LePera

Home: the place where you are supposed to feel safe, secure, and loved. The place where solid foundations for life are supposed to be laid. My story, my beginning, did not provide me this. I was born in Bricktown, New Jersey. My parents were married at the time, I was the second of three born from this marriage. I've lived in a total of thirty-five different house so far in my life, but twenty-four of them were within the first twelve years of my life. Hotels, apartments, other family members' homes, etc. None of them ever gave me the security a child needs and desires.

My parents got divorced, and shortly after, I entered the foster care system at the age of twelve. During that time, I was pressured into taking drugs for the first time in one of the foster homes and narrowly escaped sexual assault. I bounced from school to school and house to house. I never felt that I could grasp anything, I never felt smart enough to try. To say my childhood was unique is an understatement. My mom did eventually get my siblings and me back. My siblings and I. At this time in my life, I was really struggling with my identity and my confidence. There were never rules in my house; I could miss school, I could sleep in. I did not have positive adult influences in my life or someone to hold me accountable. I really struggled in school with any sort of math or reading, and I was in special education classes which affected my confidence and belief in myself. I did not feel like I belonged in school. During my Junior year of high school, it was apparent that I was going to have to repeat that grade. I was humiliated and never wanted to show my face in school again, so the next day my mom drove me to the school and signed me out. I officially dropped out of school.

At the time, my mom was going through her second divorce, and I felt compelled to help the family. I had two jobs, but the bills were piling up. We were struggling as a family and as individuals. It was at this time, at the age of seventeen, that a family member introduced me to a new world: the dancing scene. The income was good, and it quickly allowed me to helped support and raise my siblings alongside my mom. Fast forward three years later and at the age of twenty-one, I became pregnant. Prior to this, I attempted to get my GED, but I failed. I realized that I needed to make a change as I was bringing a daughter into this world, and I wanted to give her the life I did not have. But it did not happen like that, as I was sucked back into the dancing scene after a particularly tough conversation with a family member that convinced me it was my only path to take care of my daughter and family. Still, I began to feel that God was guiding me down a different path. I eventually switched to bartending to step away from the dance scene. I was bartending at a few different places over the next few years, but it wasn't until I started bartending at a local country club when I met Jean. She and I hit it off, and she asked me if I would ever be interested in working in corporate America. I took the chance and of course a big pay cut, but this is what I had to do if I wanted to create a better life for my daughter and myself. After a year of working in the corporate world, I was offered a bigger opportunity with a different company for a sales/marketing position. I loved it and quickly climbed the corporate ladder and became very successful in my sales position. However, I still felt as though something was missing from my life. One huge milestone, a positive one, was that I was able to purchase my very own home. I was able to give my daughter a stable home!

However, I was finding myself becoming extremely depressed. Here I was, creating the life I had always wanted, but found myself always being away from home traveling. I started taking depression medication and drinking one to two bottles of wine a night, but I was somehow still surviving. It was December 18, 2011 when a friend through work gave me tickets to a Philadelphia Eagles game. I tried everything I could to give these tickets away, but I guess the universe knew I was supposed to meet my husband on this day. I decided to take my best friend, Kristy, her son, Ben, and my daughter, Alessia, with me and go to the game. I noticed a very handsome young man was sitting behind me. Silly as it sounds, I also noticed that he did not have gloves on. Remember it was mid-December, so I offered him some handwarmers. This is when I met my husband, Marc. There was something about him, the instant chemistry; I felt a connection for the first time maybe ever. I firmly believe God put us together at that game. Marc is the driving force behind me finding and going after my dreams. Marc and I knew that we were meant to be together. I treated him differently than anyone I had ever met due to my past, as I struggled to trust anybody, especially men. I was that girl who always had a brick wall up. In the first few weeks of Marc and me dating, Marc introduced me to fitness, to a healthy lifestyle, one that I had never truly known.

About a year later, we started our own health and wellness business with the company Isagenix. This gave me the opportunity to leave my corporate job and run our business full-time. Marc encouraged me to go get my GED, I never had the desire to go back since I knew I would struggle. I also had the fear of failing again, especially as an adult. Delaware County Community College knew I was terrified, so they offered me a tutor to help me through the testing and I still barley passed, but I did it! I broke the family cycle: I am smart enough; I am brave enough. At the time I was actually embarrassed because I was thirty-five years old, so I never shared the great news with anyone but my close family and best friend, Kristy. However, I now realize how proud I should be of what I accomplished, and I now share it with everyone.

Marc and I got married on July 11, 2014 and decided that we wanted to make a family together. We decided to purchase our first home together and found a house in New Jersey (we were living in Pennsylvania at the time) during which we found out we were going to be parents. Our daughter, RaeLynn, was born on September 20, 2015, and because of the business Marc and I built I was able to stay home with her. I was very thankful for the life that I was able to live through Isagenix, however I knew that I was not done growing. Through building my network, I was able to connect with some amazing women. God continued to place people in my life that would help me become aligned with the purpose I had always felt in my heart. Due to my past, I realized that I needed to learn how to love myself. I threw myself into workshops, events—basically anything that had to do with personal growth and development, I did it. I began to see the more I showed love to myself the more I could help people. I realized that my beginning was going to be the key to me finding my purpose, wanting to share my story, because I knew that there were so many other women that were lost in this world who lack self-confidence and love.

As I began becoming more confident and implementing all of the self-love tools I had gathered from the work I did on myself we received a message, one that would change our lives forever. Marc and I had decided that we would like to add another child into our family and were actively trying. Through social media, my dad contacted us and let us know that my half-sister, Hope, had just given birth to a baby boy, and child services was stepping in because he was born addicted to drugs. Having been through the foster care system myself, I could not imagine allowing a member of my family to experience what I had, so we agreed to take him. This is when our son Charlie, birth name Kevin, came into our lives. Little did we know how this little boy would bring so much joy and happiness into our lives. However, having a NAS (neonatal abstinence syndrome) baby comes with some pretty major struggles. Charlie had to go through withdrawal from all the drugs. It was sad and hard for us to witness. There were many, many nights we did not sleep as we had to make sure he was okay. He is currently in different types of therapy that help him with his speech and motor skills so he will thrive in this world. Charlie was five months old when we found out we were pregnant again! So now we had Alessia, RaeLynn, Charlie, and were expecting another baby. Crazy, right?

So here we were, raising our daughters, helping our son heal, getting ready for the birth of another child, all while building our marriage. Relationships are tested often. However, through these tests they strengthened, and man are we strong! My pregnancy was not easy and brought its own number of tests. Our son, Hudson, was born a month early but healthy and happy on April 22, 2019. Six months later, my half-sister decided to give up her parental rights. We are now in the ongoing process of adopting our son, Charlie. Within five years we went from having one daughter to a family of six. Each day brings its own adventures, but we are figuring it out together as we go. I always said God wouldn't give us what we couldn't handle.

Because I decided to work on myself, and I learned how to love on me, I am able to show up for my husband and my kids in a way I never knew possible. The best part is I have realized that I can help so many people with everything I have been through and learned. God continues to place people in my life that guide me closer to my calling. During the days of going to as many self-help seminars as I could, I crossed paths with my now business partner, Penelope. A year or so later our business was formed. Through prayer, God guided Penelope and her friend Amy to me and my story. In faith I decided to partner with them and start spreading positivity into the world through our business, Inspired Purpose Coaching, and our podcast series.

All that work I did to learn how to love myself has now guided me to helping others. I am using the pain and struggle that started my story and helped me start my very own self-love business, Self-Love and Success. This March 2020, I launched my own website with 1:1 coaching and several engaging programs to help others. I am ready to help women learn to love themselves just like I did. The truths in my story that I shied away from sharing are the same ones that are going to help me change the world. I am very proud of the journey that has given me so many tools to be the person that helps others, my true calling. Always remember, we were all born with love. Fear is what we learn. The spiritual journey is the unlearning of fear and prejudices and the acceptance of love back into our hearts. Love is the essential reality and purpose on earth.

God is good!

ABOUT TARA LEPERA

Tara Ann LePera is the founder of Self Love and Success and co-founder of Inspired Purpose Coaching, a motivational speaker, podcast host, self-love coach, manifesting Mama, and co-author.

For the last five years Tara has focused her expertise on personal development, growing her self-love, building a strong mindset, and learning how to manifest her dreams into reality.

While growing up, Tara lacked confidence and viewed herself in a negative way. It wasn't until Tara learned to tap into her innermost truth and shift her limiting beliefs in her capabilities that she launched herself in alignment and co-created a life and business that makes her proud.

Tara's primary focus and joy is working with women. Her main focus is teaching multiple self-love techniques in order to build confidence while sparking the inner energy back into their lives. Tara does this through one-on-one coaching, group support systems, as well as programs and courses that are focused around professional life development, self-love, manifestation, confidence, and resetting.

Tara is the mother of four children and married to her husband, Marc. Tara and her family live in South Jersey and love to explore the world together while living life to their fullest abilities, all while creating everlasting memories.

Tara welcomes you to connect with her by visiting:

selfloveandsuccess.com
email- Taraannlepera@gmail.com
Instagram- @selfloveandsuccess
FaceBook- Tara Ann LePera

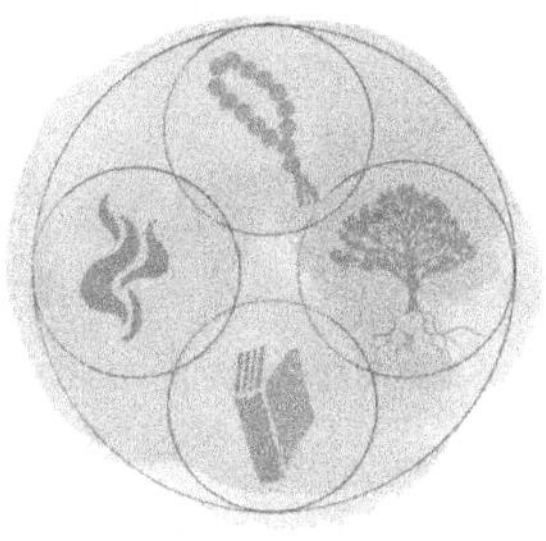

THE ART OF INTUITION

Nastassia Marie

"The strength within me is far greater than the fear, that is how I rise."
- Nastassia Marie

Early September 2018 is a period of time in my life that symbolizes strength, will-power, transcendence, and the biggest "HOLY SHIT" moment of my life thus far. Fall has always been my season of choice. The reverence I have for the crisp omnipresent air and earthy colors that appear during this time of year runs deep within my soul. Every year as summer comes to a quick end, I personally wait in anticipation for this connection to ignite within me, to embody the most creative parts of myself and most importantly to feel a total sense of peace and contentment. You see, I didn't feel this way in fall of 2018, though. Life as I saw it was dark. I was living in a constant state of fear due to the circumstances I continuously kept finding myself in, I was having major breathing complications every moment of my waking day from PTSD, and I was desperately craving freedom from a life that I felt and believed at that time I had absolutely no control over.

Since I was a little girl, I've been spiritually connected to something greater than myself. I always knew there had to be something guiding and protecting me like no other. Childhood upbringings were never a topic of conversation I felt comfortable partaking in. The emotional, physical and sexual abuse, drugs and violence I experienced and was exposed to as a child was harsh. But I truly believe that's where my deep-seated faith and trust in The Universe really began to surface. I carried this knowing that if I was able to survive that kind of childhood, I could survive anything.

This day in September was undoubtedly the catalyst for casting me into the woman I am today. I vividly remember standing in my living room, staring right through my sliding glass doors into a world that I felt completely disconnected from. Holding my one-year-old daughter tightly in my arms, my body fell weak, and I felt as though all feeling was lost in my lower extremities. I fell right down to my knees, coddled my face in between the crevice of her tiny neck and shoulder and became engulfed in the presence of deep surrender. Tears streaming down my cheeks, voice shaking and body trembling, I fully screamed out LOUDLY to My Higher Power for help: "God, please, PLEASE help me, PLEASE guide me, PLEASE show me the way!" I was ready. I was so ready. I couldn't live life like this anymore. I needed help. What I was doing was not working, my answers were not the solutions, and finally my desire for peace and contentment had superseded my subconscious desire to continue living in pain and fear. I threw my hands up in the air and connected to a power greater than myself, and within that very moment of clenching fiercely on to my newfound faith and personal power, I was given a clear intuitive vision of the beautiful and miraculous life of joy and service that was waiting for me — if I powered through and overcame this one last battle: The battle of dissociating with everything I was and once knew in return for the version of me that would finally live a life of pure freedom and free from fear. The version of me that had incarnated here to lift and inspire others through her journey. But most importantly, in return for the version of me that my child deserved more than ever to be loved, cared for, and raised by.

I had never surrendered like this before. This was the BIG surrender.

I've received signs, synchronicities, and intuitive pings throughout my entire life, but the clear vision of this version of me emerging out of the darkness was so strong and so powerful that there was no way I could confuse it with anything other than a clear and DIRECT message from God. I had been waiting, praying even for a signal, and here it was! Hello, Intuition, Universe, God, whatever you or this is. I see you. I trust you. I honor you. I'm following you. Let's do this!

See, the most beautiful thing ever about hitting rock bottom is that, that's it! You've actually hit your threshold. You can't look down any further than you already have, so your only option is to laboriously shift your awareness, look up, and find the light that's been waiting for you the entire time.

This vision reconstructed my thoughts and beliefs on EVERYTHING. It opened up a portal to awakening the untapped and unlimited potential within me. I started seeing so clearly that my life was not one by my own design, but rather molded and mirrored by the conditioning and programming I had picked up on as a child. When we are born into a world where its foundation is primed by violation, neglect, abuse, and abandonment we typically associate that kind of behavior in adulthood as normal. My intuition had been trying to communicate with me for years that something was not right in my life, but on a very deep and subconscious level, the life I was living provided me the greatest sense of "home" I had ever felt. And I craved chaos, even though the counterparts were uncertainty and an immense amount of fear.

I decided that day that "enough is enough!" I was going to start listening to whatever guidance was presented to me, even if it scared the living shit out of me. And so, that's exactly what I did. I knew what I was intuitively guided to do didn't make logical sense, but here's the thing … if I would have for one moment said "Look, I just had a conversation with God, pretty cool guy, he told me I needed to up and move across the state, completely disassociate from X,Y and Z, dive deeper into my spirituality, and figure out how to rewire my brain and heal from all this trauma to manifest into my Highest self," it probably wouldn't have been reciprocated very well, as you can imagine.

My trust and faith had to be massively bigger than my fear. So, I did it. I spent the next several months from that very day listening and following my intuition, sorting out my life, and cutting off relationships that I knew were no longer in alignment with who I truly desired to be. It was painful, and it hurt like absolute hell, but I did it unapologetically. I couldn't make anyone see what I was seeing, or understand my Why. I knew I needed to do all the things I was being guided to do, because my life would soon start reflecting to those around me the exact physical reality that was presented to me in that moment of deep surrender. Every time my ego would show up trying to convince me to stay where I was, cave in, and go back to the version of me I was deliberately trying to escape from, I'd remember that powerful vision I had of the life that was waiting for me if I just kept fighting through the resistance!

It was my job to rewrite my story. I knew that to reach the vibration I wanted to exist in, to start living the life I knew I deserved to be living, I was going to have to do some forgiving like no other. Forgiving of others for sure, but most importantly forgiving for the versions of myself that existed as I was fighting to survive from a life based solely on fight or flight. I was prepared to fully submerge myself in all the things that would be my gateway to freedom.

I began proactively ensuring I would have a full recovery from PTSD through EMDR therapy, neuro-feedback, and talk therapy with a therapist that I know with my entire soul is my angel in physical form. I started reframing and rewiring every story, thought, and subconscious belief that caused me anxiety and fear. I established a morning ritual dedicated to journaling and meditation. I began saying affirmations that were in alignment with exactly what I wanted: "Be here now", "Everything I need is already within me". I started to stick post-it notes around my entire house that reminded me of who I really was and why I was doing what I was doing. I hired multiple mindset coaches to help elevate and expand my consciousness, self worth, and connection to the abundance of The Universe I had been so disjointed from. I kept thinking to myself, "If I was able to unconsciously manifest things in my life getting so bad, then I for damn sure could consciously and actively manifest things in my life getting so good!" I just had to create new stories, new beliefs, and a new me on a very cellular and subconscious level.

From the outside in, I fully disassociated with almost everyone for an entire year. I know it looked lonely, crazy and isolated, but for the first time ever I didn't care what anyone thought. That was freedom within itself. I was finally uncovering parts of myself I had not known existed, parts of me that were suppressed and afraid to step into the light. This was such a sacred time for me. It was a rebirth. I dedicated all of my time to my child, myself, and to healing. I had finally just met myself, and I wasn't ready to share her with anyone.

Through all of this reprogramming I began to change the way I looked at the world, and then I changed the way I experienced the world, and through that the world around me began magically changing as a result. The lens through which I had viewed life had broadened. The film that was blocking my vision, banished. Everything I started seeing, I started seeing through a lens of love. I started calling in situations, experiences, and people that matched the healing vibration that was emanating from me. Life had transformed from pain and chaos to absolute light, forgiveness, acceptance, and bliss. I had never felt this kind of freedom and alignment before. I knew that I had done tremendous work and was beginning to reap the benefits from my unwavering resilience. My Crystal and Jewelry Business 'Promote Peace' began flourishing more than ever. Amazing people started reaching out to me from all over the world, asking me about my transformation, asking for guidance on spirituality and how to enhance their mindset and the very essence of their life. This was the part that wasn't so new to me. I had always been one whom friends and random people approached with life dilemmas and to discuss spirituality with, but this was different. I knew I had created a new self and more so a new mind, and with that I was showing up for these conversations differently. The tools I acquired from one year of deep transformation were what some people search their entire lives for. I had never wanted to be of service more in my life up until this point. And so, my second service-based business 'The Art of Intuition' was born.

I had built such a beautiful rapport with people through my social media platform with 'Promote Peace' that many had witnessed my transformation, and transitioning to also becoming a Transformational Coach ebbed and flowed with grace. I had so much love and support radiating towards me, because that's what I was able to cultivate within my very own self. I knew that everything in my life — all the pain, the glory, the absolute sacrifice of my old self— had led me to this. This was my purpose; this was my calling. I was actually living the very vision that was provided to me one year prior. I had never felt so divinely aligned, connected, and blessed. I now believe that our experiences are never meant to destroy us, but rather to awaken and evolve us. Since I was a little girl I've dreamed of helping, inspiring, and lifting others. Now I see that I just needed to experience my own healing transformation to its core to be able to show up fully for the world, so here I AM.

ABOUT NASTASSIA MARIE

Nastassia is a mother, multiple business owner, mentor, writer, transformational coach and a certified master practitioner in Neuro Linguistic Programming. With over a decade of helping run, train, and scale small and large corporate businesses in the restaurant industry, she knew that human connection, mentoring, and entrepreneurship would be the foundation for where her life journey would transcend.

Having always been passionate about helping and being of service to those around her, Nastassia's mission in life is to do just that. After experiencing a tremendous awakening and coming to terms that her life had manifested into a reflection of her childhood conditioning, she experienced a powerful transformation which reframed every aspect of her life. Her resilience came from the knowing that one of her soul contracts in life was to break generational trauma and change the trajectory for those who follow her. She recognizes the compelling power of what one can do when they start following their intuition, step into their self worth, and believe in their inherent ability to co-create a magical and abundant life with The Universe, both internally and externally.

With the junction of her innate and intuitive gifts, her own healing and transformation journey she now guides people around the world through her online coaching programs on how to heal on deep vibrational and energetic levels. Nastassia graciously provides the subconscious framework needed to help tackle self limiting beliefs, reach elevated states of consciousness, reframe trauma, and cultivate internal and external wealth and freedom. Her ultimate hope is to awaken as many people as she can to step into the version of themselves that is free from worry, judgment, and limitation, in addition to recognizing that there is a beautiful dimension of us that exists which is full of generous well-being and bliss!

To follow more of Nastassia's journey and learn more about how you can experience your own powerful transformation, follow the links below. She would be honored to connect and hear from you!

Instagram - @theartofintuition

Facebook - @theartofintuitionn

Theartofintuition.net

theartofintuition@gmail.com

Join the The Art of Intuition community on Facebook

https://www.facebook.com/groups/676204819578333/

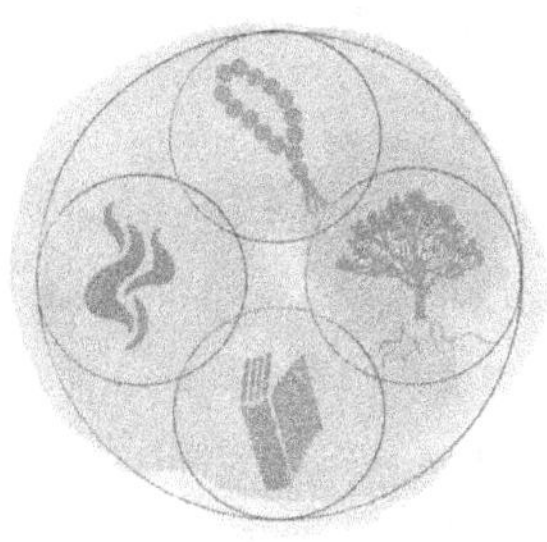

HEALING A HEART

Laura E. Summers

"Clear," I timidly said through the open cockpit window. "You have to be louder," my father snapped. "If you are going to be the first female commercial captain, you have to clear the prop before you start it." I wasn't sure it was my dream to be a pilot, but I knew it was his dream for me. All I knew for sure was I loved being with my dad and he loved flying. He was a private pilot with an instrument rating. That meant he was trained and qualified to fly in inclement conditions. He aspired and was working toward his commercial pilot's license. I was thirteen and could complete a take-off and a landing in the single engine aircraft without help (dad was sitting next to me), but I was too self-conscious to yell "CLEAR!" out the window.

A few months later, dad was working out of town when my grandparents came for a visit. We didn't get to see them often, so we loved it when they came. Dad filed a flight plan to our home in South Dakota for a long weekend from his job in North Dakota. He should be home in time for dinner. We were playing a game at the kitchen table when there was a knock at the door. Two men identified as law enforcement asked to come in. They stood inside the front door and told my mom that Dad had been in a crash. The airplane had crashed into a farmer's field; there were no survivors. The blood drained from my face and I couldn't catch my breath. I grabbed my dad's fringed jacket out of the closet, wrapped myself in its leather that smelled of my dad's cologne and headed out the door. I needed to be alone with my thoughts. I needed to breathe. I needed it to be a lie. It wasn't.

The next weeks were a blur. Family, friends, too much food and traveling to Colorado for the funeral. I sunk into the solitary depths of grief. I was angry. Angry at God for taking him. Angry at him for leaving. Even angry at my mom when she'd say, "Everything will be alright." It didn't feel like anything would ever be alright. Not. Ever.

Death, or any heartbreak, changes those left behind. Once grief entered my heart, I was never the same again. I became a different person. I fumbled and flailed for a new normal, recognizing even at thirteen-years-old that familiar me was gone forever.

My grandfather saw the way grief gripped every cell of my being. He offered me comfort of an explanation this way. "Your dad was a great pilot. He was experienced and confident in the cockpit. He probably had a heart attack. His passenger wasn't a pilot. Maybe he panicked, pushed the stick in and caused the crash." "Oh my god," I thought, "I could have landed that plane! I could have saved my father's life if I would have been there!" I didn't share my thoughts with my grandfather, but those thoughts became a part of who I was becoming.

That guilt of not being there to save his life settled into my subconscious, guiding my behaviors and thoughts from that day forward. The culpability grew inside me causing shame and feelings of worthlessness. Some days it was all I could do to survive the day carrying the weight of the self-blame that developed and grew. "If I had been there, I could have saved his life," I would think lying awake in the darkness at three o'clock in the morning.

Many years later I learned this was the moment of the birth of a shadow. Swiss psychologist C.G. Jung says, "Our shadow is the person we'd rather not be." Each of us has shadows. Shadows are the limiting beliefs we hold deep inside, not wanting to expose them to the light of day, much less share them with anyone else. They are the parts of us we don't want to acknowledge, confront, or admit to. And, in part, that's what gives them their power! They have great command over our day-to-day decisions, choices, behaviors, and actions, or inactions. Shadows are typically born during traumatic or difficult events in our childhood when we were too inexperienced to process the event. We took those events or situations to mean something negative about us or the world around us and tucked that knowledge into our subconscious where it helped to form our personalities. It's there, in the subconscious, where we decide how much success we're entitled to create or how much failure we're destined to have. Author Debbie Ford said, "The shadow is an oracle that predicts all of our behaviors, driving the way we treat those around us – and how we treat ourselves." Because none of us have just one or two shadows, I was soon to add more into my subconscious.

Ages thirteen to fifteen were challenging. I was learning to navigate grief before puberty. Then my mom, a thirty-seven-year-old widow with four kids, decided to remarry. I was already rebellious but after her wedding I dove off the deep end. I didn't agree with her choice in men. It was a mutual feeling; he didn't like me either.

Soon I was on the highway with my thumb out chasing after my twenty-five-year-old boyfriend who'd moved to Kansas City. We set up a home and began our life together. I was happy, but not for long. A new grief, loss of a relationship, was about to enter my life. Ten months into our co-habitation he was arrested for dealing drugs. I knew he was doing it, but he protected me from that part of his life. After three days in a Juvenile Detention Center, I was on an airplane headed back to my mom's house.

Mom and I had deep, meaningful conversations. She told me she made a mistake and would be filing for divorce. She was excited to start fresh in Oregon. She hoped I would go back to school. I wanted that too. We laughed together, cried together, and for the first time I saw her as more than my mom. She was a warm, vulnerable, compassionate, intelligent woman who was becoming my friend.

A week after I came home, she collapsed on the floor and violently started convulsing. An aneurysm had burst in her brain.

Eight days passed before the swelling in her brain had gone down enough for them to attempt surgery. The aneurysm gave no warnings. No headaches, no symptoms. Surgery was a painstaking eight-hour process, but she survived it. My stepdad showed up during that week and the next morning, while we were all sleeping, he was called to the hospital. Mom had taken a turn for the worst. He invited me to come and I jumped into his car.

I was holding my mom's hand in recovery when she took her final breath. In my mind's eye, I imagined my father's spirit standing on the other side of the bed. I imagined she let go of me to take my father's hand. Somehow, that brought a small feeling of peace and comfort along with the devastation of deep sorrow.

I had been on my own, yet I still felt like a child. Lost again in grief. Only this time I was acutely aware that I had now lost both parents. This is what it felt like to be an orphan. My stomach was in my throat and my heart ached. I stood against the wall in the hospital hallway and sobbed.

After Mom died, a nurse had taken my hand out of my mom's and escorted me out of the room. She told my stepdad that Mom was gone, and he went in to see her. When he came out of the room he was pissed. He walked up to me, grabbed me by the shoulders and pushed me hard up against the wall. He said, "You killed your mother! You killed her because of everything you put her through!" He pushed me once more when he let go of me and he walked down the hall.

At that moment I birthed a few new shadows. Not worthy. Disposable person. There's something wrong with me. I'm damaged. I'm a bad person. And, I'm not loveable.

It's been more than four decades since my adolescence. Grief is a part of my story, but it doesn't define me. Several years ago, I decided to search for the National Transportation Safety Board's Crash Report.

When I got it in the mail, I was surprised it didn't match the stories I was told. The NTSB Report summed it up like this, "Pilot made an uncontrolled descent resulting in a collision with the ground. Conditions at the crash site were overcast with a ceiling of 300 feet. Visibility was less than ½ mile with heavy fog and drizzle. Pilot attempted operation beyond experience and/or ability level and became spatially disoriented. Pilot's log showed no actual instrument time."

I could not have saved his life! If I had been in the plane, I would likely have died with him. What a revelation! I realized my grandfather's story was said with good intentions. He wanted me to see my dad as my hero.

Grief comes in many ways. Death, divorce, breakups, a job loss, selling a home or moving, serious illness for you or a loved one, death of a pet, financial change, miscarriage, retirement, the loss of a cherished dream, loss of safety, family estrangement, or a traumatic accident. Or even having a parent remarry.

Grief is normal even if the process itself is highly individualized. Healing through my grief with my dad's death was different than the process with my mom's death and that was different than the process of losing my relationship. There is no right or wrong way to grieve. Healing takes time. I had to learn to be gentle with myself and acknowledge my pain before I could forgive myself for carrying the guilt of not saving my dad and for being a "bad" kid.

My journey of healing led me to become a certified Master Life Coach specializing in guiding people through their shadows, limiting beliefs and healing their hearts.

Using a similar process I went through, I teach my clients how to expose their own subconscious shadows and create new empowering and supportive beliefs. I teach them how to bust through those limiting beliefs that keep them stuck and often sabotage their efforts to reaching their goals. They learn that by starting with one step and doing the work it's possible to reclaim their confidence, believe in themselves and really go after what they want in their lives.

By doing my own work, I found new meaning in all my relationships. I recognized and released my guilt, anger, and sadness, and I was able to make the shift to feeling more valued from within. My relationship with my husband began to flow with more ease and other relationships in my life changed for the better too. I'm more accepting and less righteous, controlling, and judgmental. It was hard, but I'm grateful I uncovered the resentment, anger, and confusion I held against my parents for dying. Because it brought me through the healing process to a place where I've learned what it feels like to love and be loved without conditions. And, more importantly, I learned to have a better, more loving and forgiving relationship with myself.

ABOUT LAURA E. SUMMERS

Laura E Summers is a Certified Master Life Coach, Author, Speaker, Student Coach Mentor, business owner and ordained Reverend. She holds an Associates of Arts Degree with an emphasis in Broadcast Communications, two coaching Certifications from the Ford Institute for Transformational Training and is a Certified Trainer in The Success Principles by Jack Canfield.

She uses her education and life events as well as her experiences as a former NBC Promotions Director and entrepreneur to guide her clients to overcome core issues, develop personal action plans and help them to move effectively toward achieving their goals and realizing their visions. She specializes in helping clients overcome their shadows and limiting beliefs and in healing hearts.

She enjoys speaking and teaching others how to live with intention using the Success Principles and her own examples of hope, determination, and love.

Married since 1992, she lives in the beautiful Colorado Rockies with her husband, Don, who has stood by her side supporting, encouraging, and loving her as she follows her heart. She is blessed with two (step) sons, a daughter-in-law and two amazing grandchildren. In her spare time, you'll find her challenging herself on the golf course, traveling, painting, and kayaking.

To work with Laura or to learn more about how coaching can benefit you:

Website: www.LauraESummers.com
Email: Laura@LauraESummers.com
Instagram: @rev.laurasummers.lifecoach
Facebook: Laura E Summers
LinkedIn: Laura E Summers
Wedding Website: www.LauraSummersReverend.com

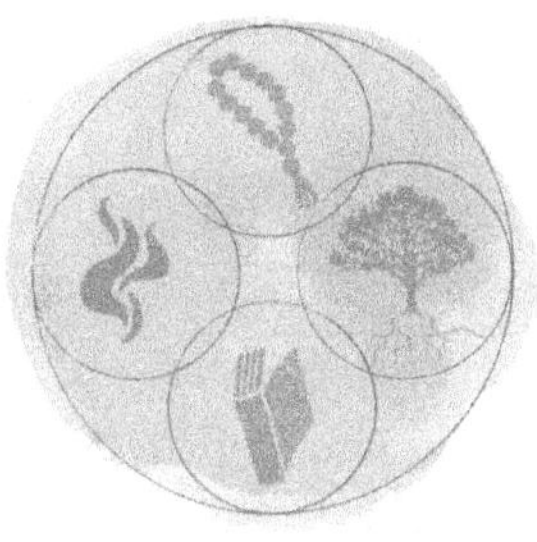

CURRENT STATE: HAPPINESS

Amanda Autry

I want to start off my story in the most appropriate way possible by introducing you to Rose, my grandmother. My relationship with her was so incredibly special. An energy healer once told me that Nan and I were soulmates, and I truly believe that. Up until her last moment on earth that woman loved me with every ounce of her being.

I was living in downtown Baltimore and working as a bartender at the time that my grandmother was diagnosed with cancer. Most nights I didn't get home from work until three or four a.m., but she never cared what time it was. She wanted to know that I was home safe every night so she would wait by her phone for me to call. Even in her illness, my wellbeing was always a priority.

The news of her cancer devastated me. I couldn't imagine a life without her, and I was not prepared to face what that would look like. Shortly after the news of her cancer, she began chemotherapy and radiation treatments and her cancer cells were shrinking. We were all so hopeful and ready for her recovery journey to begin.

One day I got a call from my mom. She told me that I needed to come to the hospital immediately because Nan was not doing well, and they didn't know how much more time she had. I remember thinking, "How could this be? I was just there last night."

I recalled a conversation that Nan and I had as I was leaving the night before. She wasn't feeling well, and I had a Halloween party to go to, so I decided that it was time to leave. She said, "You are leaving?" It wasn't what she said but how she said it. She knew that would be the last time that we would get to talk, but I had no idea. I thought I had so much more time.

I didn't have more time though. She passed away the day that I got that phone call from unexpected complications with her treatment. On that day my entire life changed.

For the first time, I understood mortality. I spent months battling the guilt for not loving her as hard as I could have or being there for her as much as she was there for me. This tragedy forced me to think about my own life and how I would have done things differently if I had known my grandmother's fate.

It became so clear to me that Nan's fate would also be my fate. I would also leave this earth one day, possibly unexpectedly. I used to believe that I had so much time to learn to play guitar, to travel to Utah, Colorado, and Sedona, and to show the people I love just how much they mean to me, but I might not.

So, the question that I asked myself then became, "What would I do if I knew that I had limited time? Would I live here? Would I work here? Would I be in this relationship?" The answer to those questions was a resounding NO.

At that moment, changing my entire life didn't feel like a choice but looking back on it, it was a choice. I honestly don't know if I made this decision from a place of courage or a place of fear, but I knew that I had to make the decision to live, truly live, for all of the people who no longer could, like Rose. I decided to leave my job at the bar that was supporting an unhealthy lifestyle, move out of my apartment and into my grandmother's home—which I had no clue how I would maintain—and I chose to leave a three year relationship that wasn't serving me, even though it felt like the only constant I had at the time. I made all of these scary decisions in pursuit of a life that I could look back on and say, "I did everything I could. There are no regrets or wish-I-would-haves. I did everything that I wanted to do."

I ripped the metaphorical rug out from underneath myself because the alternative was staying in a life that I knew I wasn't happy with, and that wasn't an option that I was willing to endure any longer.

It didn't take long after I made these scary choices for aligned opportunities to start to open up for me. Yes, it required saying goodbye to relationships that did not serve me but that opened up the space for the people and relationships that did. I quickly started connecting with people who shared the same passion for cherishing life and created a stronger support system than ever before.

I left the hospitality industry that I had worked in since my first job as a server at Friendly's when I was fourteen-years-old. Deciding to leave came with a lot of anxiety that I wouldn't find something else that I loved doing. But when I left, again, I made space for a career path that would bring me more fulfillment and allow me to serve and show up in the world at an even greater level.

Every time I took action in the direction of a life that served my highest good, the universe swooped in to support me. It wasn't always easy, and it rarely looked like I wanted it to look, but nonetheless, the universe always had my back.

I had a new career as a Realtor. I found an amazing man who is now my fiancé, and I began to create an external world that was a reflection of the love, stability, and abundance that I wanted. Life was better than it had ever been, but I was still searching for more.

My fiancé and I decided to sell my grandmother's house in the county and buy our dream home in Baltimore city. The home was a thoughtfully renovated 100-year-old home in a hipster neighborhood in the city. It was in the perfect location, walking distance from our favorite restaurants, with a yard and a big front porch perfect for our hammock swings. We were in love with this little life that we had created.

I was living in my dream home, with my dream guy, in my dream career, and I was faced with the same uncomfortable feeling that had triggered our move to the city. I felt happy but I didn't feel "dream life" happy. I knew that there had to be more out there for me.

In integrity with this pursuit and this promise that I made to myself to create a life with no regrets, I decided again to keep searching for the happiness that I knew was available to me.

In the fall of that year I took a trip to Sedona, Arizona. On my trip I met a sweet couple that had just retired and purchased an Airstream and their plan was to live in their RV and explore the country for a year. I was so inspired by their journey and intrigued by the idea of having that much freedom.

On the plane home from Arizona I sent a text message to my fiancé telling him all about this Airstream adventure. I said, "It would be so cool if we could do this one day!" His response was the catalyst for the next path on our journey to happiness. He said, "Why wait?"

I got back from my trip and we immediately started planning our own Airstream adventure. I printed out a picture of the exact RV that we wanted and stuck it on the fridge. We started to sell our belongings and we got our little city dream home ready for our future renters.

In two months' time we rented out our home, secured financing for our new Airstream, left our jobs, took money from our savings account, and embarked on a cross country adventure.

We spent our first night in the RV in Hunting Island, South Carolina. As the sun set and the sky shifted from cotton candy to burnt orange with the ocean as our backyard, I remember thinking "This is it, this is happiness."

We spent the next couple of months driving through the southern states of North America. We explored Big Bend National Park, spent an entire day watching the colors of the sky change over the sand dunes at White Sands National Monument, and explored a desert oasis at Joshua Tree National Park. We were doing all of the things that I had always wanted to do.

I was sitting in our RV one day in Twentynine Palms, California in the middle of the desert, and I felt that same uncomfortable yet familiar feeling of unhappiness. I thought to myself, "What can I do to make myself feel happy right now?"

That question brought me to a realization that put everything into perspective.

I had never imagined that I would have the luxury of having everything that I believed would make me happy. Yet, here I was with everything that I'd ever wanted, and I was still searching for more.

I was on the greatest adventure of my life in one of the most iconic recreational vehicles ever made, traveling the country with a man that had agreed to spend the rest of his life with me, with enough money in my bank account to sustain our lifestyle for months, and I still wasn't truly happy!

I sat there in that RV with tears streaming down my face thinking, "If a loving fiancé doesn't make me feel loved and wanted, traveling the country doesn't make me feel free, and having money doesn't make me feel abundant, what is the answer?"

I dropped my head and looked down at my where my heart sits in my chest. In that moment I finally understood: Happiness is not out there, it's in here.

Before that moment I would have bet everything I own that financial stability would eliminate my money worries. I was convinced that traveling the world would bring me a sense of fulfillment. You could not have persuaded me into believing that this life that I created wasn't the answer to happiness. I had to see for myself.

I loved taking bold risks, I was an advocate for adventure, and I wholeheartedly believed that it's not necessary to stay in a situation I was unhappy in. But I recognized that I had a pattern of constantly shifting and changing my external world in search of things that were ultimately an inside job.

When happiness became an inside job and it was something that I created instead of something that I received as a result of something else happening, I took my power back. No person, place, or experience can ever take away what I can create on my own.

Through embodying this realization, my feelings of worthiness stopped being dependent on whether someone else loves me or not. The abundance and gratitude that I feel doesn't have a correlation with the number in my bank account. I don't have to wait until I have my dream home to feel like I have everything that I want in life. It is not circumstances that determine whether I have an amazing and full life. My reality is created by the lens that I see my life through, and I have the opportunity to choose which lens to pick up at every moment.

I know that I was graced with the opportunity to go on this journey so I could share it with you. As a life coach I find myself asking my clients (and everyone that gives me the time of day), "What would make you happy?" Most of the time they rattle off a list of material things, romantic partners, or winning the lottery. Then I get to give them the good news: all of the things that we want are available to us right now.

ABOUT AMANDA AUTRY

Amanda Autry helps women change their lives from the inside out through writing, working intimately with clients 1:1, and facilitating retreats in Sedona, AZ.

Through her work, Amanda creates space for women to experience transformation and self-love. Sedona provides an ideal landscape with powerful energy vortexes to cultivate this type of transformation and clarity. On retreats, Amanda facilitates hikes, meditation, yoga, unique culinary experiences, and self-discovery workshops to help attendees deeply connect with themselves, nature, and others, so that they leave feeling invigorated and inspired to step into the person and the life that they truly desire.

To stay updated about upcoming retreats or to inquire about working with Amanda 1:1, visit Theseasonofbecoming.com or become a part of the community on Instagram @Theseasonofbecoming.

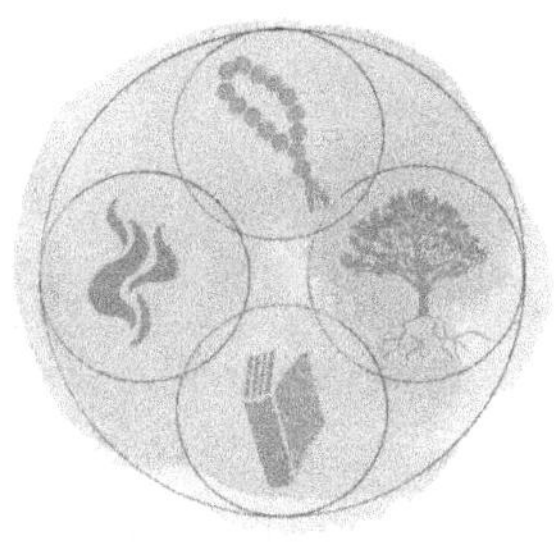

THE HAPPY GIRL

Jenn Romano-Baus

My name is Jenn and I am a Happy Girl. Over the last two years I have lost almost one hundred pounds by changing the ONE thing that I had never tried changing before: the negative attitude that I had towards the person I ignored for a very long time—MYSELF. After I was able to conquer that, everything else started to fall into place. The unhappy, unhealthy person I was carrying around for over twenty-five years started to fall off. Once I finally found my inner Happy Girl, my outer Happy Girl came easily.

My earliest memory of being heavy dates all the way back to 1996, during my Sophomore year of high school. From that moment on, my weight loss journey was full of ups and downs, highs and lows, and great successes followed by inevitable failures. In 1998, I graduated from high school, attended college part-time and began my career in the automotive industry. At this point, I was just seventeen-years-old and over two hundred pounds. As I started to make a name for myself in the industry, I quickly realized two things. First, my huge, happy, and bubbly personality hid the fact that I was uncomfortable in my own skin and extremely unhappy with my weight. Second, and more importantly, I discovered that I was a born leader. I had a natural ability to sell, manage, motivate, and lead. So that's what I did for the next twenty-two years and counting.

By 2006, I was twenty-six and felt like something was missing in my life. I was devoting all of myself to the true love of my life, the car business, but rarely made time for a life outside of work. When I finally decided to "get out there" and meet someone, it ended just as quickly as it began. We were married and divorced less than a year later. I was back to doing what I did best, excelling in my professional career, and moved on from this experience alone and somewhat broken.

In 2008 I entered what I like to refer to as the "black cloud of hell". Being almost thirty-years-old and seemingly forever single, I decided to give love another try. I was working a lot and making great money, but I still felt like something was missing. I always knew that I wanted children and found that as I was getting older, that desire was getting stronger. Despite my low self-esteem and lack of confidence, I put myself out there again. People always said things like, "You have such a pretty face!", "You have an amazing personality!", "Who cares about your weight?!?", "There's plenty of people out there!" Guess what? They were right about everything. I found someone. Boy, did I find someone.

The next few years were a whirlwind of abuse, humiliation, court dates, and restraining orders. After a miscarriage in 2009, I was lucky enough to give birth to two beautiful baby girls. My eldest daughter was born in 2010, followed closely by her sister in 2011. What should have been the happiest time of my life ended up being some of my darkest days. My daughters brought me strength I didn't know possible and I am convinced that without them, I may not have been strong enough to survive. "Who the hell will love you? Your body? Your disgusting stomach?" The mental abuse continued and eventually escalated to physical abuse. After years of being punched, spit on, tortured, humiliated, and embarrassed, I decided to take my daughters and walk away. I had two children, aged two and one, and I was preparing to start over. I was two hundred forty-five pounds and at the lowest, mentally and emotionally, I had ever been.

I briefly moved in with my sister in 2012 and then moved back to my parents' house. I was working again, and everything was falling back into place. My life was slowly starting to come back together with the love and support of my family. They helped me to refocus mentally and get my life back on track. During the summer of 2013, I managed to lose some weight and went from two hundred forty-five pounds to two hundred one pounds. In January of 2014, me and the girls finally got our own place and I was so proud of how far we had come!

Everything started moving in the right direction over the next few years. In addition to continuing my career in the automotive industry, I opened a dance/fitness studio in our town in early 2016! As a mom on a budget, I spent many years searching for affordable fitness alternatives and birthday party venues. A few pricey gym memberships and crazy expensive birthday parties later, my vision was born. I wanted to open a place that catered to all walks of life, regardless of age, shape, size, or budget! The Hip Hop Shop just entered our fifth year in business, and we are still going strong! I met the true love of my life and man of my dreams, and we were married in August of 2016. Despite all of the amazing events taking place in my life, I still hadn't found my Happy Girl. I started looking for inspiration in others and found myself drawn to Ellen DeGeneres. She made me laugh when I needed it the most. Being a mom of six now, I needed all the help I could get! Sometimes you have to look to others for motivation when you can't find it in yourself.

After getting settled into married life again, I became pregnant with my third beautiful Happy Girl, and our amazing blended family of seven (my husband had three amazing children from a previous relationship) became a party of eight by the end of 2017.

Fast forward a few months and THE EAGLES WON THE SUPER BOWL! If that isn't enough to make you smile, I don't know what is! I found myself watching and re-watching highlights of this amazing victory for our city. I was so motivated and inspired by how they overcame all challenges and managed to bring it home against all odds. My mom saw me watching Eagles highlights one day and mentioned how everyone was so shocked that I hadn't thrown a Super Bowl party. I immediately snapped and said, "I just had a freakin' baby, Mom!" Then it hit me; despite having a great family, amazing career, and owning my own business, nothing really mattered because I was deeply depressed. I couldn't believe I had let this opportunity pass me by. How the heck did I miss the Eagles winning the Super Bowl?! How did I not run through the streets?! I had waited for this my whole entire life!

Around Spring of 2018, my oldest daughter, who was seven at the time, asked me if I was going to lose weight since the baby was getting older and I wasn't nursing anymore. I was honestly a little hurt at first but quickly I felt like I was almost being tested by her. My first reaction was to call for a consultation to get a tummy tuck. Maybe that would help me get on track. After learning that I would need to lose eighty pounds before even being considered as a candidate, I laughed for a while then decided to explore another avenue. You read that right—I would need to lose the weight of an entire teenager before I would be considered for eligibility. A fire instantly turned back on inside. Is this what I needed to get myself where I have wanted to be all these years? Could this really be it? Is it finally my time? I started transforming myself day by day. I knew I had a long road ahead of me. This body has been both mentally and physically abused in the past. I grew and gave life to three amazingly perfect Happy Girls (all C-sections). I have put my body through years of crazy fad diets and tried all of the weight loss pills you can think of. Most importantly, I never loved myself. I was never happy with who I was and because of this, I mistreated my body for as long as I can remember.

I started looking in the mirror and trying to figure out why I could never tackle my weight loss in the past. I would hold my stomach up to see my potential. Lifting my inner thighs up, I would catch myself smiling at what I was seeing. I FINALLY made up my mind that I would either be happy with the Jenn that I saw at two hundred forty-four pounds or I would transform myself into what I wanted to feel and look like. I was ready to do this for myself and by myself, once and for all! Plus, after my husband told me without hesitation that I looked like I weighed around one hundred eighty pounds, I wasn't mentally ready to admit out loud that I was over two hundred forty pounds. Then I realized, nobody will ever be a better coach for me than ME! After all, I know myself better than anyone.

It took me ninety days to fall in love with myself again. To finally become my Happy Girl. I decided that in addition to transforming my body and mind, I wanted to document my journey so that I was able to share it with as many women as I could. I started a journal. I took monthly pictures and videos to track my progress. I put a plan together that allowed me, a working mom of six amazing kids - nine, eight, seven, six, six, and three-months-old, to finally be successful in my weight loss venture. The goal was simple. My plan had to be easy to follow, fun to do, and most importantly, allowed me to eat real food!

By June I was ready to go! Putting my visions and goals on paper, holding myself accountable and sharing this with the world is one of my greatest accomplishments. The thing about me is I am a born leader and motivator. I've been in the automotive sales industry for twenty plus years. I own my own business and on top of that manage a crazy household of eight. I don't have a master's degree. I live my life by experiences and that, ladies, I have plenty of! I just needed to finally figure out how to lead and motivate myself, for once, instead of everyone else. I knew once I was able to accomplish this, I would be unstoppable!

By June of 2019, I was feeling AWESOME! I was down over sixty-five pounds and it started to get really hard! I finally qualified to get a tummy tuck, so I scheduled one. I was so excited! This is what I had wanted for so long. After praying about the surgery and talking it over at length with my family, I decided to cancel my surgery. I wanted to challenge myself one last time. Even if it meant losing $500 for cancelling.

I have come so far, and I still strive to be better every single day. In

January 2020, I joined CrossFit Boot Camp Legions. I get up at 4 am Monday through Friday, leave the house by 4:45 am, push myself hard during a fifty-minute class, and make it home by 6 am before the kids are even awake for the day! I have found a way to devote time to myself and it doesn't hurt our schedule or interfere with routines. I have finally made myself a priority on my list. I wasn't even on my list before, let alone a priority. My only disappointment is that I waited this long to change. I have missed so many happy and amazing milestones in my life because I used to put on a fake smile for the world but was never truly happy with myself. I am not that Jenn anymore. I will be forty in October of 2020, and I decided two years ago I was going to love myself first from now on. It is okay to love yourself. It is important to make your health and happiness a priority. I was always rooting for everyone else but never for me. Now I root for everyone, including me! That was the main change I made. No matter what diet you are on, what pill you are taking, or what surgery you have, if you don't love yourself, the road to success is so much harder. You will always question yourself. I do it every single day. I continue to challenge myself because I want to be the best mom I can be. I want to be a cool mom! I want to make my kids and husband proud. When I look in the mirror now, I realize that I have actually changed. I see a completely different person looking back at me from the girl I saw in 2017. I was so scared to change. I changed. I believed I mattered enough to add myself to my list. You matter. Your happiness matters. You deserve to be added to your list.

I launched The Happy Girl Company in January 2019. I have a group of over sixty-five women who have decided to take this journey with me. My goal is to reach as many women as I can and be there for them! It is so important to have someone by your side during the most difficult times in your life. I want to be that someone for you.

I have hundreds of women who take fitness classes at The Hip Hop Shop and an amazing group of women who joined The Happy Girl Company! I am still in the car business and manage a crazy household of eight. I get up at 4 am because I choose to push myself. I love myself now and that self-love makes it so much easier to push for your family, focus on your job, and continue to set goals and dream big. I love you all.

Let's do this together!

ABOUT JENN ROMANO-BAUS

After walking away from an abusive relationship in 2012 as a single mom of two little girls, ages two and one, I slowly learned to wipe the slate clean and began to heal, rebuild, and trust again. I re-married in 2016 and combined our families into one big happy blended family of eight! I am a wife, a mom of six (ages ten, nine, eight, seven, seven, and two), a professional with over twenty years in the automotive industry and a small business owner. I love to dance and wanted to offer something affordable to families in my area. In January 2016, I opened The Hip Hop Shop and we have won Best of Gloucester County for Best Birthday Party Facility as well as Best Fitness Studio in 2017, 2018 and 2019!! After having my youngest daughter in December 2017, I was finally ready to change for me. I launched an online weight loss company that offers 1-on-1 support, motivation and coaching to women everywhere. Since going live in January 2019, The Happy Girl Company has helped me lose close to one hundred pounds and helped over one hundred women on their weight loss journey over the last year!

www.thehiphopshop.us
jennshiphopshop@gmail.com

www.thehappygirlcompany.com
thehappygirlcompany@gmail.com

ONE STORY, TWO HEARTS

A Mother's Hope and a Daughter's Dream

The next two chapters you are about to read are written from a mother's perspective and a daughter's perspective about the same event.

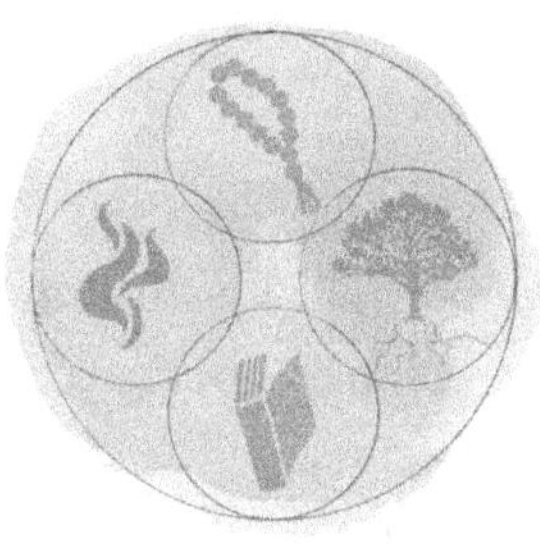

A MOTHER'S HOPE

Carol Dechen

Our story started with several phone calls between my daughter Jillian, myself, and my two other children. Jillian was up in Presque Island, ME, a small logging community which borders Canada, working as a traveling ER nurse. With each telephone conversation we all noticed that she just did not seem herself. She was very forgetful and complained of being dizzy and nauseated. It was hard to decide if she had the flu or something else. She went to the ER where she worked and was diagnosed with an inner ear infection and sent home with medications. When I spoke to her after her first ER visit, I asked her to start writing down what she did each day and the time. For examples, feeding her dog, Foster, taking him out for a walk, or eating. After a few days of this same scenario, I decided I needed to go up and see for myself what was going on. After all, for the most part, she was very independent, self-sufficient, and very responsible. She was working and traveling the country, just her and her Foster, so none of this was making any sense.

When I arrived at her apartment, I found her with a foot-drop when walking over to greet me and her left wrist was twisted inward. The temperature outside was frigid and yet she had her bedroom window wide open because she was hot. The apartment was not hot. When we took Foster outside, she had to go down twenty steps on her butt because she was to unable to walk down, even if she used the handrails. I knew then that we needed to get her home ASAP.

We packed up the car, cleaned the apartment and started our fifteen-hour trek home to New Jersey. We had one hiccup when we started our trip home — yup, a flat tire! Luckily, we found some friendly and very compassionate folks who helped us get back on the road. Our trip was delayed by five hours. She was so sick, and a fifteen-hour-plus car ride is the last thing you want to do when you are dizzy and nauseous, but we made it home with no further delays other than New Jersey turnpike traffic.

I was able to get in to see our family physician, and upon his physical examination of her, he suspected it was Multiple Sclerosis (MS). I had no idea what MS was. We did not have anyone in our family, nor any friends or relatives, with MS. We were able to get an MRI the next day where initially she was diagnosed as having a stroke. We were transferred to the stroke unit at Thomas Jefferson University Hospital (TJUH). After thirty-six hours, because of further exploration of past and recent medical history, it was determined that she had not suffered a stroke but more than likely it was MS. However, because this was the first episode, it could not be called MS but was labeled as Clinically Isolate Syndrome (CIS). She was given a three-day regimen of steroids, antibiotics, and a few other medications and sent home. This was her first holiday home since she had started traveling across the country as an ER nurse, and it certainly was not how she wanted to spend her holiday: at home on mom's couch.

Several days later, we had the family over for dinner to celebrate the holiday. It was a great night with all of the family together. The very next morning, Jill woke up with what she described as Vaseline over her eyes and she could not see clearly. We called the hospital and were told to come into the ER for evaluation. Luckily, we were met by the same neurology resident that we had seen just days before. Again, she was hospitalized and began a three-day regimen of steroids and fluids.

Not only was she nauseated and still dizzy, but now she couldn't see and had extreme sensitivity to light. So, she sat in a dark hospital room in bed and was very depressed. Her life of independence and her career were now in jeopardy with no real answers. We went home New Year's Eve day and were told to make an appointment to see a neurologist in two weeks.

Getting in to see the neurologist quickly was a feat in itself. The earliest we could get in to see the neurologist specializing in MS was three weeks away. Over the next several days, while waiting to see the neurologist, Jill's physical and mental health declined rapidly. In the morning we would get her to the downstairs family room where she would spend the day sleeping on the couch or over a trash can vomiting. In the early evening, we would get her upstairs to her bedroom, otherwise she had no strength to go up the steps to her bedroom. Soon she just slept on the couch in the family room and I knew I had to find answers when she started doing an army crawl to the bathroom because she had no strength to stand or walk.. We also noticed that her speech was becoming more and more difficult to understand. There was even a choking incident while eating food one afternoon. Things were just so unexplainable. She was frustrated and we were puzzled with what was happening.

I finally called my family physician again to ask if this was normal. Our appointment to see the neurologist was still two weeks away. Our physician made a house call that same evening and recommended I get Jillian to the ER. He agreed that she had definitely declined since he had last seen her in the office just a few weeks ago. We were in the middle of a winter snowstorm, so we were not going anywhere that night, but first thing the next morning we went back to TJUH where Jill was admitted for the third time in less than one month. We were also in the middle of flu season, so we had to spend the night in the ER waiting for a private room. I stayed with Jillian, since at this point she was unable to communicate about her present or past medical history.

So, we got to a nursing floor, however this was not the neurology floor, which was under renovation. We were on the orthopedic floor. Jill was inconsolable and screaming because they did a spinal tap, and it was very painful. There was little I could do to calm her down. Minor movements sent her off screaming. Looking back, it had to be an extremely frightening experience not to be able to tell me or anyone what she was feeling, so screaming was all she was able to do. I was embarrassed and I also felt bad for the other patients on the floor and the nursing staff trying to function yet listen to a screaming patient. I spoke to the nursing staff to ask them to give her something to help calm her down several times. After the third time, I insisted on speaking with the nursing supervisor. I said, "we would not let our mental health patients scream for hours on hours, so why are we allowing my daughter to be in pain and obviously in some type of distress?" We finally got her some medications to calm her down but also moved her down the hall where her screams were somewhat muffled. I remained with her, and the nurses were very attentive to her needs.

The next several days and weeks at TJUH were eye-opening. We met with physical therapy, speech therapy for decreased swallow reflex and risk of choking or aspiration, occupational therapy, and the blood bank for plasmapheresis treatments. There were so many doctors, nurses, and students coming and going, but we saw little improvement during this time.

Jill was in the hospital while waiting for the neurology appointment. I asked around to nursing staff and family for their opinion of going to the neurologist appointment by myself without Jillian. Everyone agreed that I should go. They all agreed because they had heard me speak of this neurologist that all of the medical staff referred to as the expert, yet he had not come to the hospital to see my daughter. I remember thinking, "Why wouldn't he want to come and examine this independent 27-year-old female who just two months ago was very healthy, but now was newly diagnosed with Multiple Sclerosis — a disease he is an expert in!" I could not wrap my head around this, and I needed answers.

Looking back and telling our story, there were many times during these months of hospitalization that I had to stand up for my daughter to get things moving in her medical treatment. For instance, her third admission when she was screaming because she could not talk, or the time when she was vomiting day after day with no real progression in stopping. I am no hero; I'm just a mom doing what moms do, and that is protecting their little ones no matter how big or grown they are. That's just what moms are supposed to do, right?

Over the course of sitting in the hospital, trying to understand this new diagnosis of MS, I did my due diligence by surfing the web to find out more about MS. There is so much information out there, it is mind blowing. MS can also mimic several other life-threatening diseases. Jill was prodded and poked, up and down, test after test, trying to rule out other disease processes, but everything came back to MS.

So, I went to that doctor's appointment, and they were not going to let me in because Jill was not with me. But we had been waiting three weeks to see the doctor and I was not leaving that office until I had my fifteen minutes with the MS expert! I was very nervous, but I got to see the doctor. The news was not good. Jill was diagnosed with the worst of the four types of MS: she had fulminating MS, or terminal MS.

I feel blessed to have had the opportunity to be with Jill throughout this ordeal. She was in no shape to be able to communicate with physicians or medical staff. If I was not there, she was not able to tell me what happened during the day or night. She was in the hospital more than she was home during those six months.

I am a retired Operating Room nurse and Jill was an ER nurse, and we both learned much more about our healthcare from the other side of the bed. We were astonished at some of the interactions we had with staff or doctors, some of them good and some of them bad. For example, inserting a Foley catheter upon every single ER admission; as a nurse it's something we all learn in nursing school. It's not hard but something that could cause a lot of trouble for the patient if not done correctly. It was hard to watch. Or the insertion of an IV. Don't stick the patient three times and then say, "Maybe I need help with this." Or the fact that there was very limited private space while in the hospital for the patient or the family. I found the bathroom and the chapel to be my solace. A place where I could shut my mind down and pray for a miracle to make my daughter better.

I remember feeling helpless and, like any mother, I thought to myself that I should have this disease and not my daughter. I did not want to talk to anyone. After all, I was being inundated with daily hospital schedules of blood draws, PT, OT, doctors, teaching staff members, housekeeping, beepers, monitors, and more. I talked to each of my children pretty much on a daily basis and my sisters once a week. I couldn't talk more than that. I was exhausted. Looking back now, I was probably depressed. Why us? We had already endured the heartache of losing a husband and father, and now one of my kids was so sick with no expectation of getting any better. We needed a miracle and we needed one quickly.

I prayed a lot, and I know that family and friends prayed a lot for Jillian. That's all we had. We had hope and prayer, which allowed us to think that things had to get better. It looked really bad for a very long time. Day in and day out with very little improvements.

Over the course of months and years of living with MS, I have learned and listened to other folks with MS. It is very interesting to hear other stories from a mom or a dad, or the patient themselves. My daughter was diagnosed with MS in January 2014 much to our surprise. Many times it is hereditary, but we had no family history of MS. Our story is unique, as are most cases of MS. No two people present the same, hence why some people have no idea they are living with MS. MS symptoms can be very subtle to very complicated, mimicking other disease processes, and therefore it can take years for an accurate diagnosis of MS.

Jillian had been so very sick and there just seemed to be no hope. She was continuously vomiting with the slightest movement, and I had had enough. I took a stand with the doctors. I said to them, "We need a change to her treatment. What we are doing right now is not working, so let's go back to the drawing board and develop a new plan because this is not working." They did. The very next day, they came back with some trial medicine for her nausea, her dizziness, and the progression of her disease. We started an infusion of Tysabri. This was so nerve-wracking. This drug is very caustic to the body, and 2% could cause a fatal brain infection. I had to make a big decision with Jill's best interest at heart. She couldn't live like this, so I decided to try something else because we had nowhere to go but up; she was at rock bottom. June 13, 2014 is the day our lives turned for the better, specifically Jillian's life.

Each day, each week, I began to see her improve. It was a very slow process but little by little she started to gain her strength and challenge herself to push harder. And push she did. She began with yoga at home, to walking to the corner with a rollator, to walking around the block, moving from walkers to a cane, to using a walking stick, to buying a recumbent bike. She continues to push herself. For instance, in November of 2016, she walked the Philadelphia Half Marathon, which is thirteen miles. In September of 2017, she completed half of the MS City to Shore bike ride, which is seventy-five miles, and now is planning another half marathon in June 2020.

Fast forward to present time, Jillian is now living life her way, married and settled in Wyoming with her new husband and three golden retrievers. She remains very active by hiking or walking daily and practices yoga for strength and flexibility. They have purchased some land and plan to build a home. The home design will have handicap accessibility because she does not know what her future holds, and planning for the worst makes the most sense for the two of them.

I am very proud of Jillian. She has been through a lot and has had to deal with learning about and living with MS. She had to relearn to eat, walk, and talk and rebuild her life around MS. It does not define her, but it is something that does not go away. She cannot work, especially as a nurse, because of short term memory deficiency, inability to balance or lift objects with both hands, and definitely a lack of fine motor skills in her dominant hand. But she can walk, and that gives her a sense of accomplishment.

I also marvel at Jillian's ability to talk to people. She will make friends in Walmart or at her infusion center or just walking down the street. She enjoys talking about her MS with other MS patients or teaching people about MS to those who are inquiring about the disease. She never gave up. Don't get me wrong, she had her moments of self-pity, because who wouldn't feel sorry for themselves? She had an awesome career as a traveling nurse and aspirations of becoming a flight nurse. She wanted children of her own. But now, her life goals needed to change to include MS.

This was my experience from the eyes of a mother and the heartache of watching one of your children suffer. You feel helpless yet invincible because you will do anything to make it right, even if it's only a little better. I watched Jill fight for herself, and she continues to fight for her dreams. She deserves all of them.

I hope this helps some of you out there with a family member, or a friend, or someone you know who has MS. It is a devastating disease which robs mostly our young women of their dreams. It is my hope that, as a mother, family member, or friend, you help them find a new normal and fight for them. We need to raise awareness and find a cure now.

ABOUT CAROL DECHEN

I am a retired Operating Room Nurse, mother of three grown children, grandmother to three grandchildren, along with six furry grandpups, five of which are Golden Retrievers, with one beagle.

I currently am an independent certified health coach trained to help other people transform their lives to optimal health. When life is hectic with work, raising a family and the stress of making sure it all works, we tend to forget about the basics of self-care. I was living a very unhealthy lifestyle and had a revelation that I needed to make some changes to my lifestyle so I would be around to watch my kids and grandchildren grow up. So, I took charge and lost the weight. Now I am living a healthier lifestyle and feel so much better, being much more active (golfing, swimming, biking and fishing).

The diagnosis of MS and living with it seemed so unreal at the time, and looking back it still feels like a nightmare. Our experience with MS came as a shock with no family history. My daughter's diagnosis was unimaginable and heartbreaking, and yet she found a way to bounce back to a new normal and live her life full of dreams. That's all a mother wishes for their children.

I am writing this story to bring awareness not to my daughter or myself, but to highlight and bring awareness to this devastating disease called Multiple Sclerosis (MS). We hope and pray we find a cure within my lifetime, but more so in Jillian's lifetime.

I can be reached at dechenc@comcast.net.

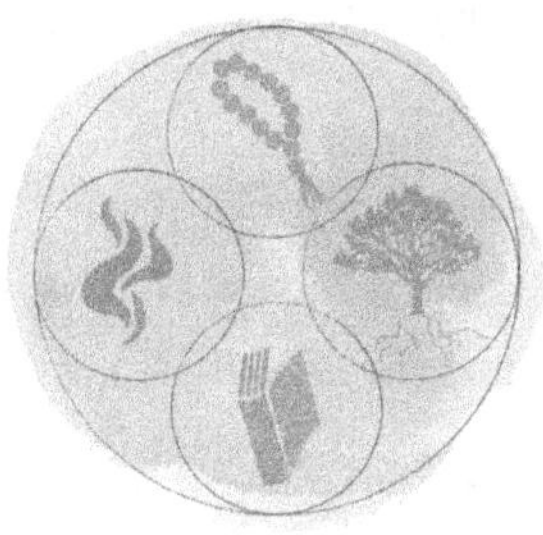

A DAUGHTER'S DREAM

Jillian Blosser

I was a normal twenty-seven-year-old, a traveling Emergency Nurse, going from state to state in my Jeep; New Jersey, Texas, Minnesota, Wyoming, Maine; living my best life with my golden retriever by my side, Foster. Then, as the Baz Luhrmann song Everybody's Free (to Wear Sunscreen) goes, "something blindsides you at 4 p.m. on some idle Tuesday" and my life changed.

I don't have a full memory of *that* year, some things are foggy, but what I do remember I call them blips. These blips are moments or images that are crystal clear. For instance, Mom standing in the door of my hospital room on the phone, giving an update to a doctor who I worked with back in Wyoming. Me being extremely frustrated with the physical therapist wanting me to stand when I wasn't able to move my head half an inch without vomiting from the insane nausea and dizziness. Imagine the worst hangover of your life, now imagine that, day in and day out, every minute of every hour for seven months, all while having the muscle tone of cooked spaghetti and now, someone has the great idea to make you stand. I remember being unable to move or talk, but I was trying desperately to communicate that the "pressure ulcer" on my heel that everyone was so concerned about, was a surfing scar from my college days – but weeks later when I finally could communicate, I realized they were talking about the opposite foot– that was my bad! I remember when I fell in the driveway at Moms house and my brother coming to the house to pick me up off the ground and he got me into my Mom's front passenger seat and the song by Luke Bryan, "Drink A Beer" came on, Matt was in the backseat and his face was in his hand and he said "I can't listen to this right now", and to this day, anytime I hear that song it brings me right back to that moment. My sister, Jaimie, would paint my toes whenever she would come to the hospital and every morning a neurologist student would come in my room for a daily assessment, he was a funny middle aged guy with a bald head and he would always ask what color my toes were that day. It is unimaginable to someone who has never been in that position to be in a hospital room, everyone around you is talking about you, not knowing if you will live or die. But I was there the whole time, I heard and saw but could not speak, I could not move my limbs, could not scratch an itch, nor tell people I was there, I could hear you but I could not respond, I could only blink on command. So many emotions–anger, fear, frustration–I would never wish that on anyone, it was probably the single worst feeling through that whole year!

It was the beginning of December. I had just taken an assignment up in Northern Maine in the ER. I started having symptoms of what I assumed was an inner ear infection. The nurse that I am, I just brushed it off–something simple, just take some over the counter medication and all will be good as new. I would take very hot showers, because when it's negative five degrees out and you are sick, nothing feels as good as a hot shower. I would get in with the idea of washing my hair and as soon as the hot water would hit my body, I did not know why, but all I could do was lean against the shower wall. I would get out and feel so exhausted that I would stumble to my bed, flop down on it and fall asleep for a bit. I would wake up and attempt to go shower again. Little did I know then, sudden exhaustion in hot water is a tell-tale sign of what was to come. Hours or possibly days passed, I am not quite sure, but dizziness and exhaustion, forgetfulness and confusion, slight foot drop and left arm weakness had presented. I was scared, I wanted Mom there with me. I took my first dose of the over the counter dizziness medication, thirty minutes later a large, flat red rash covered my chest and I had a feeling in my throat. I was a really smart nurse in my day, quick to realize symptoms or jump to action, and I knew something was not right, but I was not in my right state of mind to know my brain was not thinking appropriately and I could not see the giant flashing lights in front of me saying something is really wrong. I called Mom, as I had been talking to her a lot these past few hours or days, again I couldn't tell you if moments were passing or weeks, but I would tell her all about all my symptoms, she would try to give me advice. Now I will tell you from personal emergency medicine experience, you can sort of give guidance over the phone but it can be a whole different story when you are standing with the person and you can use sight, hearing, smell and touch to assess a situation. I was a poor historian of what was going on, so when in doubt, she said what I would have said "get to the ER", so a new friend took me to the hospital where I had worked for just two days, where I got a concoction of medication to reverse the suspected allergic reaction. I was scared, I was in a place where no one knew me for more than a handful of days. I was scared and knew something was wrong but was confused so I was not thinking properly, I was alone, confused and having to make big judgement calls on my own. Since I had only been in Maine for a week, the staff at the ER that I worked at did not know my baseline personality. For all they knew I was just an odd bird, but something serious was brewing. I was scared and just wanted my Mom.

I was released from the ER and went back to my apartment. Thoughts, dizziness, and confusion festered and turned into an emotional crisis where I actually felt everything in my life–family, friends, my career, were all falling apart and I was swirling around and could not make sense of anything, I could do nothing to save myself. I was scared and remembered being on the phone with my sister, my recruiter from work and closest friends talking, crying, trying to get out of this assignment–because of course life was so great now, that obviously, it was this assignment that had sent me into a tailspin. I was scared, I did not know what was happening. I just thought if I could get out of this assignment in Maine I could go back to Wyoming and everything would be okay. I was alone, scared, I felt as though time was passing and things were falling apart every second that I did not react to fix it. I knew but I did not know that by me trying to fix things I was only messing them up more. Hours and days went by, though it felt like weeks. All while this was going on, my family was working to get my Mom to me in Maine from NJ.

This is when a lot of the blips start to happen. I don't know why I did certain things, but I just have blips of me. It is though I was watching all these things go on, watching from above. I had the window open in my apartment, and I was holding my head and top of my torso out of the window because I was having hot flashes. I had never had them before, did not know what they felt like and they were and still are short and intense. They come on in about one to three seconds and generally last for about ten minutes as long as I can cool myself down. Over the years I've learned and, am still learning tricks to manage my hot flashes. God, bless me when I go through menopause, double duty hot flashes!

When I saw mom pull into the parking lot, I immediately burst into tears. I finally let the air out of my chest. Mom was here, Mom could save me, Mom was smart, she could tell me what I needed to do to save myself. She got to my apartment, I flew the door open and hugged her, sobbing into her arms. I was so thankful she was here.

We packed up my Jeep and drove back to NJ. We got to my childhood family doctor, Dr. Michael Rogers. He was the first to say it: "I think this is Multiple Sclerosis, but we need to do more tests to be sure." He sent me for an MRI. I laid in the machine. I remember when it was done, I sat up on the table and the radiology tech came to me and said, "You need to call your doctor right away." Immediately I thought, "Oh my god, I did have a stroke!" which would be completely plausible–all those long hours driving cross-country could have formed a DVT (Deep Vein Thrombosis) and it could have broken free and gone to my brain and caused a stroke.

To avoid going the long way around the barn here, the short of it is, I wound up at Thomas Jefferson University Hospital, or as I call it, Jeff. I was in the ER and scared. I had never been on this side of the bed before. I'm a nurse, I handled serious matters, I had never had anything wrong with me, so being vulnerable and not being able to call the shots on the human body was extremely scary, I was no longer in charge of my health. The doctors determined I needed to stay, so I was admitted. When I was being pushed upstairs in the stretcher by orderlies, they were talking amongst themselves–no fault to them, I'm sure I have done that exact same thing a time or two, not thinking, but that was a horrible feeling. I really hope every doctor, nurse, tech, orderly and CNA really hears me when I say this–I was having one of the worst days of my life and they were just chatting casually about weekend plans. It makes me think, "What if I ever did something to affect someone like that in my time as a nurse or even an orderly?" That first night in the hospital was terrifying. I tossed and turned all night with all the hospital sounds. Mom wound up staying every day and every night with me for that year, by my side at every turn. But that first night, I had to stand on my own and I was as scared as a child.

Over the next six months I spent weeks at a time in the hospital and physical rehabs. I have lots of those blips throughout this time, my life was in a whirlwind, and I thought I was never going to land on my feet. Upon January arriving I was given six months to live. Now, because I was in what I call a mental coma, I had no idea until about March that six months were given in January, and apparently that was two months ago ... so I spent two out of the six months I was given lost in my own MS brain, no idea time was passing. Can you imagine knowing that because you were in your mental coma and not really knowing that in

January you had been given a death sentence, you only have four months left to live now, and you're so bad off? In general, it's a question people throw around. What would you do if you only had a month left to live? Answers usually are something big–go to Antarctica, go bungee jumping, get married. I had four months and I couldn't even move my head half an inch without vomiting. So, what were my options?

Life was pretty dang miserable for the next six months, but June 13, 2014 was the day my life changed in a different direction yet again. I remember it was Friday the 13th, and as silly as that is, I was superstitious about that day. I was about to have Tysabri infused for the first time, not knowing what I know now, all that my Mom went through to even make it a possibility. With all the serious complications that could arise from this infusion, and my less than perfect track record with MS so far, I was not really feeling too positive. Honestly, I really was starting to give up the possibility of ever getting better. I did not care what happened to me. I had accepted that I had been given a death sentence. I do remember thinking to myself well at least I had gotten to do some big things in my life like live in Australia, go hang gliding, travel cross country, be a mom to the most perfect dog ever - but please God oh God, or even Dad, oh Dad (my Dad passed when I was just a kid so instead of talking to God, I talk to Dad), just make this painful process end. I was not so much in physical pain, but my head had been swirling for seven months. It was breaking me. I had always been a happy-go-lucky, talkative person, but this figuratively and literally was killing me.

Over the next several days after my infusion, all the sudden I could move my head without vomiting. It was still like trying to stack a mound of grape jelly– it just was not happening–though without the dizziness and constant vomiting I was attempting to sit up and actually eat real food. It was a nice change of pace from the soft diet of what my brother and I joked "looked like a can of dog food".

Weeks went by, months went by, and I went from being bed-bound to getting around in my wheelchair, to using the walker, to forearm crutches, to walking sticks, to one walking stick to walking without any assistive devices at all. Chris Taylor, a friend of the family, had gone through something similar before, having to relearn how to walk, talk, eat and all that stuff. She was wonderful to me; and to this day we are good friends. I credit her with helping me learn to walk again. We started with one block, which in a couple months went to half a mile and has now sparked a love of walking. I walked my first half marathon in November 2016 with my friend from high school, Allie Bratton. I plan to do my second half marathon in June of 2020 with my friend, Jessica Fink and our dogs.

I've struggled to find my new normal. Unfortunately, everyone has unwarranted advice about your progress. I've had jobs here and there trying to find normalcy in my new MS world. However, for one reason or another I haven't found a good fit yet. It weighs on you and as I said before everyone has an opinion, but the thing I have learned since being sick, it is my journey, and at the end of my life will I think back to the life I led and will I be able to say - I lived the life I wanted to or did I just live the life I was expected too. I have never been someone to go through the motions, I have always gone big in life, not afraid of risks.

When someone asks in general who are you, the old answer is, "I'm an ER nurse." But I can't say that anymore. I'm no longer an ER nurse, and that was such an identity I loved. I was brave, never afraid to jump into a situation and help another, could talk anyone down with kindness and understanding. But I've learned that I am not just what my profession is or was. My soul is what makes up who I am. I am who I am because of everything I have been through. And if there ever comes a day when I have to live that year again, I will be able to tell myself I did it once and I can do it again. Because even though I'm no longer an ER nurse, I'm still a smart, kind, loving, funny, outgoing, talkative, adventurous, happy girl, but I just have to do it differently now.

Tips for anyone who must go through something like this –

1. If you are in the hospital for longer than one day and are unable

to do it yourself, have someone brush your hair minimally twice a day. My hair was about to the center of my back. From being in the hospital bed like a wet noodle for months, my hair had become matted to the back of my head. My mom worked on my hair for days to get the knots out and every second was miserable. I was dizzy, unable to sit up, and the constant tugging on my scalp was painful. My mom was afraid we would have to shave my head, but thank goodness she got enough out that it could be cut to the nape of my neck.

2. I do not remember this time, but I do remember being told afterwards that my brother, Matt, came up with the idea to put a sneaker on my foot to prevent my constant rubbing of my heel up and down on the sheets, causing injury to my skin – genius!

3. Keeping the head of my hospital bed below thirty degrees in elevation prevented bedsores on my bottom. However, on the other hand, keeping my body supine for most of the day for days and weeks at a time (for comfort against the dizziness) actually made my dizziness so much worse in the long run. It is six to one half a dozen to another, but just know these possibilities and do your best to alternate.

4. If anyone has ever had steroids intravenously infused, they know the terrible taste it creates in your mouth – it is like melting a Tylenol tablet on your tongue. A very kind nurse told me this trick upon my first infusion. Put a piece of chocolate on your tongue and let it dissolve. It is incredible, the taste goes away completely! Something I have figured out on my own is, if you must take oral steroids, take it with chocolate nut milk--again, works like a charm.

Dedication --

I know if it was not for my Mom's love for me, patience, stubbornness, compassion, and nursing background, I would not be where I am today. Mom was amazing that year, she saved my life. I will never forget what she did for me that year.

ABOUT JILLIAN BLOSSER

I grew up with my dad, a police officer, and my mom, a nurse, and two siblings. I got my fun, outgoing personality from my dad and the bug to be a nurse with big aspirations from my mom. I currently live in Wyoming with my husband, Ken, and our three golden retrievers, otherwise known as my three walking partners.

I always wanted to go back to Wyoming to settle down even before I got sick. At one point, while living in New Jersey, something was missing and I felt this everyday: *this* was not the life I wanted. I could no longer strive for my dream of being a flight/trauma nurse and could no longer have children. I really fought with myself about what I felt obligated to do versus chasing my dreams. One day I just realized and said to myself, "I don't want to wake up when I'm eighty and realize I never got to do any of the things I always wanted to do." My then boyfriend (now husband) said, "Okay let's do it!" So, Ken and I moved cross country to Wyoming and bought two acres of heaven facing the Big Horn Mountains. We got married in a very small ceremony at sunrise in Jackson Hole in January of 2019. Life is not what I thought it was going to be, but have you ever heard that quote, "Tell God your plans and hear God laugh." I have always been a planner, but I realize you've just got to roll with the punches. So, I used to think I was living my best life back before I got sick, but Ken and I get to live in Wyoming with our three boys, and I'm grateful for every single moment.

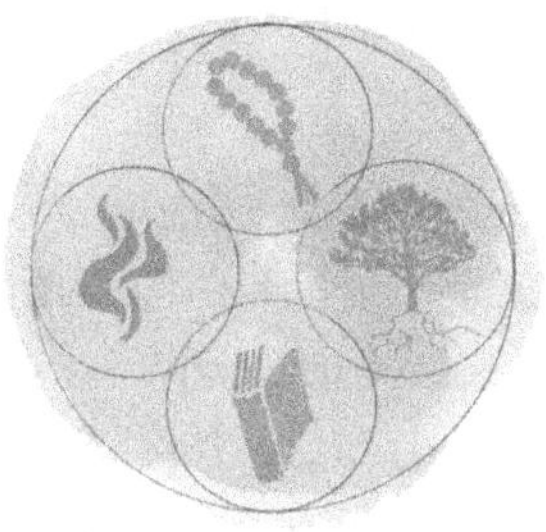

CREATE YOUR POTENTIAL

Rebecca Chalson

Before you can create your potential, you have to first unlock it. Let me explain. Have you ever had a dream that painted a picture of your reality? Even more noteworthy, is when it takes you through the subconscious evolution of what has been versus what can be for your life. This was that kind of dream.

PART ONE: GOING THROUGH THE MOTIONS

My Dream… I find myself in a crowded room full of people walking around aimlessly.

Heads down, arms swaying, and everyone acting as if they are alone in a crowded room full of walking zombies. With my head raised and looking around, I cannot help but wonder, "Why are we here, and why is everyone acting this way? This is not where I belong."

Yes, there was a time in my life when that was exactly how I felt.

My Reality… As the oldest of ten children and with an unorthodox education, I grew up wrestling with self-identity and limiting beliefs regarding my potential.

To add to this challenge, at fourteen-years-old my family joined a religious conservative lifestyle. This isolated community was especially oppressive towards women, and obtaining a college degree, let alone a career, was frowned upon. I often felt like I was simply a number with no sense of individuality. However, I always felt in my gut that I had a unique purpose just waiting to be set free. Be that as it may, I was going through the motions of what was expected of me and felt caught up in a world of walking zombies. Aimlessly hoping for change, but I felt powerless to create it.

One night, I was looking up at the sky, admiring all the stars shining brightly. Living in "farm country" made seeing the Milky Way Galaxy possible. I thought about the names of the various constellations and the millions of years they have bravely stood their ground. People of all backgrounds and experiences have been able to look up at the same night sky that I was. For a brief moment, I felt connected to a bigger world and people whom I had never met. I was struck by the extensivity of the universe in comparison to the little corner of the world I was living in.

By age nineteen, I could not suppress this nagging feeling any longer. I concluded that if I was not willing to step out of my comfort zone, and interact with the real world, I may never discover my full potential.

An especially defining moment was when I was working at my minimum wage job and gave my two weeks' notice. "What makes you think you can make more than $7.25 an hour without a college degree?" my boss said, as if to echo my own fears. **This would be the first of many milestones where I would choose to step beyond complacency and evolve as a SURVIVOR.**

The first night on my own was especially memorable. I recall lying in bed looking up at the ceiling of my apartment. A rush of fear and excitement flooded over me. I could not see the sky, but for the first time in my life, I felt like a cloud had been lifted. The future was unknown but thinking about that night under the stars gave me hope. The only limitations were the ones I put on myself.

For years, I felt like an alien who had landed on planet Earth but determined to learn the language of the locals. Pop culture, traditional dating, and learning the social cues of society were all challenges that often left me feeling more like an outsider. I was determined to fit in and appear "normal". Socially awkward in my personal life, I built my sense of worth through climbing the corporate ladder. Over the next twelve years, I applied my work ethic and sheer determination to become a leader in corporate America. Eventually, I started earning opportunities that typically only those with a college degree achieve.

I was evolving from a once zombie-like existence and now morphing into a living and breathing soul. **No longer just a number, I was carving out a sense of individuality and belonging. I felt like I had finally graduated from survivor to THRIVER status.** Be that as it may, my life was about to unfold to reveal that, even though my external circumstances were no longer holding me captive, limiting beliefs were still preventing me from tapping into my full potential.

PART TWO : BREAKING FREE OF LIMITING BELIEFS

My Dream… Observing the room full of zombies in my dream is like recognizing the "walking dead" of my past belief system.

Turning my attention now to myself, I look down at my hands. They appear normal, until I start flexing my fingers. Small sparks of electricity flash from my fingertips like lightning bolts building strength. Looking around the room, I now see others discovering the same phenomenon with their own hands. No longer zombies, we form a circle of connection. With one uniformed gesture, we raise our hands to engage our superpower strengths and create a huge electromagnetic force field dome around us. It occurs to me, "How is it that such powerful beings can be imprisoned?" I look to the far end of the room and see a larger-than-life padlock on the door of our captivity. **Interesting to note, the lock is on the inside.** My first thought, "Every lock has a key, so where is it?" This was the same question I often asked myself while wrestling with setbacks in my own path towards self-discovery.

My Reality… During my twenties, I searched for this mythical key that would magically unlock my success and happiness.

Can you relate? How many of us go through life thinking that if we could just read one more self-help book, gain more education, earn that promotion, or find that missing relationship …THEN we will feel more empowered. However, it took repeated disappointments and betrayals for me to recognize the brainwashed sense of my potential was based on a distorted perspective. It took time, but I eventually began to realize that the only obstacles to my success are limiting beliefs. I can create my potential. **Once I realized that the lock to my success was on the inside, in my mind, I was able to take control of my reactions to life circumstances and begin to manifest what I wanted to see in my reality. I became intentional about not playing the victim to my pain and instead chose to create my potential through it.**

An example of this was when I lost my "dream job" after climbing the corporate ladder.

By thirty years old, I had a corporate management job that made me feel that I had finally reached my potential. However, after moving to a new city for a big job promotion, I unfortunately became one of nationwide layoffs. **Despite wrestling with disappointment, this set back was a blessing in disguise. Now I was free to discover my personal brand.**

Let me explain…

Have you ever felt like you dodged one bullet, only to find yourself in the war path of many more? Referring back to my "zombie" dream, I had found myself going through the motions of yet another era of "proving my worth" in the midst of corporate politics and popularity contests. Not only that, but I had sacrificed my health and personal life by isolating myself in the world of workaholism. **Though I had made a significant improvement in my environment compared to the restrictive lifestyle I once knew, I had subconsciously traded my sense of freedom for a false sense of identity and security.**

When I lost my dream job at an age when I was supposed to have it "all figured out", the domino effect questions unfolded. "What's next …why am I here …what is my purpose …who can I trust …how do I rebuild my sense of self-worth?" Fears plagued my mind, similar to when I first moved out at age nineteen. Despite wrestling depression, I channeled my sense of vulnerability into a greater sense of self-awareness and determination.

I'd be lying if I said it was easy…

For a time, all I wanted to do was zone out in front of the TV or sleep. I was depressed about being depressed. However, I realized there is a time to mourn loss but also regain strength. The movie, *The Secret*, based on the book by Rhonda Byrne that sold thirty million copies worldwide, made a life-changing impression on me. It explains how the Law of Attraction works when you are intentional about building a positive mindset that manifests your reality.

I realized that the Law of Attraction is not magic. It is a progression. My mindset affects my reactions, which in turn, affects the outcomes that become my reality.

First and foremost, I chose to become purposeful in the reality I wanted to create by changing how I was being influenced AT HOME. I created a Dream Board, wrote daily affirmations on my mirrors with a dry erase marker, decorated my apartment with motivational quotes, and implemented consistent meditation practices.

Second, I took the time to develop a positive circle of influence and support ONLINE. I became intentional about what I was feeding my mind with social media and streaming a positive newsfeed full of motivational speakers, entrepreneurs, and teachers. Peta Kelley, Marie Forleo, Gary Vaynerchuk, Ruby Lee, Selena Soo, and Jason Silva being amongst some of my favorites.

Finally, I recognized my need to develop a strong circle of influence and support OFFLINE. As I started making it my full-time job to connect with local networking groups, non-profits, and influencers,

I began to uncover the universal need that everyone shares regardless of their background or career. **We all have the need to create REAL connections.**

After identifying the steps I took to grow my network, I created a systematic approach for expanding one's network as a resource for others. When I told a friend about my plan to create events, and a networking resource hub, she said, "What makes you think you can do this when you just started attending networking events yourself?" I did not know exactly how I was going to do it at the time, but knowing that it was needed for the greater good, increased my determination. I shared my idea with others and my intent to create a launching event on a Monday night so that it did not conflict with any other networking groups that I was intending to help promote. The response, "Don't ever do an event on a Monday night, because no one will come," could have stopped me …but like the naysayers of my past, it did not.

On October 5, 2015, not only was my signature Full Circle Networking™ launching event on a Monday night, but it also had approximately 200 people in attendance with twenty-two networking resources represented there. The theme "What Is Your Super Strength?" and ice breakers helped guests network based on who they are, and not just what they do. I could not have done it without having a strong circle of support and friends to help make it happen. (Too many names to mention here, but you all know who you are, and I am forever grateful for you believing in me.)

Through creating masterminds, workshops, and events, my sphere of influence grew. I became known as Your Networking Navigator™ and created a networking hub to help professionals "turn online contacts into offline connections".

In 2016, I was awarded 40 Under 40 with South Jersey Business people for my impact on the community, and then in 2017, was featured in Forbes as a networking influencer sharing my tips on "How To Network Effectively In The Digital Age". I felt that I had finally tapped into my "super strength" as a connector and community builder, and enjoyed empowering others to do the same.

It was a very similar experience to the progression of how I recognized my superpower in the dream that I once had. However, there is another part to that dream that I have yet to tell you. Remember that larger-than-life lock on the door? Believe it or not, while I was still making big strides in my professional life as a Networking Navigator™, it would take yet another setback for me to recognize where the ultimate power to unlock my potential comes from.

PART THREE: WAKING UP

By 2017, I had begun to crack the code in creating a business model around helping professionals learn when, where, and how to network more effectively. Unfortunately, my growing success started to attract those with ulterior motives. Betrayed and taken advantage of, I again wrestled with depression as my sense of identity and purpose felt threatened. Thankfully, a couple of my friends, who were no stranger to depression themselves, were able to provide a light of hope. It was recommended to me to read Brené Brown's book *The Gifts of Imperfection: Let Go Of Who You Think You're Supposed To Be and Embrace Who You Are.* It explains how **it's the vulnerability of our humanity that connects us as people, not our perfection.** I became obsessed with Brené's books and videos. Like drinking water during a drought, she made a big impact on helping me process pain and map out a formula for changing the narration of my story. **I realized that it's through PAIN that we can tap into our PASSION and rebuild our sense of PURPOSE.**

It was through this time of self-reflection that I came to the following realization: People can steal what I do, but they cannot steal who I am. I concluded that it was not my Full Circle Networking™ business concept as a Networking Navigator™, but rather my "personal brand" that was the source of my strength.

My business or service is what I do. However, my personal brand

is how I SHOW the world what I do.

I realized that my true passion is much more than networking. It is empowering individuals to learn how to discover and spotlight their core strengths in order to grow a more authentic circle of influence and support. **I realized that I wanted to focus my service around helping business professionals and entrepreneurs unlock and create their personal brand. Ultimately, this would help them rise up to their unlimited potential.**

I also realized that there is a much bigger "why" that fuels my sense of purpose. The "politically" correct story of Full Circle Networking™ had been summed up in the following way. I moved to a new city … was laid off work …had to find a new job … started networking … and wanted to empower others in their networking endeavors. For a long time, I had been ashamed to tell my more vulnerable "why".

I was afraid to talk about the pain of having once been an alien zombie raised in a world of limiting beliefs and isolation. I was afraid that if my REAL story was revealed, that people would see me for who I really am: an outsider. Ironically, when I shared my bigger "why" story in 2018 through the launch of my website www.CreateYourPotential.com, more people wanted to connect with me, because to some degree, they could relate. Feeling "lost" is a challenge that everyone wrestles with at one time or another. Immigrants trying to create a sense of "home" while adapting to new surroundings and circles of influence. This was my experience, and it was through vulnerability that I was able to harness the power of my true strength, release my most authentic self, and create REAL connections that count.

PART FOUR: UNLOCK YOUR POTENTIAL

My Dream… The last part of my dream is especially significant. Realizing that an external "key" is not required to unlock my potential, I use the full power of my internal super strength instead. With fingers outstretched, I zap open the larger-than-life padlock, blasting open the door to my captivity. All those who are in the room with me flood out. Before leaving, however, everyone grabs an item from the room that could also serve as a weapon in case we are met by outside forces who threaten our freedom. Last in the room, I start searching for something less likely to be used as a weapon, but rather as a tool. I find myself searching for a pen and paper.

When I awake, I conclude that this is a dream meant to be shared. On May 18, 2016, I write, "I had a dream last night about having a superpower. However, in the beginning of the dream, I have not yet recognized it. I am not alone. I am in a large room full of people who have superpowers too, but who have also not yet discovered them." It would take years for me to fully understand and interpret the dream's meaning.

IN CONCLUSION

As you can see, it took a series of stages for me to progress out of a limiting belief system and create my potential. I was once a SURVIVOR, existing as a walking zombie going through the motions of what was expected of me. Then I became a THRIVER, progressing in growing my skillset and circle of influence. The power to unlock my greater potential came when I discovered how to "super charge" my personal brand by sharing my more vulnerable "why" and thus became a REVIVER. This is the stage when we are able to revive that which was hidden, break free into creating our greater potential, and help others do the same.

Now, I enjoy teaching people how to network and develop their personal brand through events, workshops, online training, and one-on-one coaching. I share my story as a reminder that regardless of our background, **we ultimately control our potential and can create the life of our choosing.**

ABOUT REBECCA CHALSON

With over ten years of professional sales and marketing experience, Rebecca's go-getter and personable approach to business development has earned her recognition with Forbes, 40 Under 40, and several other regional awards. As an author, podcaster, trainer, and personal branding strategist, she enjoys helping professionals build their brand and grow their network.

Rebecca's services include website and promotional video design, social media strategy, and event planning support. Her training curriculum includes practical guidance in influencer marketing, social media engagement, and building authentic relationships. *Unlock Your Potential: Discover Your Personal Brand* is one of her signature online training programs that helps individuals explore their unique core strengths and communicate their value proposition more effectively with their target audience. Learn more at www.CreateYourPotential.com/Discover

Rebecca states: "Regardless of the career path we choose, how we project our core strengths and effectively grow our sphere of influence directly impacts our level of success and happiness. That is why the sooner we can hone-in on what makes us unique (aka Personal Brand), and understand how to communicate that from a place of authenticity, the more effective we can be in creating connections that count."

Rebecca invites you to download your FREE Social Media Branding Checklist by subscribing to www.CreateYourPotential.com She can also be contacted at the following:

rebecca@createyourpotential.com

Listen to the "Real Talk With Rebecca" podcast on Spotify and iTunes: www.CreateYourPotential.com/RealTalk

Connect On Social Media:

www.facebook.com/networkingnavigator

www.linkedin.com/in/rebeccachalson

www.instagram.com/rebeccachalson

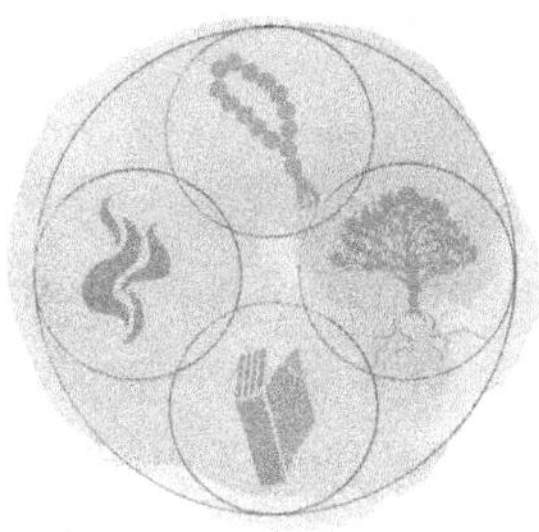

FINDING FAITH THROUGH MY FATHER

Solina Feliciano-Gonnion

It's three days before my 43rd birthday and four days shy of two months since losing my dad. I've been reflecting a lot on the past year, the past two years actually. Gotta say, it has been quite a challenging couple of years. You ever have moments in life where it feels like someone keeps ripping off every Band-Aid from every childhood wound you have ever had? Yeah, that was pretty much how the past two years felt overall. The emotional storm began with my second parents divorcing after thirty-three years of marriage. Biologically, they are my aunt and uncle, but emotionally and spiritually they are every bit my parents. This triggered a lot of memories and wounds from my biological parents' divorce, and boy did they resurface with a vengeance. Shortly after learning of the impending divorce, my (biological) dad was diagnosed with stage 4 liver cancer. We would lose him a little over a year later. And so, the crazy storm of the past two years would force me to face every ache and every pain in my life in a way I never expected.

As I've been trying to navigate through the healing process of all this, especially losing my dad, there has been one moment that keeps coming to mind. It took place about a year ago. It was the first time I took my dad to his chemo treatment. As we were sitting there waiting for the nurse to bring his meds so he could begin his treatment, we somehow ended up talking about his surprise over my second parents' divorce, which then led into his divorce from my mom. In my mind, I thought we were going to have this epic conversation where all of the missing pieces to the puzzle were put together once and for all. I thought I was going to finally have a clear picture as to what happened and why we lost touch for so many years. But that was not what happened. I honestly couldn't even tell you what was said for the most part. The only thing I remember my dad saying was, "I always knew one day God would bring my children back to me." He then closed his eyes and laid back in his chair looking extremely peaceful. And just like that the conversation was done. At that moment I realized two things. First, the conversation I thought we would have was probably never going to happen, and second, I was totally ok with that. I actually had an overwhelming sense of peace about it. I have reflected on this moment so many times over the past year because in that moment my dad taught me what true faith was, and I am forever grateful.

In that moment and since his passing I have begun to realize it's ok to not have all the answers. Choosing to let go of my need to have all the answers for the past in that moment freed us. We were able to just be together. There was no expectation or judgment, just us. We were truly present for each other. This moment has trickled into how I view all parts of my life. It made me realize that it is ok to say, "I see you here and now," and that's all that really matters. It's ok to say we may have different experiences and different perspectives on the same situation but we can meet in the middle and still celebrate our common ground and the beauty we see in each other. It helped me realize how I needed to not only accept people for who they are in the moment, but that I also needed to be kinder and more accepting of myself. I needed to rewrite the narrative of my life experiences.

You see, growing up I experienced sexual abuse before I was even in school and emotional abuse throughout my teenage years and into my early twenties. Not to mention I just felt completely lost and broken after my parents divorced when I was a child. I blamed myself. I thought somehow it was my fault. I thought if I was a better daughter, did something different, was just more of whatever it is I should've been, I never would have lost my dad for all those years. I never felt a sense of belonging anywhere or with anyone. I was a chronic people pleaser. I was always trying to mold myself to fit any situation I was in and please the people around me. I had no sense of self. I had no concept on how to handle my emotions other than to suppress them and numb myself with self-destructive behaviors. I constantly put myself in toxic and negative situations that would give me the destructive and negative outcome I thought I deserved. I had no self worth.

Now don't get me wrong, I have been working on all of this since meeting my husband and becoming a mom. Doing anything and everything I can to improve myself emotionally and spiritually. There is nothing like having children to really give you a wake up call to the messages you are sending out into the world. You start thinking about what behaviors and lessons you really want to pass on to these amazing little beings. No matter how much I worked at accepting what had happened in my life, I never really stopped feeling broken or damaged. I never truly valued who I was. That began to change during this last year I spent with my dad. The seed was planted during that conversation at chemo. That is when the shift really began for me. There was so much knowledge and love in that simple act of faith. There was a beautiful peace and acceptance displayed that struck me in a way I never felt before. There was this sudden ability to let go and trust in what is and what will be that began to blossom. What if I stopped questioning why all of these things happened? What if I just trusted that in the end there is a reason greater than any explanation that I could ever rationalize or come up with? What if I just needed to shift my perspective?

I began to realize my experiences don't define me. They are not who I am. They are not why I am broken. These experiences are actually why I am kind of amazing. They have not broken me. They have actually given me my superpowers. It is because of these experiences I have so much compassion and empathy for others. It is why I can look at a "negative" situation or someone most people would judge and turn away from and still find something good. It is why I know my daughters won't have to struggle emotionally the same way I did. They will always be allowed to have whatever emotions they need to experience and know they have a safe space to work through it. It is why I will always create a space for them to know they are not just loved but valued. They will always be seen and heard and have a space where good, bad, or indifferent, they can come to and know they are accepted and loved just as they are, always.

This simple act of seeing the possibilities, coming from a place of love, in any given situation is transformative. It has truly allowed me to have compassion for myself. It has given me the ability to finally start to honor my spirit and trust that all I have ever needed has always been inside of me. I was always a kind and empathetic person before, but the way I can show up for others now because I am finally showing up for myself is different. It is deeper. The connections I am able to make are on a different level. I can see someone and see his or her struggles in a different light. I can offer them a compassion and kindness so pure because I have been able to give it to myself. There is no longer any judgment attached to it. It really is an amazing thing to be able to honor yourself, to be able to honor your journey and where you are in it. Being able to now trust in who you are and who you will grow into. All of this will translate into the ability to honor those around you while being able to hold space for them, exactly as they are. When you free yourself you give others the ability to do the same. It is definitely not always the easiest thing to do. Some days can be extremely difficult. There will also be days where it is effortless. I know I have all of those days and everything in between, but there is a beauty in being able to surrender and trust in something greater than yourself. In these moments, I always try to remind myself that things are not happening to me but for me. And when it is one of those days where it seems almost impossible to believe that, I remind myself to just take a moment to sit back in my chair, close my eyes, take a breath, and have a little faith.

ABOUT SOLINA FELICIANO-GONNION

Solina is a licensed skin care specialist and makeup artist who believes skin care is more than skin deep. She works with people to help them feel beautiful from the inside out. Solina's mission in life is to help people identify their self worth, honor their inner beauty, and care for the external, believing anything is possible. She believes there is good in everyone and that a simple act of kindness and compassion can change someone's life. Solina is married to her college sweetheart, Joe, and is the mother of three amazing girls, Isabella, Aureanna, and Sabrina. If you would like to connect with Solina you can reach her at solinasskincare@gmail.com.

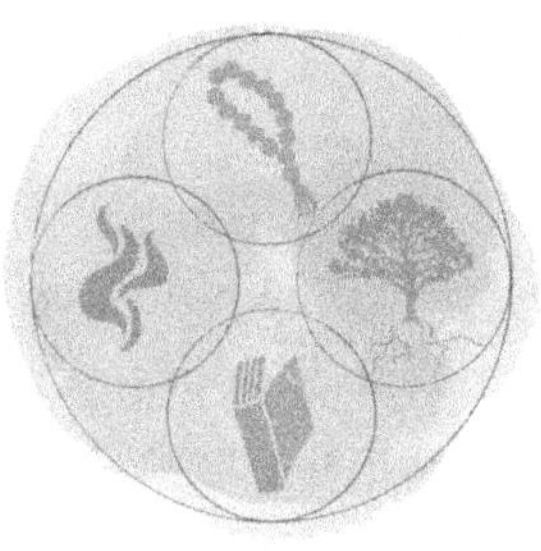

ONE SEASON

Pamela Harris

There have and will continue to be seasons that come and go in my life. Seasons which are challenging along with the seasons that bear great fruit. The season I am sharing with you has been the most challenging of all.

It started on a wonderful Friday. It was a wonderful day because Mike, my husband, was promoted to Captain in the United States Army and we went out to dinner. We celebrated with a few friends we had made since arriving in Germany the next evening.

Saturday had come and was now ending; it had been a busy two days. As I tucked my four-year-old son into bed there was an unexplainable joy. I can still see his small white teeth as he laughs. His whole face was smiling. I felt his excitement. He had a special day prepared for tomorrow; he and his dad were going to go on a father-son outing. I can remember the feel of those tiny little perfect arms as he hugged me with all his might, and I kissed his forehead and said good night.

As I got into bed, I felt so loved, safe, and secure as Mike pulled me close and tucked me in closer to him with his strong, loving arms. As I closed my eyes, I knew I would rest well, for my safest place was in his arms.

I heard the alarm go off at 6 am and I went into the little person's room (this is my son whom I often lovingly refer to as the little person.) I gently pulled back his soft blanket and caught the scent of his clean aroma. I hugged him and pulled him out of bed. "Son, it is time to get up." I can see him now, brushing his teeth and dressing himself, showing that independence which he will carry for life.

The three of us hurried through breakfast so the two of them could get on the road. I smile even now as I can see my son, Marcus, jumping around asking, "Dad, can we go?" Mike in his usual loving manner said, "Yes, son." He picked Marcus up and put him in the backseat with his seatbelt on.

Since it was Sunday and Labor Day weekend, I dressed and hurried off to church. The house was quiet as I returned home. I started reading a book, took a nap, and waited for six o'clock to see my family.

Six, seven, and eight o'clock came and passed. I walked back and forth to the kitchen window watching, waiting, and praying they were ok and would be home soon.

"It is not like Mike to be this late returning home," I thought. Since there were no cell phones, or at least we didn't own one, I couldn't call. All I could do was wait.

It was now 8:45 PM, and I will never forget that time. I was standing at the kitchen window in tears and so worried that they were still not home. I started quietly asking myself, "Where are they?" I asked myself the same question repeatedly as my voice was getting louder and louder, and I could feel my heart pounding. Then I saw some car headlights turn into the parking lot. With relief I started to breathe easier, just knowing it must be them. My body was starting to relax and became less tight with stress. "They are home!" I thought. As the car approached, I realized it was not them and the anxiety and sadness quickly returned. My fear that something had happened was back. I was now telling myself, "It will be ok."

I noticed two men in military uniforms getting out of the car and approaching our building. One looked like Mike's commanding officer, James. My heart stopped beating for a second as unbearable fear surrounded me. The doorbell was ringing. I answered the door and the trajectory of my life was changed forever. I had no control over anything at that moment. I couldn't breathe, all I could do was cry.

I found myself in a cold room which looked like a chapel, and I was so afraid and lost. I didn't know what to do. I still couldn't remember how I got there. I couldn't stop crying. "I don't know how I got here. I really don't know what is happening or what I am supposed to do," I thought. A man with a clergy collar approached me. He asked in a very calm, smooth voice, "Are you ready to see your husband?" I shook my head 'yes'. "Where is my son?" I asked. "I will take you to him soon."

Mike's lifeless body was lying there on the table. The room was so quiet, all I could hear was me sobbing, "Oh Mike, oh Mike." My legs were weak, and I was now sitting next to him. I looked at the corner of the room and I saw his shoe covered with blood. I covered my mouth as I cried. "I have to call my mom and his mom." All I felt was sadness and fear. I heard the man's voice in the room saying, "We will call Captain Burleson's family." In my mind I heard a voice saying, "Their son and my son's father is dead." My heart was broken. I was feeling pain in my chest and I couldn't feel myself breathing. I knew Mike's mom's heart would be broken. So much was going through my head. "What do I do? I don't know what to do. I am confused." The chaplain had some papers and explained that my son needed emergency surgery. I signed the papers. The next few hours were a blank in my memory.

Feeling as if I were in a dream, I told the chaplain, "I want to see my son." They took me to another unit in the hospital and the sign read ICU. I saw my beautiful, perfect baby lying there, his tiny forty-pound frame was now broken and bandaged. There were tubes and machines over what appeared to be his entire body. The helplessness I felt is unexplainable as my son fought with all he had within him to survive. All I had was my faith and I pled, "Oh my baby! God, I need you, God I need you. Please Lord save my son." As I was praying, I heard my grandmother's voice in my head saying to "pray with faith", and my prayer changed to, "God, I know you will save my son. Father I need you; you will save my son." I saw the physician coming into the room. He called my name, I heard him, but his voice sounded so distant. "Mrs. Burleson, I am Dr. Weather. Your son is in critical condition. He has a broken left arm, a fractured pelvis, and most serious is the skull fracture at the base of his skull, which has penetrated his brain." I could no longer stand; my legs couldn't hold my weight. I was helped to a chair by somebody in the room. He continued, "We had to repair the skull fracture, his broken arm, and pelvic fracture. We will keep him sedated a few days because we don't want him to be in pain. He will need physical and occupational therapy; his recovery will take time."

The bandages I saw on Marcus' head were for covering the wound and adding pressure to control the bleeding. All I could do was pray as the tears continued to run down my face. My son and I were alone, and I was holding his little soft hand. A comforting hand had just touched my back. Looking up, I saw it was the nurse. She was just gently touching my back. She was standing there with me and my son. How comforting it was to know that someone who didn't know us saw us as valuable enough to care and have empathy for our loss. My son and I were lost and alone in this unknown country, and someone cared enough to comfort us.

My life had fallen apart, and I couldn't think, I didn't know what to do. I asked the nurse if I could call my mom and dad. She was going to set up a phone call for the next day. She told me they had a room for me across campus and I should get some sleep. She told me she would be on duty all night and Marcus would be sleeping from the sedation. I went to the room but couldn't sleep. The next morning when I arrived, she was in my son's room. God had sent me an angel to watch over my son.

A week had passed and my son was moved to a different room. Most of the days that followed over the next two weeks were the same. I didn't think about much because it was too overwhelming. My thoughts were all about Marcus. I didn't have the energy to think about anything other than getting Marcus back home. Getting him well enough to travel was now a priority. So, I got up each day and walked one half mile to my son's room and concentrated on helping him regain his ability to hold his fork so he could feed himself. Helping him practice repeating his words so he could speak again. Helping him balance so he could walk again. These were the things I was totally focused on. This is what was important.

At the end of week two, Marcus was well enough to travel by Medivac back to the United States. We were loaded on a very large plane with many other patients for our return home. The military had already packed up all our household items and returned them to Mike's parents' home.

Once we arrived home, my son was hospitalized for continued treatment. My family and friends, my tribe, surrounded me with nothing but love. Now, I needed to find the strength to plan my husband's funeral. The funeral was finalized but it still felt so surreal. I would have never gotten through the funeral without the duty officer assigned to me. I am so grateful for the Army sending him to help me. I buried my husband and my son's father on a Saturday. I can't believe how abruptly my fairy tale life had ended and now I was in the middle of a nightmare.

It was now Tuesday, and my son had been discharged from the medical unit with orders for outpatient therapy.

Knowing Marcus was home and Mike was buried, I felt like I was in a space where I could breathe. However, I still felt like I was in a dream and would never wake up. Each day I looked out the window, knowing Mike was going to drive up and come through the door. I felt tired and had no energy. I felt very depressed. All I could do was cry, but often there were no tears. I had no energy and felt like I couldn't move. My tribe was offering me food, but I had no appetite, I couldn't eat. All I wanted to do was sleep but my sleep was intermittent and restless. I had a sadness like I had never known. I kept asking myself, "Why did this happen? Why didn't I stop them from going on that outing?" I felt like

I was responsible for all that had happened.

Then one day my father-in-law brought me a letter from the department of the Army. The letter was the accident report. I read the document and I became more and more angry as I read each line. The person who had killed my husband and severely injured my son was a drunk driver. The letter stated that my son had been "thrown out the hatchback of the car into a tree." Being thrown out of the car had saved his life. The car was destroyed, and Mike had been killed instantly on impact. The motor of the car totally crushed his abdominal organs as his body was pressed into the back seat.

Day after day, the feelings of heaviness and hopelessness became more overwhelming. These feeling had just taken over my mind, heart, and body. I was no longer the person I used to be. My bright smile, happiness, and joy had totally disappeared. My state of mind was not good.

Mike's parents had taken over the care of my son. My son was in the house and he came to see me every day. He told me, "Mommy, I love you," and I told him, "I love you too." Oh, I felt so unworthy of his love. "Just look at me, I am a mess," I thought.

My friends and family surrounded me every day. I was so physically weak and emotionally broken that they had to help me out of the bed. They were so dedicated to helping me back to a place of wellness. They had this unconditional love for me. They had developed a daily rotation schedule and posted it in my room, so I knew who was coming. Each day I heard them praying for me and they continued to encourage me, telling me, "You can do this, you can do this, just try." They prayed for me because my faith in God had faded. I felt like I was in a deep hole with no bottom and I was falling deeper and deeper into darkness. My grandmother called me every day and one of my spiritual sisters would hold the phone to my ear. I can still hear my grandmother speaking words of healing over me. Declaring, "The devil is a lie, Devil you will not have my child."

Finally, after months of living in a very black hole which was diagnosed as grief and depression, I had the strength to have a talk with God. I said, "God, why me? Lord, help me. Lord, I just need the strength to take the first step. If I can stand and make the first step, I can make it." God gave me the strength to take the first step. God answered my prayer and I have been taking those first steps since that day.

It was very difficult watching my son as he struggled to recover over the years. I wished every day I could have taken his place. All I could do was hold him and tell him how much I loved him.

After years of physical therapy, my son is almost whole. He will always have some deficits, but he is alive. I was never sure how much he remembered about the accident and over the years we have not discussed that night often because the memories are so painful. However, last year during my son's visit at Christmas he told me, "Mom, I remember two things about the accident. Dad told me 'Hold on son, son, hold on.'" These are the last words my son heard his father speak. At death's door, Mike was still trying to protect Marcus. My son also told me, "I remember how my body hurt; I was in so much pain. Mom, my body really hurt."

I would not be in an emotionally heathy place today without a renewed faith in my heavenly Father, or the strength and resilience of my ancestors which is deeply ingrained in my DNA. My recovery is truly credited to my family and friends, my tribe, their courage, perseverance, and unconditional love.

The unforeseen will happen. It is just life but when it comes—death, heartbreak, violence, and devaluation—reach out. Don't try to handle the trauma alone. Find the presence of God and reach out to your tribe, whoever that might be. Please don't give up. Find the strength to get up one day at a time and take your first step, then the next step, and soon you will be standing again.

Here are some lessons I have learned through this experience that I would like to share with you.

- When you find yourself broken into a million pieces, trust your tribe because they are the water and the clay. They are the builders and through love they will stand you up when you can't stand on your own. They breathe into you when you can't breathe on your own.

- It is ok to cleanse your system and tears help you with this process.
- There are others of you out there who have suffered the same loss as me. Some of you still find yourselves in a place of darkness from a deep emotional loss. Don't give up.
- Don't rush through your healing process.
- Love is the beginning of healing.

Many years have passed and my healing process continues. The memories of this life-changing event are still present. The pain still has a place where it lives in my heart. The trauma, the healing process, and the lessons learned are forever a part of me, and I proudly carry them from season to season.

Writing my story has been emotionally difficult. Putting this season of my life on paper has reminded me:

- I experienced a trauma, but I am not a victim, I am a survivor.
- I am still in my healing process and that's ok.

Each day I continue to take one step and others follow. This experience, this season, although painful, prepared me for other painful experiences and difficult seasons that have and will continue to come in my life. I am standing, healing, and still surviving.

ABOUT PAMELA HARRIS

Pamela Harris MHA, BSN, RN is a public health manager and leader who lives in Elk Grove, California. She is a wife and mother of one son and one beautiful daughter-in-law. Her greatest pleasures in life come from helping to enrich the lives of people in her community and all over the world. She is a motivational speaker, educator, mentor, and teacher. Her healthcare career and community service have afforded her the opportunities to touch many lives. At a young age while a junior in high school she discovered the personal satisfaction of ministering to others in words and actions. She knew her life's work would be dedicated to the betterment of others.

Graduating from college with a nursing degree opened her eyes to a multitude of many needs in her community and the world. Over the years, through her experiences, profession, and faith she has been able to minister to the emotional and healing needs of others. Through her profession she has also been able to teach, lead, and advocate in the world of health. Through her community service she has been able to reach so many people who just need to know how to take the next step to healing or success. As a mentor she has been able to guide, motivate, and help those around her reach their goals. When she is asked, "What do you do?" she will often reply, "I help to build people."

Pamela has not been without her own struggles and trauma but uses her life experiences to assist others during their journey to a better place. When you see her, she has a smile she gives to everyone for free.

Pamela can be reached at harrispk0320@yahoo.com

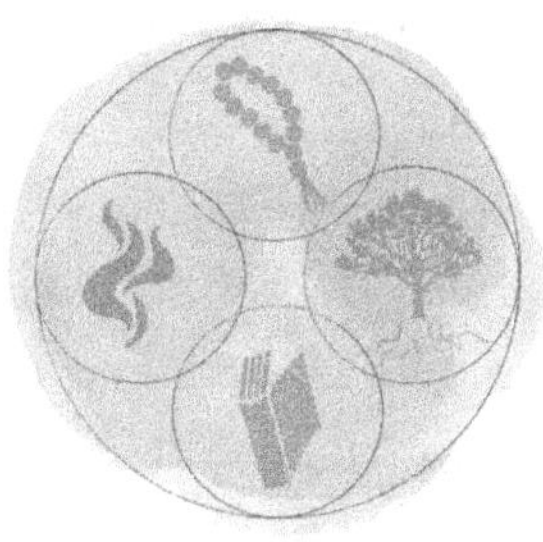

PRESENT OVER PERFECT

Cindy Kelly

No one can predict the day their life will forever change. For some there may never be a significant event when the Earth stops moving and everything stands still, but for others, like me, you remember every second like an hour, ticking off the clock in that moment when the unthinkable happens.

It was a beautiful, sunny day, September 26, 2015. I always remember it was the day the Pope was in Philadelphia, and since we lived in a South Jersey suburb not far from the city, this was monumental. However, while others poured into the city for a glimpse of His Holiness in the Fiat Popemobile, across the river we packed our minivan with chairs, snacks, and water bottles in preparation for my 10-year-old daughter Morgan's soccer game. This was routine to us, the frantic search for her jersey that may or may not have been washed from her last game, a missing soccer cleat and 6-year-old twins complaining about going to the game. Only bribery of candy would get them in the car. Nothing out of the ordinary here.

As the game was underway, we cheered the girls in a hard-fought competition, but then something happened, the moment that would forever change our lives. The ball came toward Morgan and as the play shifted and went one way, Morgan went the opposite direction. It caught my attention as she appeared to be disoriented and her coach recognized this and called her name to get her off the field, but she couldn't move, she was frozen and staring. We all watched quietly from the sidelines very aware something was not right. Slowly, she came out of whatever happened to her and was taken out of the game. Confused, dizzy, and exhausted on the bench, she was like someone with a concussion that never was hit. These events would soon become our new normal and happen multiple times daily. This was our introduction to seizures and epilepsy.

There is no way as a mother that you are prepared when your child has a medical condition, but you find an inner strength you didn't know you had and saving your child's life becomes your only job. When I was two-years-old, I was diagnosed with a rare kidney condition and my parents were given no hope, but miraculously I overcame my illness to live a healthy life. As my life began to parallel my mother's when I was ill, I pulled from her strength and guidance to be an advocate for Morgan and a role model for my other three daughters, like my mom was for me. I believe there was a reason I did not succumb to that kidney disease as the doctors believed I would. Even at two-years-old there was a plan for me, something I needed to live for, a story to experience and one that needed to be shared to help others.

The journey that began on the soccer field was not only about seizures, but many life changing events that would follow and shape our story as a family and individually. Things that were a big deal the morning of that game, like a lost cleat, an unwashed soccer jersey and gummy bear bribes were not so important anymore. For Morgan, they were now replaced by extensive neurological testing, numerous hospital stays, an unexpected heart surgery, academic gaps spanning four grades, and the culmination of it all, brain surgery that could give her life back and stop the seizures that were isolating her from life as a middle school girl.

As a mom, one of the hardest parts on this journey was the social impact for Morgan and our family. Although not true for everyone, but the more school she missed the more friends disappeared. Girls at this age are tough to begin with, but when you are in and out of school people forget who you are. At one point I wrote a poem called "I'm Not A Ghost" because that's how Morgan felt going to school, as girls that were previously friends and teammates looked through her as if she wasn't there. Party invitations and invites to hang with friends dwindled, and it broke my heart to watch this once happy child with a huge heart and big smile now dealing with medication side effects and a disease she couldn't control, crying over friendships lost and being left out. We never expected anyone's lives to stop for us, because everyone has their own things to manage and burdens to carry. This was our situation to experience as a family; it was just a piece that had a profound impact on the situation. I realized in this time how people take for granted healthy children and the life they lead carpooling, making plans and staying busy with activities.

Just as relationships changed for Morgan, I stressed over my relationships with my three other daughters and my husband, Scott. Taylor, my oldest was twelve-years-old when this began, and my twins, Riley and Reagan, were six. I was still working in pharmaceutical sales and trying to be successful at my job, a health advocate for Morgan, and the mom and wife everyone needed me to be. But I kept questioning if I was giving enough to all of them. I had tremendous mom guilt. I would take turns with Scott on the weekends attending Taylor's AAU basketball tournaments just to be with her. Taylor doesn't even know how important that time was to me, even if she would put her earbuds in and fall asleep in the car. To me that car was a place where we were together and even without talking, I was present only with her. I hoped when she looked in the stands, she was happy I was there and knew how much I loved to watch her play and how proud I was to be her mom.

As we saw success from Morgan's surgery and began to move into a better place, I found myself thinking, "Now what?" Life took an unexpected turn when my husband lost his job just weeks before Morgan's surgery and he had just started back to work after months of unemployment. I no longer had a successful career with independence, financial security and an identity because I stopped working to care for Morgan. Friendships had changed, and my soul and marriage needed repair. WOW ... that's a lot!

My journey shifted from Morgan and began to be more about pulling my life back together. I had to let go of so much to put myself in a better place. I had anger that Morgan was sick, anger about Scott's unexpected job loss, anger about how our lives unexpectedly changed and disappointment in friendships for us and Morgan. I was also not happy with myself and how I looked and felt about who I was. I stress ate during this time and the scale loved to remind me of that. I cried when things didn't fit, and I hated the person looking back at me in the mirror. I had guilt about the years I felt I missed with my other three daughters and searched for a way to make up that time. There was so much that transpired during this journey, how could I not have strong emotions? I was a poster girl for therapy!!

I needed to be present for everyone, but I didn't know how to do that. My husband went through his own struggles after his job loss and emotionally it was hard for him to be present in a way that I needed him to be, so I moved forward with blinders on and shut off that part of my life. I couldn't help him when my children needed me, and his choices were hurting me. I knew I needed to pull my life back together, but how? I was tired and honestly didn't have the motivation to do what I thought was necessary to dig out from all the emotions that were suffocating me. To the outside world I smiled and moved forward, acting like everything was ok, but the reality was, it wasn't fine at all; I felt alone, exhausted, unhappy, and it sucked! It took me awhile to be truthful and say that, but once I did, I felt better. How couldn't it suck when we had been through so much in the last five years and were still recovering?

It was time to pull up my big girl panties and start the healing process. Thankfully, I have the most amazing and supportive parents in the world and every summer they rent a house for two weeks in Ocean City, NJ. The summer after Morgan's surgery, I needed time at the beach with no expectations and no schedules. I wanted to enjoy the time with my family, but also put me first for a change. I enjoyed late beach days with the setting sun and getting ice cream at night with the kids. I read books and in the early morning found peace walking on the beach before the crowds descended. I prayed and meditated, looking for answers. I left after those two weeks feeling like I had been to an island retreat.

Coming back to the routine, I tried to hold onto that feeling and sat in my backyard every morning searching for peace and calm. I have a small pond with a waterfall, and it was the perfect back drop in my quest for healing. However, I knew this summer euphoria would not last forever and I had to make changes and shift my mindset. Starting therapy was by far the best thing I did for myself. Having someone other than my girlfriends validate I wasn't crazy was a huge relief--well maybe just a little crazy, but in a good way. Therapy was a safe place to be truthful, vulnerable, and to let the tears flow. I was surprised how many things came out that I didn't realize I'd been holding onto for years and weren't even a part of my current situation. For example, I mourned the four miscarriages I had years previous and recognized the pain I endured during the years I struggled with infertility. Now having four healthy children I thought I had moved past all of that, but clearly it was still weighing on me.

The weather changed and months flew by. I worked as an assistant in Riley and Reagan's school while I tried to figure out what was next for me, but also as a way to be present and to give them more security after so much turmoil. However, when things got rough, I tried to put myself on that beach in Ocean City and listened for the waves to guide me. Unfortunately, sometimes the peaceful waves were not what I needed on this healing journey of trial and error. Sometimes I was angry, and it was just a bad day. That's when I would get in my car and drive, but it wasn't just a Sunday drive in the South Jersey farmlands that surrounded me. It was a drive to let off steam and to blast music, music that felt as angry as I did; "Straight Outta Compton" became my song of choice. I know, it's not your typical minivan driving mom music, but it gave me an outlet and it felt good. The lyrics were lost on me, but the angry tone set me free. I shared this one day with a girlfriend at work who was going through a divorce. She laughed so hard and told me she did the same as I only she played Metallica!! From beach waves to rap to heavy metal, there is something for everyone on that drive to nowhere in search of clarity.

Although I'd love to say there was some big profound thing I did to change myself in that year, there wasn't. It was a change built on many little things like therapy, the car rides, taking a bath with relaxing music, and small activities personal to me that gave me calm, if only for a moment. At the time, I was also working with many strong women going through a variety of personal struggles and friends dealing with life changes of their own. We slowly opened up and supported each other. On the days we wanted to cry, we found humor in our situations and made each other laugh, a laughter that made you forget your problems and almost wet your pants. Honestly, at our ages and after having kids, you wet your pants when you sneeze, so this laughter was a full blown Depends emergency, but much needed! That was when I realized I needed to figure out a way to share my story and the stories of others to help people know they are not alone.

As we arrived at the beach the next summer, I had a new purpose and was in a different place. It was now time to figure out my next chapter. I repeated many of the things from the previous summer, but I had a different energy. I knew that although difficult, we had been gifted this journey and these experiences for a reason, and I couldn't not share our story if it would help others. As I walked on the beach, I looked at the footprints in the sand and wondered about the people who walked before me and their stories. Did they walk this same beach looking for answers to marriage, careers, and family? I was sure I was not alone in my feelings and it continued to become clear I needed to share and help others. This summer was different because I was creative and I wrote each day and began to think about creating a blog, writing a children's book, or doing motivational speaking. Prior to pharmaceutical sales I had a career in public relations, and I knew that was calling to me again. I needed to put that into the Universe and open myself up to signs and follow where they took me.

Since last summer, in 2019, I have slowly learned to give myself permission to let go of things, and trust me I am a work in progress, but aren't we always? This was something my strong and inspirational mother always preached to me, but I needed to have my own experiences to understand what she meant. Permission to let go of things like the wash or straightening up the house like a lunatic before bed. Trust me, I get how hard this can be and I would not recommend letting the wash go for weeks, but one or two days to sit and watch a movie instead is ok. I am as Type A, detailed and organized as they come, many times to my own detriment, so this was a new concept to me.

Typically, I would have been crazy shopping before Christmas and jamming in holiday activities to fill the calendar with things I felt I HAD to do. However, two years ago Hallmark Christmas movies changed my life! They sucked me in, and we had fun family movie nights by the fire. I sat on the couch lost in a fake world of predictable holiday cheer and didn't stress over creating a Clark Griswold holiday to-do list. Who was I? Movie time and cookie baking was fun because we were present together as a family. I still shopped and things got done, but at a different pace. And guess what? Christmas still happened. And this year when I waited a week after New Year's Day to take down my decorations and enjoy the lights on the tree a little longer, no Christmas Police showed up with a citation; it was ok.

For anyone who has been on a journey of life that includes illness, being a caregiver, job loss, marriage crisis, or whatever has knocked you down (it could be all the above), you will find a way to survive. In the middle of it you think you'll never get out and it sucks and don't let any Pinterest Perfect or Facebook Flawless person tell you differently, because they are LYING! The reality is, it's ok to be angry about your situation, so take a breath and realize you are human and not perfect. You should not feel guilt or shame about your feelings because it's YOUR pain and YOUR struggle and YOUR emotions are very real.

When you decide you don't want to be angry anymore, find a way that works for you to heal and make yourself happy again. I started walking and then began working out. I'm not always consistent but I'm getting better because I like that I feel healthy again. Take baby steps and be present in the moments so you don't miss the good things. It has taken me a lot of time and therapy to recognize this and I am evolving every day. You can only work on one part of yourself at a time and learn to let things go piece by piece to find clarity. Don't let other people put pressure on you to follow THEIR plan, it's your soul that needs healing and it must be on your terms and in your time, and if you have setbacks, that's ok too. There isn't a handbook to tell you the right or wrong way to handle your pain, frustration, or grief.

Sharing my story in this book is the first step in the next chapter of my life. I hope to find more peace and calm in each day and set an example that makes my daughters proud. Most importantly, to not forget what we went through because that shaped who we are but move forward and enjoy the time we have together and choose to be present over perfect.

ABOUT CINDY KELLY

Inspired by many strong women in her life with different stories to tell, Cindy feels passionate about giving each story a voice that can touch lives and help people know they are not alone. A series of God Winks have put Cindy on a path to reinventing herself and sharing life experiences, not only about how seizures changed her family, but all the other things that life throws at you and how to reset, refocus, and find renewed possibilities. Cindy aspires to build a series of inspirational talks for children, caregivers, and adults, as well as to create online resources to help people who need inspiration without unrealistic expectations and humor to keep from crying.

Most of all Cindy would like her four daughters to see what can be accomplished with determination and a dream, no matter where you are in your life. She invites them to be a part of the creative process as they grow and build their own life experiences.

Cindy resides in South Jersey with her husband, Scott, and four daughters.

You can find Cindy on Instagram @cindykellyinspired

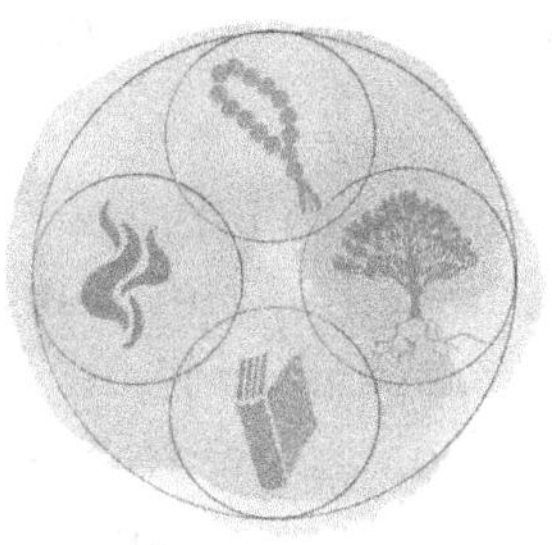

THE POWER OF CHOICES

Mona Meland

The decision was made: my marriage had come to an end, there was no return. And I, I had to start all over again, find a place to live, make a new home for my children and myself. Three of my five children, at ages three, ten, and fifteen were still living with me. The other two were grown and had settled down in their own homes.

I felt so sorry for myself, hitting rock bottom, at the age of forty-three. In the process of starting all over again. It's not the same when you're in your forties as when you're in your twenties or thirties.

I felt like a failure and a disaster. How could I overcome this? How could I summon all the energy and strength to do what's necessary to move on? The packing and unpacking, the washing and cleaning, getting an apartment that was suitable for us to live in, furnishing it and finding a source of income—all of this in only four weeks!

I had put myself in a terrible situation by not securing my finances responsibly. The lawyer had told me that I had no rights, not having legally signed a contract regarding the money and finances within my marriage.

After deciding to end the marriage, I was holding my son in my arms; he was not handling the break-up well and was about to have an anxiety attack. I guided him to breathe into a plastic bag and showed him how to do it if he was ever alone and had this experience again.

An hour later we were in bed and my son said he wanted to stay in bed with me, so he felt more calm and safe. We were talking about all the changes that were happening, that I was getting a divorce from his stepfather, that we were going to move and start a new life.

Earlier that afternoon, his stepfather had been shouting angrily and the police and childcare had come to the house. This really upset all of us. But just before he fell asleep, my son said, "Mom, it's going to be okay. I know it, everything is going to be fine. I know it. I can feel it, I really feel it deep inside my body."

I kissed him goodnight and told him that I was also sure that everything would be okay, and as he fell asleep, I looked at him. He had the face of an angel. He was breathing calmly and quietly.

I felt worried thinking of my son's words and knowing that even though I couldn't see the road ahead, this was the first step to a new life. Even though we didn't have a new home yet, even though I were going to have a financially breakdown after leaving my husband and I knew it had to happen.

This was not what I had dreamed of in my childhood, my third marriage ending in divorce.

As a little girl I hoped that when I grew up, I would meet a man, fall in love, get married, have children, that we grow old together, and have everlasting love.

Life had to be better, and to have a better life, this decision was important, important to make and important to follow through on.

I was in bed, thinking about my financial situation. How would this turn out? I was in huge debt! I was now responsible for more than 2.2 million! How could I manage all of that on top of my health issues (caused by a traffic accident back in 1997)? I had been unable to work since then and was living on government assistance.

Who could I ask for help while I strived for this new start? I felt so lonely.

As I was lying in bed, listening to the sound of my son breathing in the darkness, I suddenly remembered my neighbor, Olav, from my childhood.

He had become a good friend again recently. I met him by coincidence at the popular gardening store and invited him over. He was ninety years old and a widower. He seemed like a very lonely old man. Most of his friends had died, or were hospitalised, or had been put in elderly homes. We started to visit Olav regularly and also invite him over for dinner. He still lived in the same neighborhood I had while growing up.

The last time he came to dinner, he told me, "Mona, remember this: whenever you are in need of anything, please ask me for help." I remembered Olav's words and made a decision to call him the next morning.

After the children went to school and I took my youngest to kindergarten, I sat down in my living room and called Olav. He sounded happy to hear my voice, but I told him this was not a happy call. I asked if I could visit him—I needed to talk about a serious matter.

We met and I told him everything. We agreed on a deal. He would let me borrow money from him and I would pay him back by cleaning his house every week. It had been a long time since everything was cleaned. The windows, the ceiling, the walls ... they all needed a deep clean.

I started to look for an apartment. I asked friends and family members if they had heard of anything suitable for me and my three children.

Two weeks after meeting up with Olav, we were moving into our new apartment.

It was completely empty—no furniture, no electric appliances, nothing. I cried because I knew that we were going to have a more peaceful life even if though it was in an empty apartment, the first important steps had been taken.

I felt so much gratitude to be in this apartment by the ocean, to be able to feel the ocean breeze in my hair and the fresh smell of it all. I fell into tears and I knew that this place would heal me. The view of the mountains one way and the end of the horizon the other was like medication to my soul.

Olav also helped me get a refrigerator and dishwasher, and I borrowed a stove from a friend. I got a sofa for the living room from my eldest daughter, who had wanted to replace her sofa with a new one.

The first months in this new apartment, I washed our laundry at my friend's house or my mother's house until I saved up enough money to buy a laundry machine.

We had brought with us the children's beds, our clothes, bookshelves and books, toys, some lamps, a cupboard, and a dining table. This was much more than a lot of people in the world have, and I felt so much gratitude.

About four weeks after we moved, my doctor called me. "Mona, you need surgery. A hysterectomy. If you don't, you will develop cancer. We need to hurry."

I had the surgery and decided that I was going to be a survivor. I was going to live a long-lasting, healthy life and do my best to support my children. During the recovery time I was reading about self-esteem and I decided I needed a new mindset. One of focus.

I discovered that I had to work to do in all areas of my life—finances, health issues, and relationships. I realized I had been viewing myself as a victim. I felt hate and anger, I felt life was unfair. I wondered how I could break free from all of these circumstances.

I knew this had to change, this had to stop. My negative behaviour had to come to an end.

I had to take control and be in charge of my life. I wanted to be happy, healthy, strong—it was vital that I start dreaming and then make my dreams come true.

I began to meditate and to change my mindset, which I'm sure lead to me no longer needing painkillers or prescription drugs to ease the pain in my body which was the result of the car accident in 1997. (It was a miracle I had survived!)

I continued to focus on relaxing, using new mindset skills, meditation, breathing techniques, affirmations, visualizations, gratitude practices, and also self-love practices in the mirror.

I took action by making payment plans to the bank and credit card companies for all the debt I was responsible for.

In my marriage I had borrowed money so we could expand my husband's carpentry business. He had not forced me to, it was my own decision to show him how much I loved and cared for him and to show my support.

Two years before our separation we had almost lost our home. At that time, I went to the bank to borrow more money to save our home. My husband could not be approved for the loan because his business was struggling from an economic downturn in Norway at the time.

I was now responsible for this loan that saved our home, but I was never registered as the owner of our home. I was solely responsible for the loan payments. This was a scary financial situation to be in after our divorce, and because I didn't own the house, I couldn't sell it. However, my husband and I agreed that he would make the payments and pay interest on the house as long as he lived in it.Then I could afford all of the other debt

I made a strict household budget, making dinner lists for the month, what groceries were needed for all the meals, then making them as cheap as possible. In this way I was able to save more money to pay off the debt.

After a year without painkillers and using meditation and breathing techniques daily, my mindset changed, and I spoke to my doctor about the possibility of getting back to work. Maybe I could get an education in self-development?

I already had an education in being a nurse, a hairdresser, and a personal trainer, but none of these were really options for me anymore. My doctor thought it would be a good idea to go into self-development and he said he would support me in the process.

In Norway we have a governmental care program which supports people getting back to work or getting an education in order to find suitable work.

With an optimistic attitude, I scheduled a meeting with the agency to ask for support to get an education in self-development so that I could then work in the area of my interest and expertise.

Unfortunately, they denied me. Even though my doctor reported all of the progress I had made in the last year, the agency told me, "You are not in any state to be able to work. After reviewing all of the notes about your health condition, it is decided that you are 100% unable to work. We will not support you."

Hearing these words was like being hit in the face.

I felt so sad, like a disaster. Again, I felt worthless, which I had been told I was so many times during my life. How could I make my dream come true? How could I make someone believe in me? Later that night I lay in bed, searching for a solution.

Who did I know who would support me? Is there any company out there who would be willing to take a chance on me and teach me personal development and coaching? Suddenly a quiet voice came into my mind … what if I could be that company and support myself?

I investigated what industry I could start my own business in without too much starting costs. What did I love to do that would earn money and help me take classes in personal development?

To make a long story short, I decided to train in relaxing massage, which became the start of my own business.

Five years after I hit rock bottom, I had risen again. I moved into my own newly built home. Five years after taking the first steps of putting myself first—from leaving a destructive relationship and getting my own apartment—I had built my own business, built my own home, and learned how to dream in my adult life. Even though at first, I couldn't see the road forward, I just continued taking baby steps until I was comfortable taking even bigger and bigger steps.

I set big goals. I had a lot of faith, and through my own courage I continued to find inspiration in my own inner guidance system—the inner voice that speaks in the silence, the voice from my heart.

I also was inspired by others who had taken similar steps. I read books, watched movies, followed inspirational and motivational famous people, traveled to their seminars, and listened to webinars. I learned through their actions and examples and then implemented all of it into my own life.

Over the last few years I have gotten more training and have evolved from a massage therapist into a holistic therapist and a transformational life coach. I have taken classes in my home country of Norway and abroad in England and the US.

In my own business, I am still learning. Life is such a great learning experience, and my desire is to help others do the same. I admire people who are developing and learning from their own life experiences.

Practicing self-respect, doing affirmations, setting goals, visualizing, practicing self-care and self-love are all important. But most important of all what I have learned is the practice of gratitude. It is also important to understand that we are all learners in this life, with the ability to improve and evolve.

I surrendered, and I survived. I already had happiness in my life—love and charity, too. It was always there, I just had to take action to discover it. I finally discovered my own value and worth, how to be there for myself, so that I could then be there for others. After years of neglect, I started to love myself, and I still do.

By making use of different self-development tools, I learned a big lesson: you do not need to see the end of the road, you just need to take the first step in faith, and then the next. This will lead you to the life you desire.

I live in gratitude every single day for having this beautiful life, for living through all of the experiences that have made me who I am, and for my wonderful children, my family and friends who love me and who I love to infinity and beyond.

ABOUT MONA MELAND

"I do have BIG plans and goals for the future, and as a holistic therapist and a survivor of a serious bus accident as a passenger in '97, my mission is to inspire and motivate others to open the door to transformation." - Mona Meland

Her wish to work with people led her on a path to a holistic approach and in 2013 she started her company "Hjertero og Livsglede (heart of peace and life of joy)", where she is strengthening people from the inside out through the power of personal care, love, gratitude, joy, and peace. She creates magic with tools like sound drums, singing bowls, meditation, mindfulness, the vibration of crystals, therapeutic touch, massage, and breathwork.

In her twenties Mona was studying to be a nurse. Right before her finals, the unexpected happened ... she was involved in a serious accident as a passenger while riding a bus. All doctors agreed it was a miracle that she survived! Serious head trauma and neck damage caused her pain from hell, and she was unable to work for several decades. Through goals and dedication she has taught her body to manage reading, living through the days instead of only existing and doing what she could manage in her daily activities as a mother and wife. Her biggest lesson is gratefulness to life, love and joy.

Mona's list of achievements include:

Educated PT,

NLP practitioner

Crystal and touch-therapist by Marianne Behn, Rafael touch.

Massage therapist, including Medical fibro-, relaxation-, classic- and cupping massage Balanze, Sandefjord Norway.

Certified speaker & coach in the methodology by Jack Canfield

Facebook Hjertero og Livsglede and Mona Meland

e-mail monameland@gmail.com

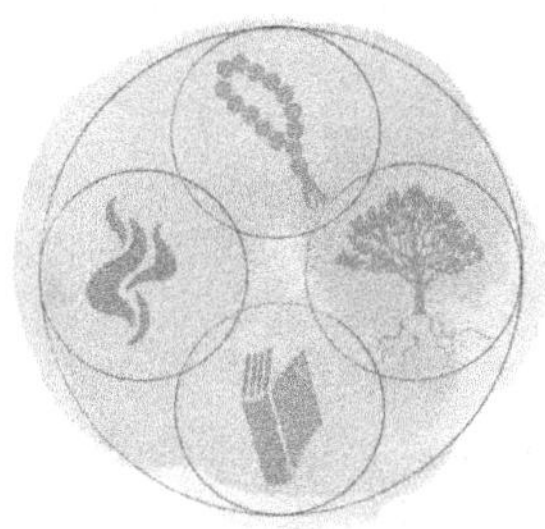

MY FEARFUL WINDING ROAD TO TRUST IN GOD

Adrianne Murchison

I'm a pushover for love. And for me, God is love and only love.

I was one of those children who made room for my guardian angel in bed at night as I prayed the prayer, *Now I lay me down to sleep.*

Early one Christmas morning, at about age eleven, my parents, brothers, and I were surprised by the new snowfall since there was no snow on the day before, and none had been expected. But I instantly thought and said out loud that it must've been because of a prayer by an unknown person, longing for snow on Christmas day.

"Because God answers prayers," I said to my cynical older brother, Jeffrey, who had a scientific explanation for the sudden snow.

I used to wonder, did my love of God come from my late mother, or was I born this way? My mother had a pure love for God, and I loved what she loved. I grew up Catholic, and Jesus was introduced to me as a completely loving figure.

I've come to realize that I was indeed born with this knowing love of God. One of my good friends says that when God made me, he gave me an extra dose of love, as love is so important to me, to convey, give, and receive.

MY GOD CONNECTIONS

I connect with God in numerous ways. I think it's because of my willingness and desire to know Him as much as I can. And his blessings have come to me regardless of whether my mind has been in fear or faith.

When I was growing up, I had frequent intuition. The kind where you think about someone and they call, or you think about a friend and you run into them, or someone crosses your mind and some situation happens around that person.

It happened so frequently that, frankly, it scared me. At one point, part of me wished it would go away because I didn't know what it meant.

Now I know and welcome the variety of ways I can connect with God. Sometimes I'm instantly guided to take a specific action. Or He places me in random places at essential moments.

On occasion, I have tangible, spiritual experiences with God, or a loved one who has passed away. One of the most profound occurrences is when I experience the presence of God, or a late loved one within my spirit, and I am able to converse with them in my mind consciousness. It's surreal and an absolute blessing.

It first happened with a late boyfriend from my teen years in my hometown of Buffalo, NY. He was diagnosed with cancer at age eighteen, just as he was about to leave for college at Georgia Tech, and died three years later.

In my mid-forties, I came across my old journal from when he and I were in a relationship. I was sixteen, naïve and engaging in adult behavior. I was insecure about my boyfriend leaving for college and other girls that he might've been attracted to at home in Buffalo, and I showed it.

Then when he became ill, I reacted with way too much emotion.

My boyfriend and I broke up soon after his diagnosis, and we weren't in communication when I went off to college in Atlanta, or later when he passed away.

Reading my writings in my journal and recalling the events had me wanting to apologize to him. I could see that I was just a naïve sixteen-year-old child, who didn't fully know myself, much less how to be, as we say, *grown*.

So, I asked God if He would allow me to talk to my old boyfriend, would he make a way for that? I asked in prayer and let it go. It left my thoughts.

A few days later, during my work lunch hour, I was driving down the road and suddenly, I felt the presence of my former boyfriend in my spirit. It was sort of a bizarre sensation. I knew it was real, and I didn't know how long it would last. So, I started talking to him and apologizing for how immature I was as a teenager and wished that I could have shown up differently when he became ill. He simply said that it was all alright and conveyed that there wasn't anything to apologize for. "It's all okay," he said in the kindest manner. I engaged with him for nearly ten minutes and then his presence left me.

It wasn't the first time that I had such an experience. Still, it was startling.

I have felt my mother's presence within me and nearby in the room. About a month before she passed away from a heart condition, I asked her to always stay close to me in spirit. I told her that I already knew it was possible, because of my Dad.

You see, my father died when I was twenty-one-years-old, and God immediately kept us connected through my dreams. The dreams helped me to realize that he is always with me, as well as the power of God.

I've come to understand through my father's continued presence in spirit, as well as my mother's, and even that of my brother, who passed in 2014, that a continued spiritual relationship with someone after they have died is a two-way street. I have to choose to engage with them, just as I have to choose to engage with God, or even a good friend.

For much of my life, I've come to feel and experience God's love and profound blessings while coping with heartache, and at times grief, over the death of a family member.

Each loss in my immediate family was life altering.

My father's death occurred at the brink of me evolving as a woman. The foundation to help me make healthy decisions in my romantic relationships was gone. It created a sense of abandonment that I have worked to heal through God and writing passages in my journal to him.

My brother Jeffrey's passing, at age fifty-five from cardiac arrest, broke my heart. His health and alcoholism concerned me for years, and I doubted his will to live. Yet, I pleaded with him to choose life and take better care of himself. He knew me well and how much I loved him. By dying, I felt he said, "No," to my pleas.

He was unconscious for eleven days before he died. His wife, adult daughter and son, and I slept in chairs each night surrounding his hospital bed. When he died, I stood in fear beside his bed for a few private moments before he was taken away. I realized that with him gone, I wouldn't know who I was. He was one of my two older brothers. I felt lost by the reality of one of them being gone. He knew me so well that I didn't know what his absence meant for my sense of being.

We hear about twins being connected and the devastation when one dies, but we don't hear about the connection between traditional siblings and how it feels when we think that's broken.

I was laid-off two days before Jeffrey died. For months afterwards, my grief and heartache left me exhausted. Worried how I would make ends meet financially, I would go out to meet someone about potential work and come back feeling low with no fruitful results. I'd just crash on my couch in tears.

I was in surrender to God, because I was too tired and weary to be anything else.

It felt like in that space of surrender, God gave me the time I needed to grieve. Every month, I worried about having full employment, but work eventually came in abundance.

Coming to grips with him being gone has helped me to stay in-tuned with the roots of all my heartache.

At that time, I was single, and met two men, months apart, that I dated for a while. As my heart opened to them and our connection grew, I experienced heartache and would start crying out of the blue if we started kissing or intimately embracing.

I'm usually very in-tuned with myself but I didn't understand what was going on with me. I just knew that I was a grieving sister.

Later, I came to realize that my heart wasn't differentiating the love. My brother, who I loved greatly, and wanted to choose life, said *no*, nonverbally, and allowed his health to decline. My human spirit feared that these men would break my heart too. My subconscious was already braced for abandonment, as a result of my father's death so many years earlier.

Through God and writing to my brother and father in my journal, I'm a long way down the healing path. I've written to them about my pain, love, and anger with them being gone, and expressed my wholehearted willingness to forgive them.

In my brother's case, I am just coming to acceptance that perhaps he was meant to leave this earth when he did. Perhaps his greater work must come from the other side. Where he is now in spirit, I know he would never leave his two adult children. And perhaps he can most help them from where he is now.

CHOOSING LIFE

My mother died less than two years after my grandmother (her mother) passed. The three of us lived in very close proximity in Atlanta, and Mom spent her final year living with me in home hospice.

Two years after she was gone, I was still saying to God, "I can't believe that you left me here all alone."

I began to realize that in order for me to move forward without my mother I would need to live authentically; and that, I believed, would bring me to happiness.

For me, living authentically meant fulfillment at home, with friends, and in my work, as well as a deeper connection to God. For a few years, I had been studying the book, *A Course in Miracles*. It speaks to that one truth, for me about God – that He is love and only love.

I joined *A Course in Miracles* discussion group that's held on Sundays in a private home. Before going, I decided that I would be real and as honest with myself as possible with anything that I shared. That was thirteen years ago, and the group remains a central part of my life.

But before that first Sunday, I was not living an authentic life at all. I was unhappy and I couldn't share a full scope of me with most close friends, beyond work and continued grief over the loss of my mother.

The missing link of truth was that I was in a long distance, years-long relationship with a married man. I couldn't share that information, so I somehow talked in generalities when I spoke about my long-distance relationship.

The good news is I knew that getting to my authentic life, and hopefully happiness, meant ending the relationship.

I was involved with this person, who I will call Michael, for two years before he told me that he was married. In reality, he and his wife lived in separate cities. He owned his home where he lived, and I would visit for days, unaware of the truth, and he would come to visit me.

By the time Michael told me that he was married, I was in love and thought he was mine. So, after shedding many tears, and hours' long conversations with him, I continued in the relationship. But make no mistake, he was not separated, he was in full union with his wife who just happened to live in a different state than he did.

I loved him deeply. But as I tried to navigate life without my mother in it, I knew he could and would never give me what I wanted. Nor could I be happy with him. And honestly, I didn't see the love in his eyes that I wanted to see from the man in my life.

In my mind, I kept hearing Meg Ryan's words to an oblivious Carrie Fisher, as they walked down the street in the film *When Harry Met Sally*.

She matter-of-factly said, "He's never going to leave (his wife)."

Although I didn't know that I was with another woman's husband for those first two years, after I learned the truth, I felt increased angst in my gut. I didn't like what I was doing, or who I was doing it to—a woman—even if she was unaware. In my mind, women are sisters.

Eventually, the relationship ended, and it was a short while later that I joined the Sunday *Course in Miracles* group. From the first day attending, I decided that if I were to be a part of the gathering, I would show up authentically and be honest with myself on this spiritual adventure to fully knowing God.

This journey has been difficult, yet healing, loving, and amazing. The greatest thing that I have learned is that God is inside us, and I can connect with Him inside and experience an exchange of communication.

For me, prayer leads me to a meditative state where my thoughts slow and stop, and I am in a place of listening.

I am so in awe of this truth.

Through the trials of my adult life—failed relationships and overcoming low self-worth, financial hardship, and grieving the deaths of loved ones—I have clung to that knowing that God is only love. And being only love, He loves me unconditionally.

Admittedly though, during low times, I have thought that everyone on the planet was entitled to God's love, except me. Yet, my faith has taught me to be vigilant to the truth of God's love, even when I feel completely alone and doubtful.

THE ROAD TO RENEWAL

I started 2019 without stable employment. I've been a freelance writer and journalist for several years, with mostly stable income, but that changed at the end of 2018 when the magazine publication, in which I was a contract editor, closed.

While in fear of losing financial stability, God brought me many blessings throughout the year, including timely, freelance writing gigs. Assignments started slowing down, however, around summertime. Panic set in. Would I be able to meet my financial commitments and keep a roof over my head, I wondered? It wasn't the first time in my adult life that I had been in financial straits, and I wanted this to never come up again. I wanted to learn whatever God would have me learn.

For a couple of years, I held in my heart a desire to trust God 100 percent. My trust level was actually at about 85 percent. My spirit knew that trusting Him fully would change my life.

So, I decided while in this space of fear and doubt that I would trust God fully. While experiencing my deepest fears, I knew that I could share my feelings honestly with the Holy Spirit, God, and Jesus. And I did, often coming to a feeling of comfort.

I've learned, though, that many times when we ask God to change something, such as in my case, to help me to trust Him in all things, He brings opportunities for me to accomplish what I prayed for.

I wanted to trust. He brought me opportunities to trust Him. My finances seemed stark. Several friends told me about job openings at their place of employment or where they had connections and contacted the person they knew with my resume in hand. You would think that would give me an automatic in for an interview, at least. In nine out of ten cases, I never got a phone call or an email. There was no interest.

It felt like I was in a space where things were not going to work out for me. I was terrified at moments, but somehow also willing to be in surrender mode.

I had many blessings. For two months, I turned to others for help with my rent, including a charitable organization.

I asked for help from my *Course in Miracles* group. Our group has funds, which has helped people in need if everyone generally agrees to it.

It's not easy to ask for help. That Sunday at my Course group, the facilitator and I agreed that I would make the request during announcements at the end of our regular discussion. I arrived in total trust that no matter what the consensus was, God would work things out for me.

Everyone was loving and went above and beyond in their support of me and my circumstances.

Separately, friends and family sent money, or came by with a check.

I was out dancing one night with some girlfriends and the next morning, I found one of them had placed $40 in my purse.

Although a secure job hadn't come my way, two separate friends hired me to help them with books they were writing.

I just kept moving forward in trust.

Earlier in the year, I started a spiritual podcast called *Let's Start Healing*, where I interview people of all different faiths and walks of life about their spiritual path and relationship with God.

Talking to guests and publishing the podcast is indeed healing for me.

By September, I landed a part-time job with a host of business podcasts, as his producer and show page writer. That felt divine, as it was right up my alley.

I felt God's blessings pouring in.

I could finally pay my rent without any assistance in October. But something happened that showed me the level of terror I can shift into.

The day before my rent was due, I had several checks to deposit from my many gigs that amounted to my rent. Totaling them up in my car, outside the bank, I became confused because it appeared that I was short $300. I literally felt a wave of fear come over me.

In that moment, a friend phoned about us driving together to *a Course in Miracles* discussion group being held that night. I was so flustered, I could only say that I couldn't make it, and was trying to figure out how I had messed up and thought I had enough for my rent.

We ended the call, and as I sat there, I remembered that a client was to send her weekly payment to me via PayPal that night. I had taken myself into a tailspin of fear and disappointment over an illusion that I made up.

That's the truth of everything around my fears in 2019. Looking back, they were just fears that I manifested on my own. None of them materialized. God always brought me through. My fears were just that – fears. They were really wasted energy. God had shown me over and over in my life that I can lean on Him and trust Him. He's not going to drop me. And yet, I've been afraid. When I get down to it, God plays a role in every aspect of my life that is good. He's the hope that I cling to. But when I'm in fear my imagination tells me that if I trust Him completely and I crash and burn, it will be game over and I'm doomed.

So, one afternoon, I felt anxious as I kept my eye out for some pay to come in that would help me in a big way. With this client, an email would generate from my bank to let me know that a wire was coming and would appear in my balance the next day.

I walked my dog along the lawn and admonished myself for not being in a place of peace and full trust considering all of God's blessings. I should be ashamed, I thought, as I was constantly checking my phone for the email notification.

In that moment, the email came.

LESSON LEARNED

There's a lesson in *A Course in Miracles* titled, *All things are lessons God would have me learn.*

The message of the lesson is *Forgive, and you will see differently*. And forgiveness must start with self.

I've come to understand that it's the punishment and doubt of myself that brings about my fears.

My faith tells me that we all are back with God in full remembrance of Him and who we truly are in the end. I believe this can happen while I'm alive or when I die. It's my choice.

My sensibilities tell me that from God's perspective, a hard or easy life will bring me to true awareness of Him.

Because He is love, I can experience an easy life and run the bases straight through to home plate as if I hit a home run, or I can allow life to be a grind, and keep slugging. In the latter case, they are simply lessons that God would have me learn to know who I truly am.

I started 2020 in a new place of confidence and surrender, and a stable job opportunity that meets my financial needs. I stay connected to the Holy Spirit. I talk to Him, and ask Him to lead me, and show me what to say and do. This helps me to be present, and remember who I am, a wholly loved child of God.

I have my moments, even hours during the course of the day when I leave myself, as I like to say, and forget who I am.

But lately those gaps of forgetfulness are decreasing, as a result of talking to the Holy Spirit, or taking a time out for prayer, meditation, or reading pages of a spiritual book that speaks to me.

I am trusting in the unknown, as a friend suggested to me, knowing that He's got me, one way or another.

I'm learning to listen to my heart because God is there.

ABOUT ADRIANNE MURCHISON

Adrianne Murchison is an Atlanta-based journalist and host of the *Let's Start Healing* podcast where she is in conversation with guests who share their spiritual journey and relationship with God, or Higher Power.

Under the *Let's Start Healing* brand, Adrianne has started healing events that range from movement and yoga classes to inspirational speakers.

She is driven to connect people. Journalism, and separately, spiritual discussion groups that Adrianne is a part of have revealed that people are more alike than different and can indeed connect. Her platforms demonstrate this.

The Buffalo, NY native's sixteen years in journalism include roles as a reporter, editor, and content producer for *The Atlanta Journal-Constitution.*

She is author of a book on the relationship dynamics between African American men and women titled, *Kalieding on the Road to Happiness.* She has moderated author conversations for the highly reputable *Book Festival of the Marcus Jewish Community Center of Atlanta.*

As a spiritualist, Adrianne incorporates God in all things in her life, and turned to Him for help in the training and completion of two triathlons, five marathons, and six half marathons.

Listen to her *Let's Start Healing* podcast on Apple Podcasts, Spotify, iHeartRadio and YouTube.

Email Adrianne at letsstarthealingpodcast@gmail.com

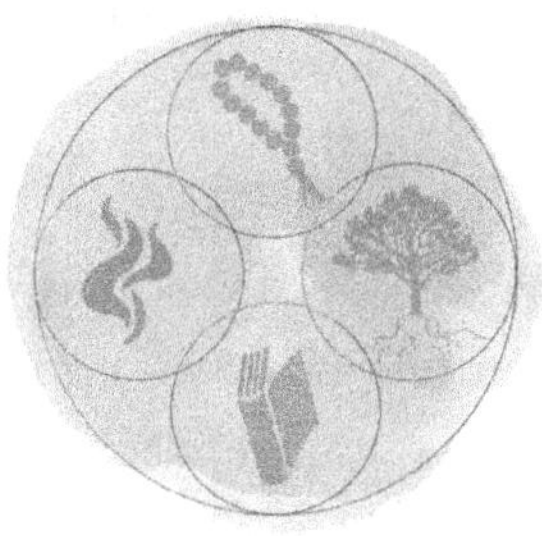

LOVE IS ALWAYS THE KEY

Tatjana Obradovic

I spent my high school years living in "Zmaj" orphanage in Belgrade, Serbia and I was never truly happy until then.

When I was two-years-old, my father received a Fulbright's scholarship to study abroad. He was the first person from the tiny republic of Montenegro to ever receive this highly reputable scholarship, and his family encouraged him to take advantage of this opportunity. When my mom realized that my father had departed without a plan for us, or even an explanation, she decided to end our lives right where he left us. My mom never talked about this event to me, however, what I have learned from my grandmother and my aunt over the years is that, about a week later, when my aunt came to visit us, she found us in the basement sitting on an old mattress and the only food available was rice cooked in water.

That was a tremendous story to inherit. Although I don't remember it cognitively, those memories are imprinted in my soul, and from that moment on my soul was ready to elevate from that living situation.

My mother's family assisted us and for the next several years my mom and I had a beautiful life. We traveled, we had a tailor who made us matching outfits, and I was free and joyful. I loved dancing, drawing, and reading; my teachers and family adored me and life was so magnificent. My mom was the center of my Universe and profound feelings of love, connection, and unconditional support were flowing unrestricted between us. It is that early on, secure attachment with my mom that gave me the strength to endure what was coming next.

My mom was strongly encouraged to remarry and move to Belgrade, Serbia. At that time in Montenegro, it was not the best reputation for a woman to be divorced with a young daughter living on her own.

I was left to live with my grandparents without any explanation of where my mom went, while my mom was sent to the capital to get married to a man eighteen years older than she was. I lived with my grandparents until I started school to give my mom's new marriage a good start, without the burden of a child from a previous marriage (as my stepfather and my grandparents believed was best.) I could not show how much I missed my mom during the day, therefore I waited for nighttime to go to bed, look at my mom's photo, kiss it, and cry silently under the covers.

My mom and my stepfather welcomed their first child, a boy, and life was good for them for the first two years of his life. At the age of two-and-a half the boy was diagnosed with autism. From a very well-developed toddler my brother started to regress in terms of all his daily living skills. He became fully dependent and until now he has been living the life of a non-verbal person with autism.

When it was time for me to start school, my grandparents insisted that I begin living with my mom. My stepfather strongly refused. He hid my existence, completely out of shame that he had married a woman who had previously been married. Nobody from his family knew that my mom had a previous marriage or a child.

My aunt took care of me during first grade in elementary school, and I only visited my mom on weekends. In first grade I learned to travel using public transportation and traveled alone for over one hour just to be able to see my mom.

I was seven-years-old when my mom and my stepfather locked me in a tiny room and ordered me to be silent, hiding me so that the neighbors who came to visit would not know I existed and that my stepfather had married a woman who had a child from her first marriage. In that moment, I decided that I would shine so brightly that no one would be able to hide me, that it would be impossible to ever hide me again, and that I would go on to create a business where I would help other women who ever felt hidden away, invisible, or non-existent; to heal that wound, to understand why the wound was needed, why what happened was a blessing for them, and then lovingly guide them to find their light and remember where they tucked it away. And finally, to give themselves permission to shine again, brighter than ever.

My mom and stepfather later welcomed two healthy girls, but given the life with a child with autism and the stigma it carried at that time in Serbia, there was rarely a happy, quiet moment in that family. Altercations became a regular occurrence, while I lived a Cinderella life until I started high school. The feeling of closeness and unconditional love between my mother and I slowly disappeared and I grew up next to her, but was actually estranged from my mother. During my elementary schooling I changed to five different schools, lived with my aunt, two different families from my mom's work, and lived in two different states–all the while remaining top of the class, in every school, in every new living arrangement. Life was unpredictable and it seemed that every time I would adjust to a new school, new family, and new living arrangement, I would be uprooted again. I always kept the smile on my face and a positive outlook on life while in school. All my friends from all those schools who connect with me nowadays via social media say one thing, "I remember you as always smiling, always being happy." School was my happy place. I had developed a love for learning and enjoyed the care and encouragement from teachers who were proud to have such a bright student in their class. Deep down I felt that knowledge was my power, and although I could not control where and how I lived during that period, I knew I could control my grades and that knowledge would be my salvation from that living dynamic.

When I was ten-years-old I decided I would study psychology, intending to use that expertise to find a cure for autism to help my brother and understand people's minds better. I hoped psychology would help me understand why I was living this deeply disturbing life and that it would give me the tools to heal myself. I also decided that my children would have a different life, and since I did not have adequate role models at home, I thought learning from books would be the best way to ascertain how to have a happy, harmonious family life. I simultaneously attended two different universities: one where I studied psychology and another where I trained to become a pre-school teacher. I never intended to work as a pre-school teacher, I simply needed to learn how to properly raise children from day one. I prepared myself for twenty years to set the best possible path for my future children. I kept my body, my mind, my heart, and my spirit the purest possible. I had an agreement with God that if I did all of that, I would have wonderful children and I would know how to raise them and create a harmonious life for them.

Once I was in high school, my stepfather decided to completely kick me out of the house. A psychologist at school helped me and arranged for me to be admitted to an orphanage in Belgrade named 'Zmaj'. That was such a blessing for me, truly a blessing in disguise and I can honestly say that those seven years I lived in the orphanage were my best years in Belgrade, until I moved to New York. Many people would think of Oliver Twist when an orphanage is mentioned. But for me that was truly, honestly a paradise. For the first time since my early childhood I had my own room which I transformed into a sanctuary. People who worked at the orphanage recognized my creativity, drive, and talents and allowed me to express them freely. I was allowed to take the spotlight and shine. At the orphanage, there was a theater, dance and art school, and fairy tale writing workshops with the best Serbian contemporary writers. I took part in all those activities. I helped the counselors in the orphanage with the younger children. With my friends from college we created a small not-for-profit group called "Zmaj" (meaning "dragon" in Serbian). We hosted students from Europe, Japan, and the USA for three weeks during the summer. The morning schedule included helping with small repairs throughout the building and activities with younger children. In the afternoon a psychologist would offer various workshops and seminars with plenty of time left to explore the city and culture. We ran beautifully for three years. My friends from different universities offered math, history, science, and foreign language homework help to the children in the orphanage while I personally offered counseling. I called it "The School of Life". I felt I was useful and helpful and that what I did mattered and made a difference in my world, while I was still doing what I loved and enjoyed. Even in those situations that many would find grim, I was able to find light, I was able to keep that inner joy and gratitude and acknowledge my blessings and emanate that joy back to the world.

As my schooling and the time I was entitled to live at the orphanage was coming to an end, I kept thinking what my next step was going to be. There was no solution, I had no place to go once I graduated, but I kept envisioning a miracle.

One Sunday afternoon, the director of the orphanage had asked me to assist him with a group of visitors from the USA. Since I spoke English, that was a common occurrence; every time we would have international visitors, I would take them on a tour of the building. During that specific tour, one of the gentlemen with a lovely southern accent, now the late Mr. William Murray, made me an offer to come to New York and finish my studies there. I politely thanked him, not really thinking the offer would come true. However, six months later, I received a parcel with all the documents I needed to come study in New York, including a letter that I had received a full scholarship from the Samuel Freeman Charitable Trust and Marymount Manhattan College. Just in time, my miracle had arrived in a DHL envelope!

One profound realization that comes to mind when I look back at those years is that when life is taking us somewhere, and that place is not aligned with what we planned or visualized for ourselves, if we fight that process, we lose so much energy, so much light, and that resistance makes us feel like we are failing in life. Instead, we should preserve the energy, allow the flow, and glide to that unknown place or situation. Once we arrive we need to be truly present in that place, time, and reality and see how we can make the best out of that situation. Now, don't get me wrong, I love short and long term plans. We all need them, but sometimes when we are truly aligned with our path, we might find ourselves in a very different place from where we imagined ourselves to be. I never even thought I would live anywhere abroad. I never saw myself living outside of Serbia, I wanted my children to be born in Belgrade, but look where I am now! I still ask myself what was the higher purpose of me moving to another continent and establishing my life in New York? I think this path of healing and helping people, writing this book, and spreading the word worldwide is the answer to that question.

If we hold onto the way we think life is supposed to go, the way we believe life is supposed to be, then we are getting into a pattern of resisting where life really wants to take us.

If I had been stuck in my story, I would still be stuck in my story.

Because I was not stuck in my story, I allowed grace and more miracles to enter my life.

It might be a hard concept to live with for a while, because there is no guarantee, it is all in the future. I had to have faith and hope and trust, but since I lived in that space, I did trust. I had to trust.

I recognized what was happening to me, I never denied that my mom was in a really dark place and that she took me there with her. I recognized that it was a horrible thing to be hidden away and made invisible. I recognized even then how that shattered my soul in those moments. I was not ignoring what was happening to me, I never said these experiences didn't occur; I admitted to myself that these were hurtful events which were damaging to my soul on many levels. However, I am saying that even though these incidents did happen, I still chose to see them as a blessing and as a result of that perspective, I was able to welcome in new blessings. Therefore, I was able to invite in even more. I kept going and I continued to live in grace.

Because I was in a place of gratitude and in a place of being open to miracles, not stuck being a victim, I intended to make the most of the situation, intended to look for all the blessings I could find. That allowed more blessings to come to me, which led me to the place I am in now, and all the blessings I can offer to other people at this place and moment.

We all have a life purpose, but if we get stuck in our story, we might overlook the signs, might get lost in survival mode, forgetting that we are all born on this planet with a wound. We all came here to heal, forgive and love, find our soul family and live our true life purpose, which always involves doing something for others, helping others; it always involves selfless acts of love. To lovingly remind myself and everyone I work with that love is always the key to all our healings, I founded The Key of Love.

ABOUT TATJANA OBRADOVIC

Tatjana Obradovic is the founder of The Key of Love, LLC. Tatjana is a mom of two happy teenagers and she has over fifteen years of experience supporting people with autism working as a Behavioral Psychologist.

Besides Behavioral Therapy, Tatjana is versed in and has a passion for Energy Psychology, Karmic astrology and integration, healing with doTerra Essential Oils, Astro-healing with planetary, gem, and flower vibrational essences—which she absolutely loves to create and personalize for her clients—Astro-meridians therapy, Twin Flames journey, transcendental meditation, Awakening and Healing Divine Feminine with her signature program for Sacral chakra healing, Timeline Healing, Deep PEAT and Usui Reiki.

Tatjana is a certified Intuitive and Success Coach who trained Dr. Lea Imsiragic, Jack Canfield, and Kate Butler. She believes that healing is a natural gift of all people. Tatjana is an avid world traveler, therapist, healer, and coach who lovingly guides her clients in-spirit to remember that gift. Tatjana enjoys awakening unconditional love in her clients. She does this through one-on-one counseling, group workshops, live events, luxury retreats on main energy centers of the world (especially Egypt), and online programs.

Tatjana is a graduate of the University of Belgrade and Marymount Manhattan College, where she majored in psychology. She received her Master's degree from the School of Professional Studies in New York City.

To learn more about how you can connect and work with Tatjana, please visit her website at TheKeyofLove.org, where you can find resources and information about her programs.

Facebook: @TheKeyofLove

Instagram: @thekeyoflove_

Email: Tatjana@thekeyoflove.org

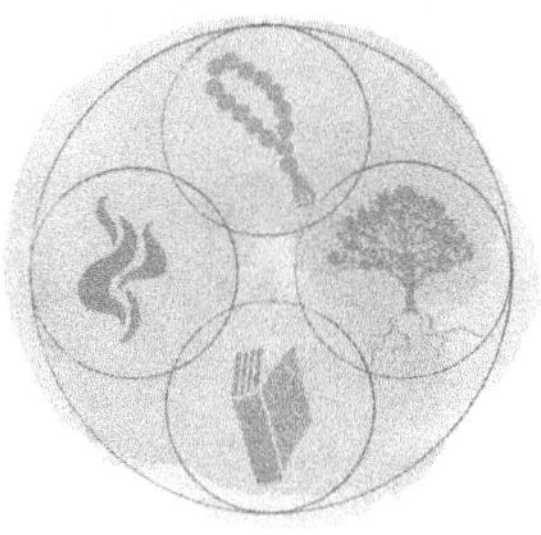

DEFINING MOMENTS

Jeannette Paxia

"It is during our darkest moments that we must focus to see the light."
- Aristotle

My eyes fluttered in a deep dream state. I could see the choices in front of me, the two roads; which one should I choose? Which way do I go? Please help me! I am angry! I am frustrated! I am sad! Why did this happen to our family? I could hear my niece screaming, "NO," and holding on to my mom's hand, lifeless as she had already taken her last breath. I could see my sister in the background, quiet as tears slowly streamed down her face. I could feel my mom's wrist in my hands as I desperately tried to find a sign of life. I could hear my dad crying in the background as he realized that his other half –"his better half" as he would say–for the last forty-one years was now gone, and I could see in the shadows my nine-year-old son, confused as to what was going on.

June 2010 – earlier that year.

I checked my list again for what felt like the hundredth time. Could I possibly have everything packed into the Jeep, everything that I would need for a new life? I looked up at my 2000 square foot house and realized that all I really needed was already packed into my car. My sons were there and that was all that mattered, the rest was just stuff. I pulled out of the driveway and saw the man peering through the window at me, a look of sorrow across his face. I tried for so long to please him, I felt if I was the best me that I could be, he wouldn't have to turn to alcohol and drugs. I wouldn't have to hope that each day I'd be safe from his rage, the person he became with each vice he indulged in. It was in these times that I understood the meaning of Jekyll and Hyde. I set out on a journey that would be what I thought was the most defining moment in my life: I was leaving Ohio, leaving him, and heading home to California. This was a huge step, one that I had been attempting for years. I knew it was now up to me to take care of the boys. I hoped just maybe this would be his wake-up call and he would change his life. My mom was supposed to have surgery and I knew she wouldn't unless someone was there to take care of my dad. This was my opportunity to help my parents, while also giving him a chance to see what life was like without us. Maybe he would then change.

I didn't know what was ahead of us, but like the 3000-mile journey that was ahead of me, all I could do was take it one step at a time. With my eight-year-old and one-year-old strapped into the back of the Jeep, in the background I could hear "Blue's Clues" playing on the portable DVD player. I drove mile after mile, confused feelings swirling through me. I was happy to be getting out but sad that our family would be broken apart. When I said those vows, I intended them to be forever. I felt like a failure as a wife, a mother, and a daughter. I hoped that what I was doing was the right thing. Pacing myself, I would drive four hours then stop for lunch, drive another four hours and stop for the night. At times during that drive I felt free, at other times I was scared to death. We hit a huge storm where I couldn't even see the road in front of me. In those times I gripped the steering wheel and prayed. Five days after we set out on our journey, we pulled into the driveway at home. Although I had lived outside of California for most of my adult life, it would always be home. I safely arrived and I was now safe in so many ways; I was home.

The next few months continued to challenge my strength. He constantly called and asked what I was going to be doing, was I staying or was I coming back to Cleveland? I was so focused on my life and what was happening to me that I missed signs that I shouldn't have, signs that my mom was sicker than any of us knew. One time he and I were arguing on the phone about Christmas, and my mom, weak as she was, stood up and yelled, "My grandsons will be here for Christmas!" and sat back down as if that was the only choice. I would accompany my mom to the doctor's visits, preparing for a routine surgery that the doctor kept delaying. As a nurse, I started to slowly notice signs and symptoms in my mom that I had been missing. But somehow, I still didn't realize how little time she had left. She was seeing an oncologist, but no one had diagnosed her with cancer. It was due to her thinning blood, they said. The surgery being postponed didn't raise any warning flags. The small dots of petechiae (pinprick hemorrhages on the skin) that I noticed on her arm were just a part of having thinning blood. I remember like it was yesterday, the moment I stopped focusing so much on my situation and realized that she was sick, sicker than I ever imagined. My mom, who never was sick, the one who took care of my dad who had Parkinson's and a lifetime of injuries and illnesses. How could she be sick? The thought had never even crossed my mind. My mom and I were sitting in the car after leaving the doctor's appointment and she said to me, "A few months ago they said I may have Pancreatitis." My reaction was one that I have regretted ever since that moment. "What?!" I yelled. "Pancreatitis is extremely painful; you would know if you had that!" She just looked at me, she looked like a child and said, "Oh, I must be wrong then, it must have been something else." I reacted with fear, but now know that she probably did have Pancreatitis and suffered alone. She tried to reach out to me, and I wasn't there for her.

I spent much of my time searching for jobs. My sister had let us live with her while we figured out what was next. When everyone was sleeping, I would stay up most of the night applying for jobs. I had to find a way to support my kids, I couldn't take advantage of my sister's generosity. She already had four kids and with us in the house, there were nine of us.

I started my new job on September 27th, 2010. I was so excited about the opportunity I had found. It would be good for my career and allow me to be able to support my children. In the weeks before I started my job, my mom had been ill, nauseous, and couldn't eat much. She was losing weight quickly. Tired of the doctors, she refused to go anymore. The day I started the job, my sister and I decided that my mom needed to go to the doctor. My sister took her while I went to my first day of work. This day happened to also be my parent's 41st wedding anniversary. The doctor told my mom and my sister that my mom just had the flu. "Grow up, go home and drink some Gatorade!" Wow!

When I got home from work, I noticed how pale she had become. She couldn't even keep down the Gatorade. I looked at her and said, "Either I am calling 911, or you are coming with me to the emergency room, this is more than the flu." She could barely even stand up. That night at the emergency room the doctors checked her into the hospital. They couldn't believe that her doctor would let her walk out of the office. That was the last time my mom would be out of the hospital until we brought her home with hospice. October 28, 2010, at 2:10 PM, she was pronounced dead in the house she had lived in for forty-one years with my dad, the house we grew up in.

Back to my dream and my choices and the two roads I could take. Losing my mom was and still is the most defining moment in my life. Nine years later, I still cry; in fact, I am crying as I write this. I still miss her, but it is what I did with that pain that changed my life completely. I realized life is too short to be unhappy. The road I chose to take was the road that would help people. Instead of drowning myself in sorrow, I thought of what she would have done. My mom helped so many people that there was standing room only at her funeral. People I had never met came up to our family and told us how she had helped them. Focusing on why I do what I do, because of losing my mom, is what gets me up in the morning. It is my WHY!

I began changing my life by changing my relationships, the relationships that weren't adding to my life but were making my life worse. At first, I thought that I should try again with my partner. I didn't want my children to lose a grandma and father all at once, but I quickly realized that it was better for all of us if he and I were apart.

I decided that I needed to examine my health habits. I researched to find out ways to become healthier. I started slowly, by adding in exercise, I began eating whole foods and decreasing the processed foods I consumed. I had the doctor run tests to see what foods I was allergic or had sensitivities to, and I cut those out of my life. It took a few years, but I lost over sixty-five pounds.

I worked on my career. I enjoyed training and coaching people, but thought that instead of training medical personnel, which was my current job, I could help others implement healthier habits. I became a health coach and then certified Canfield Success Principles Speaker and Trainer. I love what I do, helping people truly makes me happy. If you are happy in your career, it affects your whole life. Even though life is short, I want to enjoy it as much as I can. Reflecting on your life and what makes you happy and identifying parts of your life that you may need to change is important for not only you, but those you influence.

We all have defining moments in our lives. A defining moment can make you or break you. How are you going to move forward? Which road are you going to choose?

ABOUT JEANNETTE PAXIA

For as long as she can remember the basis of Jeannette's life has been what can she do today to help the most amount of people? Working in the medical field for over twenty-five years, she held many different roles, always striving to help more people. When her mom died, the way Jeannette helped people changed, realizing that "Life is too short to live without happiness." What better way to reach her goals than to be trained by *Chicken Soup for the Soul* co-author Jack Canfield? Jeannette is passionate about helping everyone live the life that they want to live, no matter what age they are. Through her companies Pax Coaching and Living Mindfully, she provides clients the confidence and tools needed to transform their lives. In addition to speaking and coaching she is a children's author. Her "Superhero" book and presentation will not only guide children in discovering their unique qualities but will also engage adults. Additionally, Jeannette will have completed her Ph.D. by the end of 2020, and she is certified as a Culture Transformation Tools Practitioner and as a health coach through the Institute for Integrative Nutrition.

https://paxcoach.com/
https://jeannettepaxia.synduit.com/CL0002
https://youareasuperhero.net/

IG JeannettePaxia_Coach

Video Link
https://www.facebook.com/677062188/posts/10156982052947189/

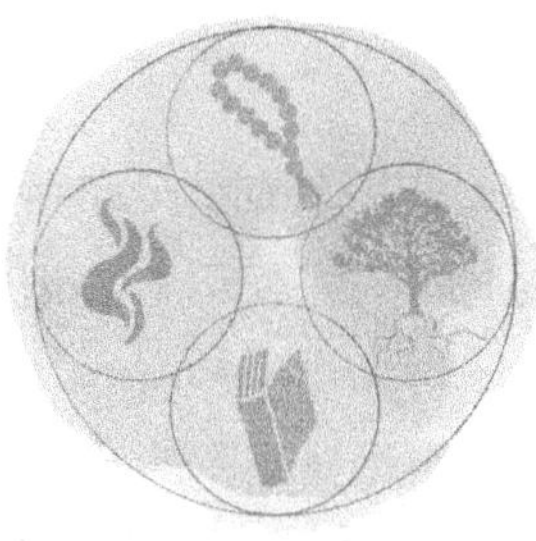

CHOOSING A DIFFERENT PATH

Ashley Richards

Life ... such an interesting journey of wins, losses, challenges, celebrations, and so many milestones in between. Many of my memories along this path were not unicorns and sunshine (probably like many of you), but I guess you can say I didn't think I would be where I am now, in a troubling but amazing sort of way. My childhood was not traditional, and there were a lot of dark times, but there was another plan for my life. A plan to help me rise from the drama and chaos and build a new life full of love, fun, and most importantly, living intentionally. Many people don't know a lot about my past, simply because I am not the person I was nearly twenty years ago. But I am ready to share it now, and share it to help encourage others to rise against their odds and thrive in a new life they can build for themselves.

As a young girl, I always knew I wanted to be in business. While many girls my age were playing house, I played office, full of file folders, papers, and even an old phone. It was so fun to make-believe an office and a busy lifestyle full of the hustle that any business brings. Even though I have some great childhood memories, like my play office, I also have a memory full of drama and dark that came from alcoholic parents who divorced when I was three-years-old. I remember the yelling, the back and forth for holidays and weekends, and the constant battle that took place over my two sisters and myself.

My life changed dramatically when my mother passed away from lung cancer when I was thirteen. I will never forget the moment my stepmother told me she died. My father and stepmother were not equipped to help us kids mourn our loss. They had their own internal battles they were fighting, so we were left to fend for ourselves. We were used to the heavy drinking, the verbal abuse, and the very little parenting that took place when we needed guidance the most. This life of chaos was normal. I just didn't know life any other way.

My confusing world got a little darker when my sister passed away unexpectedly during my senior year of high school, creating an even darker home life as we all mourned the loss of an incredible person. Losing one close family member when you are a child is hard enough, but two was unbearable, with no support or tools to help us cope. I remember feeling so alone as my father and stepmother chose to drink away their emotions. So, at the age of eighteen, I mustered up the courage to move out and started a life on my own. It was scary, surreal, and unknown territory as I rented my first one-bedroom apartment. I struggled to pay my bills with my small income, leaving only a few dollars each paycheck for food before the next pay period. In the difficult days, I remember my father's words, "My home is not a revolving door, when you move out, you are out." Those were replayed in my mind as I chose to push forward. It was an empowering few years that taught me to work hard, stay focused, and continue to strive for my goals.

I remember getting my first big break and getting a glimpse of that beautiful office life I pretended to have as a kid when I was recruited from my entry-level, a-little-above-minimum-wage job to becoming an account executive for a large commercial real estate firm. I felt confident, I felt needed, and most importantly, I surrounded myself with people that pushed me to become a better person. Successful individuals that showed me that hard work CAN pay off, and to continue to push the needle forward to accomplish any goal I wanted to achieve. It was my lightbulb career moment as I became a self-taught professional, edging my way through a male-dominated, intense industry. I had become a confident, thriving professional, and was on my way down a new path, one I chose, one that would fulfill my dreams, or so I thought.

In 2008, the market crashed and the entire real estate industry went down with it. Very quickly, I found myself at the bottom, losing my career as the layoffs began and not really knowing where to go from there. I could have chosen to drink my sorrows away like my parents did when times were tough, but instead I picked up my things and chose to march on. I was determined to stay on track to break the mold and develop a new lifestyle that didn't end with drinking or drugs as a means to overcome a challenging situation. It was from the very beginning again, but I was ready, really ready to find that right path.

I went back to college to finally finish that degree I so longed for, while working a job where I made a quarter of what I did while I was in real estate. But it didn't matter, I was filling my cup with things more important than a title or a financial status. I chose a path less taken that was full of grit, hard times, and humbling moments, but it was the perfect path for me. I hit the books hard, finished my bachelor's degree, and learned more about myself and my path along the way. My outlook was different than before. Instead of chasing status, I chased my dream job in the marketing field. It wasn't about the dollars, but making a difference and climbing the corporate ladder.

As I was beginning my bachelor's program, I met the love my life and was welcomed into a family that was full of faith, love, and acceptance. It was eye opening for me to experience a family full of grace and deep appreciation for one another, in stark contrast to what I was so used to in my childhood. I always longed for love, but I gained so much more than just a husband. I gained a family that loved and supported me in a way I have never felt before. It was, and still is, incredible and something I do not take for granted. Although I was not born into the ideal family, I was welcomed into this one, giving me an incredible foundation to make even more path changes in the future.

After finishing up school, I started my career in marketing. It was a dream come true, and my little make-believe office days became a reality as I set up my office with fun décor and photos. But my path was about to shift again, as my husband and I longed to start a family. We soon got pregnant, and after having our sweet baby girl, I decided my focus wasn't on work or that career path. That was an escape from my broken home life, the one thing I chased for oh-so long. The one thing that filled most of the hours in my days when I was alone. But things were different now. I had an incredible family foundation, and after the doctor placed that perfect little girl in my arms, my path shifted. It was no longer about my career, but about this little girl and breaking the mold that was created before her. It was a path that focused on happiness, faith, and balance while striving to keep our family a priority before anything else.

Within two years we had two children, and although I absolutely loved this mom-life, I knew I was made for more. My path was made to extend much further than my own home, and I made the leap into entrepreneurship. I wanted to a raise a business and my babies at the same time. I was ready to have what I never did, which was a foundational family dynamic, but still with the satisfaction of pursuing a career that I worked so hard for so many years for. This was my path. The path I was MEANT to be on. I truly believe we should not have to choose a specific path, but rather create one, that has all the elements of your life that are important to you. So, I did. I chose to start a business that allows me to put my family's needs first, while offering a valuable service to businesses, and it has become my mission to offer this balanced life to my team members as well.

So often we focus on how things were done before us, what memories we experienced during our childhood, and keep our eyes set on a narrow path in our life. I am here to tell you, and to challenge you, that no path is straight, no path is easy, and no path is set in stone. It is okay to veer, shift, change, create, and even slow down. As long as you are moving forward, navigating through the hardships and challenging times, you will find that perfect path for you. Widen your path to include all the things you love and are passionate about. Narrow it in times of trouble or shifts in your life. But remember, ALWAYS remember, that this is your legacy, your life, and your opportunity to live it any way you want to. As long as my path takes me to places full of laughter, family, hard work, and drive, I am on the right path.

ABOUT ASHLEY RICHARDS

Ashley Richards is a dynamic and versatile marketing executive with fifteen years of experience executing digital strategies to totally transform businesses. Her past clients include large Fortune 500 companies, fitness facilities, physical therapy offices, and large shopping centers. Ashley's extensive experience—combined with her passion for marketing—allow her to bring her clients tremendous success in the online world.

In 2017, Ashley launched E Squared Marketing to provide creative digital marketing solutions and heightened value to small to medium-sized businesses. Whatever your needs, Ashley provides a fresh perspective and creative yet pragmatic leadership to guide your business to success.

E Squared has now grown to ten dedicated marketing professionals who take their clients' goals and knock them out of the park. They bring a personal touch to everything they do—and they're just as committed to having fun as they are to flawlessly executing results-driven marketing strategies.

Ashley is a graduate of the University of Phoenix. When she's not working, you can find this Arizona native enjoying hikes with her husband of nine years, Brandon, and their two adorable children, Ellie and Eli.

Esquaredmarketing.com
@ashleyrichardsaz

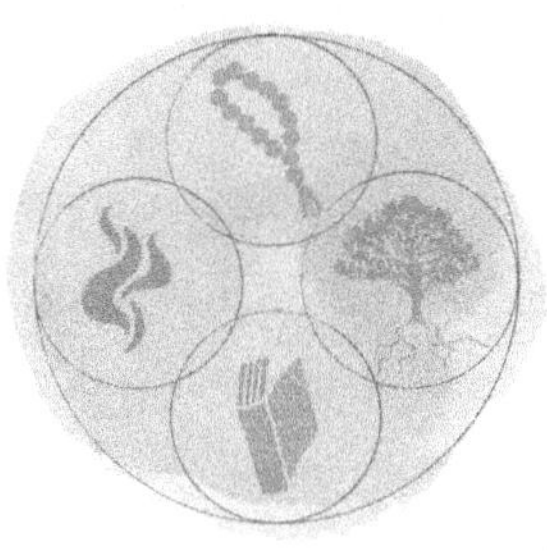

SEIZE THE DAY

Kristen Riddell

The event that caused me the most pain became a pivotal moment in my life. Pregnant with my second child, my mindset was one that after I raised my children and retired, I would then have the opportunity to enjoy life and travel. I was working at a stable job with an incredible pension. The work was interesting, but I craved to spend more time with my five-year-old son. Daydreams often floated through my head about finding a position working from home where I could have the work/life balance that I craved while my children were young. I pushed aside these thoughts and would remind myself to be grateful for the stable job that I had.

The slow decline of my father's health had crept up on me. Vibrant, energetic, and always the most handsome man in the room, my dad was now a shell of the man that I grew up with. Over time, the emails that he sent were gibberish and he was slowly losing his memory. He started to hunch over and his skin looked dry and mottled. I often drove him to his infusion treatments at the hospital. On the drive, he would always express his gratitude and I could tell that he was trying his best to be upbeat as he laughed and participated in small talk with the nurses. His knack for listening and asking questions was one that attracted others to him. I remember looking at the other cancer patients in their chairs beside him and noticing that some of them looked grey, as if they could slip away at any moment. Although the mental and physical signs were there with my own father, I did not think death was in the near future; he was only fifty-nine.

Watery, crystal blue eyes darting back and forth. That was the last exchange that my dad and I had. After receiving the voicemail message from my aunt that changed my life, "Kristen, we need you to come to the hospital right away, sweetie," how I got to the hospital was a blur. Pulling up my maternity jeans, I waddled down the hospital hall, warm, salty tears streaming down my face. The next moment I remember was repeatedly telling my dad how much I loved him. His response was a small shift from right to left with his eyes. I know that he loved me and that was the last time we communicated before his body shut down and he slipped away. That moment that he breathed his last breath was one that is in my mind forever. A sharp wheeze that sounded painful, and then complete silence.

My heart felt as though it had exploded, and I had experienced a heart attack. My body felt like lead, my shoulders ached, and I experienced a shortness of breath. The following morning my mind felt foggy and I drove to work. Numb with emotion and on autopilot. I replayed the last moments and his last breath over and over in my head as I made my way to the office. I crumpled into a chair across from my manager and promptly broke down sobbing. Looking back, I don't know why I went to work that day. I certainly could have been excused but I think I pushed away the pain and used it as a temporary distraction. After an hour of uncontrollable emotion, I left and made arrangements to take a few weeks off. I knew that I had to retreat and get away for the weekend to escape. My family drove to Lake Tahoe and soaked in the majestic views that provided a moment of relief from the hurt that I was experiencing.

There was no time to grieve and my family dove right into planning the memorial service over the holiday season. Leading up to the memorial, I sat with my mother in a dark funeral home as we made decisions about the gravesite and type of casket to purchase. The process of picking out a casket was one I had never even thought of before. It felt like the strangest purchase. Did we buy the simple pine box that was practical? Was it better to honor him with a gravestone that was exquisite and ornate? Would he want that? My dad always appreciated things that were simple and classic. I know that he wouldn't want us to spend thousands of dollars on an ornate casket. We didn't cry and I didn't feel emotion as we selected the proper burial arrangements. It oddly felt like a business exchange and the process of planning gave us all moments of relief from the pain.

The memorial service was a blur. There was a venue to book, announcements to publish, music to choose, so many details to manage. My family was hosting an event for hundreds of guests which was keeping us preoccupied as the sadness was temporarily stuffed inside. I sat in the front row and as his work colleagues, friends, and brother made their way to the front of the room, I broke down. It made me realize that he touched so many lives with his warmth and smile. Employees that worked for him each had a story about how they loved working on projects with him because he would greet them with encouragement and that warm, loveable grin. I promised myself I would try and make this impact on others I interacted with as well.

Christmas was a couple of weeks after his death and we all took on new roles in the family to fill the gaping hole that my dad left. The holidays have never felt the same. Making the coffee, infusing the room with laughter and warmth, filling my mom's stocking, we all needed to step in as our family dynamic had changed. We had to reshuffle our family roles that we had become accustomed to. I remember one moment when I was in the back of my parents' house and opened the garage. The musky smell of sawdust filled the air and my dad's tools were scattered in his workshop as if he had stepped away for just a moment. Everything was untouched, and I felt a heavy thickness in the air as if he was somehow in the room at that very moment. I fell to my knees and wept uncontrollably. I couldn't fathom how he was actually gone and how I could go on living as if this huge piece of my life wasn't missing. How could I wake up and go about my day when one of the best people I knew was no longer alive? How could I go back to work in what now seemed like such a meaningless role in the scheme of life? The grief was heavy, and I started to entertain thoughts of angels. Every week or so I would do a double take as I thought I saw my dad pass by, but it would only be a strange man in his fifties with dark hair driving by. I also wrestled with questions about the purpose of life. Why was my dad, who was one of the kindest people I know, taken from the earth at age fifty-nine while others lived to over one hundred? I couldn't wrap my head around it and put all of my focus into the birth of my second son that spring.

Days became weeks and weeks became months. I stopped replaying his last breath in my mind every hour and it spread out to every week. Guilt consumed me as I forced myself to keep rerunning the scene that encapsulates my dad. He opens the door to my parents' house with the smile and welcomes me in with his soft hug and says, "Hey, Kris." He is wearing his uniform of navy jeans and a black tee from the Gap. He has worn, beige slippers on and smells like soap as if he has just showered. This is the scene that I still to this day rerun in my mind when I think of him. I noticed that I had stopped replaying this scene in my mind as frequently and I grasped desperately for the memory. I felt guilty that the loss of him wasn't consuming my thoughts any longer. Guilty that my life was moving forward, and I was leaving him behind. I wrestled with this guilt and finally came to peace with the fact that he would want me to move on and live the life of my dreams.

After slowly emerging from grief, I had a transformative moment as I reflected on my dad's life. He had worked so hard and lived a life much shorter than I had ever imagined my own. I realized that life is short, and I needed to act on my dreams. If I passed away tomorrow how would I feel about the life that I had lived? Would I have made a positive impact on the world around me? Would I have spent quality time and created special moments with my family? Had I lived life to the fullest? I had always been a dreamer, but I had pushed many of them to the side and told myself that I could accomplish my dreams tomorrow, or when I retire.

Irish to the core, my dad had always talked about taking a trip to Ireland someday, but his health declined to the point that when he had time to take the trip, it was too late. Every day I thought about how my dad would never meet my second son. I thought about the trips that he wasn't able to take and how hard he worked to enjoy his retirement. Watching someone die was something unforgettable and I would well up with tears each time it replayed in my mind. I thought to myself that my dad wouldn't want me to wallow in sadness, but he would encourage me to live my life as if tomorrow wasn't promised. I made a vow to myself that going forward I would seize the day and it transformed how I lived my life from that point forward.

Deep conversations with my husband followed about what was truly important to me and what type of legacy I wanted to leave when it was my time to leave the earth. I knew I had to make some decisions to spend precious time with my young children while I had the chance. I quit my job and eventually found a position with flexibility and fewer hours so I could spend the time with my newborn and older son that I was craving. I took the mother/daughter trip to Paris with my mom and sister that I had always dreamt about. I took my son to concerts and enjoyed the moment.

What does my life look like today? I am now a better mom to my boys as I realize that each moment is precious. I prioritize heart to heart talks with them and our family focuses on quality time together. We spend time volunteering in the community and thinking about the legacy that we will leave behind. I am also taking more personal risks like writing a book that I always dreamt about. I constantly remind myself that life is about people and not things and focus on making time for people that

I love. There are times I get wrapped back up into the business of life or start putting off things that are important to me, but I now know that life is short, and I push myself to make things happen, today.

I wouldn't have experienced this transformative moment without the pain of losing someone as kind, warm, and loving as my dad. In some ways, I feel the obligation to seize the day to honor him. Life is short and today is the day. Make your dreams happen, you won't regret it. Why wait?

ABOUT KRISTEN RIDDELL

Kristen Riddell writes books that motivate and encourage. She has a passion for making a difference in the lives of women and children. Kristen was born and raised in Davis, California. After completing college on the west coast, she headed to New York and spent the next decade in the New York City area. She is the proud and adoring mother of two incredible sons, Alex and Charlie. She currently resides in California with her husband, Dan, and her children and loves to travel in her spare time.

Kristen's transformative moment led her to write her first children's book. You can follow her progress and updates on the launch of her new book at www.kristenriddell.com and on Instagram @kristenpriddell.

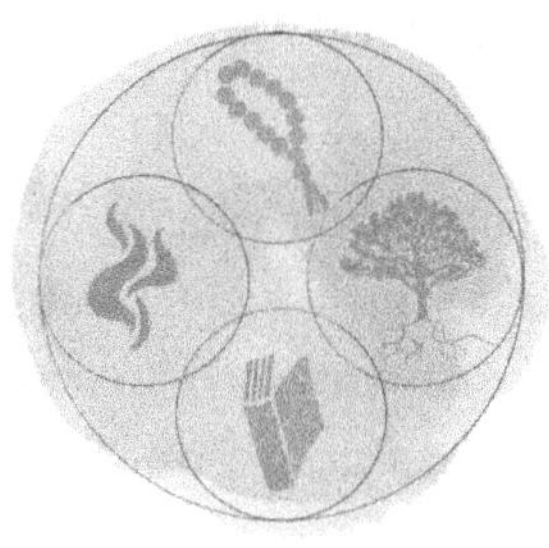

FINDING MY VOICE

Jaimee Roncone

The details are foggy. I left my body and saw only darkness. I heard a scream, my own scream, as I dropped the phone. I heard, "You need to get to your oncologist immediately. You have a bone tumor." My husband stared at me. Had someone died? (Now I realize a part of me had.) He picked up the phone and talked to my doctor. When the call ended, I fell into my husband's arms with convulsive sobs, yelling, "NO! NO! NO! I REFUSE THIS." That moment was my rock-bottom. Black out, collapse. I could not form words through my tears and the heaving of my chest. I could not find my breath. My throat raw, it felt like a cattle prod had seared my heart, my voice.

In this moment, in total darkness, my true healing began. It was the moment I lost my voice for the last time. I knew that healing from my pain would not be neat and tidy. The moment I said "I refuse …" the cancer was the moment I decided it would not be an option for the return of cancer to take over my life. But cancer did take over, for two more years.

Back in 2017, I had just begun to recover from my losses from breast cancer: the loss of my breasts, the loss of my physical strength, and the loss of my life as I knew it before cancer. Fear, guilt, shame, and pressure to do the right thing all rose to the surface. I thought, "I should never have had breast cancer in the first place." I was healthy, and I was a healer–meant to help others with cancer. I could not save my aunt, who had died at age fifty of breast cancer years earlier, but I could create a space where others with cancer could find comfort and solace, a space to heal on their own terms.

Prior to my initial breast cancer diagnosis in 2015, my husband and I purchased a building to house my wellness center. At the time, I was having many unusual sightings of owls, which for me was a sign that my aunt was trying to message me from the spiritual realm. The message I was receiving was that creating a place for healing was the right thing. As a massage therapist and bodyworker, my long-held dream of owning and operating a wellness center was becoming a reality! The center quickly became a success, with a cohort of amazing healing practitioners. Little did I know that just as my business got going, a seed was planted to set me up for my own success, in my own fight still to come.

By spring 2016, owls again began to appear. During a routine mammogram call-back for a second look, I asked the technician to stop the test because nothing was found and as they continued the mammogram, I could feel the radiation pulsing through my breast. I was relieved that the images appeared to be clear, and a voice in my head said, "Phew! They found nothing–but if I didn't have cancer, that radiation could cause it!" But, knowing breast cancer ran in my family, I decided to have thermography screenings so that I could still follow tissue changes without the pain and radiation from mammograms.

It was between my initial and second thermography scans in 2016 that a palpable lump appeared in my left breast. And suddenly, my messenger owl began showing up again. My heart sank. By this time, my kids were on summer break from school and it was nearing our family vacation. I decided to wait until my kids returned to school in September before I returned to a breast clinic where a biopsy was done, resulting in my first cancer diagnosis. I intuitively knew I needed to create space and time for what was to come. Still, even knowing I needed to create space, I went on as always, making sure everyone was taken care of.

I received the call with my biopsy results as I was headed to see a client. I knew the diagnosis before the nurse even spoke the words. I didn't skip a beat; I had to get to work for my client. I was a loyal healer–thinking of everyone else before myself. The nurse repeated, "Did you hear what I said?"

The first oncologist I saw recommended a lumpectomy and then radiation on my left breast just to be sure they got it all. As my breath shallowed and my body shuddered, I felt a deep repulsion rising. I put my hand to my heart and whispered, "But that would be radiation over my heart." I knew deep inside that this was not the route I wanted to take, even though in the moment no other options were put before me. I didn't know what to ask. Before I could articulate even how I was feeling, my body knew there could be another way. I had to dive into the darkness and find my right course. I did, and against all rationale or conventional medicine (including a second opinion), I chose a double mastectomy with reconstruction–because it was best for me and my conscience. In this choice, I found my voice for the first time.

What stands out to me now is that even in the face of devastating news of my own breast cancer, I did not pause. I had trained myself so well to put my own wellbeing aside, even in the face of trauma, in order to be of service to others. At a young age, I had created a belief that when a traumatic experience occurs, I should tuck it away in a tidy box. I even chose silence to keep peace around having been sexually abused by a neighbor, after my father denied me my truth and stole my voice. This trend of choosing silence carried on into my adulthood where I always put my own issues aside to serve others as a healer, mom, and wife.

After my physical scars from breast surgery healed, I returned to work. My appointment book filled quickly; my clients had missed me. I was back to "normal", back to the flow of my life–until one day a few months later when I heard my soul speak. My hands lifted from the client on the treatment table in front of me, and a voice inside me said,

"You cannot continue to work the way you always have."

I stopped doing massage with clients–work that I was passionate about and loved–in order to dive more deeply into my own healing, which led to the work I knew I was supposed to be doing. I grieved the loss of connection with my clients, many who'd been with me for fifteen years.

But during this break, another voice spoke to me. I never want any other woman to feel as I have–isolated, alone, and riddled with panic, anxiety, and depression after breast cancer treatment, waking each day wondering what 'normal' is. I decided to become a health and life coach.

Four months into my program, I attended a live event in Dallas, Texas. For four days I sat in a room of 700 people. I learned; I wore heels; I danced. When my anxiety propelled me, I went for a run in the city.

After the event, filled with euphoria and a renewed insight and vision for my life, I boarded my flight home–but I could no longer ignore an aggravating hip pain.

I had multiple massages and visits to a chiropractor who wouldn't do adjustments on me. She wanted me to have an MRI; I think she intuited what we were dealing with. I had more massage and chiropractic appointments but still had no relief. Again, I was not listening to my own voice, even as I kept telling people that the pain was "unreachable" and "deep in my bone".

Accompanied by the pain, I went to my one-year, post breast cancer oncology appointment and got a clean bill of health. I was on my way past breast cancer. Yeah!

But, the nagging pain in my hip would not subside. I stopped working out because lunges, squats, and burpees weren't helping the situation. Finally, I got an appointment with the pain doctor recommended by my chiropractor, but it was a couple of months away. I continued to see my chiropractor, still getting no relief–so, I called the pain doctor again–and felt the stars align. They had a cancellation, one hour from the time I called!

They did an x-ray immediately. The doctor thought it was my sacroiliac joint and wanted me to return for a cortisone shot the next day. I was desperate for relief, so I agreed. At this point I had been doing bodywork almost twenty years and I knew deep down that my sacroiliac joint was not the issue, but I decided to jump through the hoops of the system, hoping to get my MRI. The doctor tried calling me an hour later, but I missed the call. He called my home later that day, after 5:00 PM. In my gut, I knew something was wrong; he'd said he would call with the x-ray results the following day and schedule my shot.

This was the call. There was a tumor in my bone. This was the call.

This day changed everything. My hope of being "cancer-free" was no more. Eradicating my cancer was not an option. Metastatic breast cancer has no cure–only treatments; I hoped to outlive the treatments and the cancer. One day I was a survivor of breast cancer, and the next I was forced to learn how to live with cancer in my body. But, how would it be possible? I lost my own identity at first as the "cancer girl". This title, metastatic breast cancer, put me in a whole new arena. Treatment, every day, for the rest of my life. No cure. Average life expectancy, five years. I go down every road, looking for answers. But research is slow, and funding is rare.

After many sleepless nights, tests and scans, and research, I began the rigorous path to healing, utilizing conventional medicine as well as multiple natural healing modalities with the guidance of a naturopathic oncologist. I woke, telling my husband that the only way for me to survive conventional methods is to include healing modalities that I knew would support my health and counter the side effects of the rigorous drugs. I came to a place of mercy and surrender, choosing fear as a motivator to live rather than paralyzing me to death. In that place, I found my WHY. My greatest motivator of all is looking into the eyes of my children, wanting to see them graduate, get married, and have children so that I can be a grandmother, never wanting them to be motherless through all of life's greatest triumphs of youth. For them, I realized if I had to make peace and live with cancer in my body for the rest of my life, I would learn not just to survive, but to thrive.

Over time, I have learned to find the answers the only way I know how. Inside. Inside myself. I learned to listen to the voices within. They aren't the cure to cancer, but they certainly guide me in how I choose to live my life with cancer.

Healing became more than healing the cancer alone. It became about healing the wounded and damaged girl within me–the girl who was sexually abused as a young child. That girl whose truth was stolen and whose voice was silenced at the age of four. I had to find her within myself and heal her pain in order to heal my own body and reclaim my voice. I began to realize that alignment is key to healing. Whether I agree with my doctors or not, my path must be aligned with the whispers of my soul. Alignment would happen in part with the healing of my relationship to my little girl within.

Two years later, as I write this, 20/20 vision in the year 2020 has shown me a deep trust and faith in myself and the plan the universe has had for me all along: peace within myself. I wake each day finding my own rhythm in life as I move on, past the removal of breasts, past the removal of my ovaries, past the treatments–and I choose how I live each day. I listen to my inner voice and I advocate for myself. I live with cancer in my body, with no cure in sight, but it does not define me.

Each day I rise to life. I choose where I want to focus my energy. I remain in alignment as much as I can. I have the power to create a new experience for myself–and empower others to do the same. I am hopeful again and passionate to support others to find their own voices in alignment with their souls' whisperings.

I have learned to change my mindset on a daily basis and, while I still have cancer in my body, I feel stronger than ever. I have found my voice through rest meditation. I have become a Daring to Rest Yoga Nidra certified facilitator, and this is what empowers me to help others find their voices and advocate for themselves and their own healing paths.

ABOUT JAIMEE RONCONE

Jaimee began her Daring to Rest journey along with her metastatic breast cancer diagnosis. It quickly became a tool that dissolved her panic and anxiety, making life and medical decisions grounded in rest instead of stress. She found herself doing it during her medical scans, other treatment therapies, and to be at peace in her home. She quickly realized the need for rest to heal and certified as a Daring to Rest™ Yoga Nidra Facilitator in order to offer rest medicine to others dealing with a cancer diagnosis. Jaimee, already an owner of a wellness center, received a soul whisper to build a one-of -a-kind rest cave at her center where people can lay down to rest and heal.

Jaimee has been a healer for over twenty years and is trained as a therapist in massage (including oncology massage), in craniosacral therapy and in lymph drainage therapy. She is a wellness navigator (as a health and life coach) as well as owner and operator of her own wellness center where she is a creatrix of connection and creator of a welcoming energy and space.

Jaimee believes that when you create space to deeply rest, you can dive deep into the dark and discover the strength to transform and realign with your path.

Jaimee resides in the hills of western Massachusetts with her husband, son and daughter, as well as two dogs and a cat. Her eldest daughter lives in Atlanta. Jaimee spends her free time finding stillness in the woods and overlooking a nearby lake. She enjoys laughter, dancing, hiking, and connecting with close friends for tea or coffee on her couch.

Contact: jaimee@rockstarnavigator.com
https://healingtreehealthandwellness.com/
https://www.facebook.com/TheRockstarNavigator/
https://www.facebook.com/healingtreehealthandwellnesscenter/
https://www.instagram.com/jaimeeroncone/

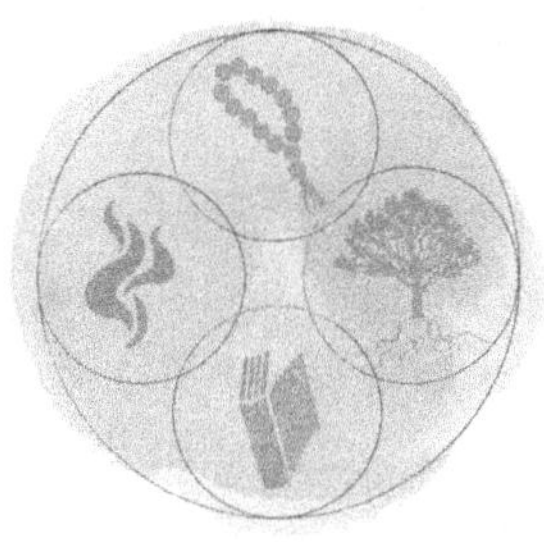

A ROAD LESS TAKEN

Jennifer Somers

October 4, 2006.

I remember the clouds that day. The sky was the most perfect blue. A faint breeze was the only thing that gave me any sort of comfort from my inability to breathe, almost like the earth was breathing for me, forcing air into my lungs.

I remember the look in my siblings' eyes—expressing fear and horror—and I remember the desperation I felt for them. Twenty minutes prior we were told my brother had been shot, so we raced against time to the hospital.

While horns screamed and my mom looked just how you think she would look, I focused on the clouds, and I told my brother I loved him, just in case he didn't already know. I was sixteen-years-old and I prayed to whatever was up above to protect him.

When we arrived at the hospital my father had to identify his body. The next two weeks I had to stay home from school. My body had shut down from mono. I couldn't understand how someone could shoot a person they hadn't even known.

Two years prior I had begun using drugs. I remember the confidence that it had given me as it shimmied up my nose. If only I had understood how it swallows you whole.

I read a poem once written by Robert Frost about two paths diverging and which path he chooses to take. I had always admired the symbolism within it and the power within every choice we have. On the other hand, I continued down the path of getting high. I had known better, but I ignored it, and for seven years I experienced much pain. I would think it could never possibly get worse, and then, just like that, it would.

I became a puppet in a play; a slave to a devil. A destroyer of myself by my own hands, not realizing that I was the one who controlled the strings.

In the beginning, I would attempt to go to meetings, where these people exclaimed that they were just like me. No, they weren't. These people used needles and had been homeless and in jail. This could never be my story.

Eventually, through many tragic situations unwritten between these lines, I switched from over the counter prescriptions to snorting heroin. I justified it, of course, and told myself I was having fun. That life is short, and I was young.

Life continued on, and one day, in the mix of my own insanity, I met Adam.

A group of us went out and I was warned of his current struggles. I'm not sure what happened really, but before I knew it, he and I were dancing on the dance floor, and I had never danced before, not even a day in my life.

And while we danced, everyone disappeared but us. Just him and me. Me and him.

It felt magical. Straight out of a movie but better because it was real.

He became everything to me. Our relationship started off beautifully, if you were to ask me back then. I saw so much good in him and knew what we could be. A year later he asked my father if he could marry me, and we named our future daughter Brooke.

We planned a beautiful life together, but we had one thing to overcome—and that one thing would change everything. That thing WAS everything, and that thing began burying all of our friends.

We tried anything to get clean but failed at every attempt. I heard my parents arguing that I was at the place of no return. I went to rehabs but left shortly after on a bus. Within thirty minutes of leaving I was high. I stole my parents' most valuable possessions, but what's worse was I stole their health, their sanity, and replaced their rest with sleepless nights. All of the doors in our home were locked, and an ominous fear lingered.

One beautiful afternoon that I couldn't even stand to admire, Adam asked again if I'd try shooting up and said I was wasting it by snorting it. I couldn't deny it any longer. Just like 2+2=4, it just made sense. Inevitably, time made me more willing. I was scared, so I pulled over and he did the deed for me.

And … done.

Arrested over a dozen and a half times, the pain getting worse with each round. I didn't know how much longer I could go on like this. I started to battle secret thoughts of suicide, because I didn't see a way out, and I didn't want to stop.

When I was a little girl running around with a Barbie doll in hand, I never imagined I'd grow up to face this person in the mirror. I didn't believe this could happen to me.

Adam and I would go off on our own adventures, not coming home until we were entirely defeated. We sold everything and had nothing but each other. We broke into hotel rooms and slept on benches, just so we wouldn't be far from heroin. We chose drugs over food and walked with the same sadness, in the same clothes, every day, for miles and miles on end. We switched our socks because we couldn't bear the pain, and we said that when tomorrow came, we would go home and get clean.

But tomorrow never came.

Shortly after, I ended up in jail. I was flabbergasted. I promised I'd never be back, yet here I was, experiencing night terrors that paralyzed me once more. I awoke drenched in sweat, fearing the future to no avail.

My parents wouldn't answer my calls this time. I realized I had to try harder now to stay clean. I was under its spell so much so that it had everything it wanted from me except my life, and I would have preferred that it took that, too. I wrote. I cried. I read the Bible, looking for any sort of hope within those pages. I thought of things I wanted to accomplish in life if I were to actually get clean.

I dreamed of becoming a writer or maybe a poet. I dreamed of speaking and inspiring. I dreamed of creating beautiful things that made the world better, so that this didn't have to happen to anyone else. I said that one day I'd be an entrepreneur. I laughed at the idea of someone like me being able to get better and accomplish ANY of these dreams. But I said if I made it, against all odds, that I would make sure of it.

I knew then that if I could get clean after this, that I could do anything.

I was bailed out on the anniversary of my brother's death, followed by another span of using, followed by another arrest.

I remember next lying in the hospital because the paramedics had said that my heart tissue had died. I was in big trouble again, and I told God that I couldn't fight any longer, and that I was ready for whatever he saw best fit for me. And I meant it. I was ready for even the worst outcome, if that was what was best. Shortly after the officers came in and told me that if I promised to go to rehab, they wouldn't bring me to jail. I needed help and that's not what jail had to offer. I felt the miracle that had just happened. Although I was so far into the woods, I acknowledged the sign and knew I had to begin to walk out.

The next day my dad came to get me for rehab with a few trash bags full of random articles of clothing. He wouldn't allow me in the front seat—he didn't want to look at me. He had always believed in me until then, so I was the only one left to believe in myself.

The song "Let Her Go" by The Passengers played and I realized that I hadn't heard music in months. The song touched my heart in more ways than anyone will ever know, and I sobbed the entire ride there. The words were so beautiful, freeing, defeating, and although I was a disaster, they sparked something inside of me. I knew I could do this.

I knew there was more.

So, I sat with myself, the person I hated, and forced myself to look within. I committed to a new life, one that I hadn't yet understood, but made it known that it was coming. I listened in group meetings, I shared pain and hope when my heart told me to, and I took in every word from people whom I respected. I made a formula and took every suggestion.

I had to tell Adam that we needed to work on ourselves so we could be together again in a year. I knew we could overcome it all. He was angry and wouldn't speak with me. A few weeks later I received a missed call from the pizza shop we used to go to. I knew something was wrong. The next day, I received the phone call that he had overdosed and left a note.

My world collapsed. To say the next few days were hard is an understatement. I couldn't sleep, I couldn't breathe. Regret filled my entire being. How could I live through this? I tried crying, and even when I could, it didn't help. I couldn't eat. I started fainting and the night terrors resurfaced. I tried praying, running, talking, and I dived deeper into step work. Everything hurt. I did anything I could to replenish that seed that began growing.

On my six-month anniversary of being clean, I put on my black clothes and attended his funeral service that was in the same room as my brother's. With my family all around me, we mourned again. When I left, I left with a hole in my soul.

I thought back to the time he said he saw me getting older and how beautiful I looked. I wanted nothing more than to see him, too. I re-read his favorite book he had given my mother about a golden retriever's life, who eventually reincarnates as a young boy once his time as a dog was over. At times it was so painful, other times it was what I needed. I tried remembering everything and wanted to continue to improve, in honor of him.

My roommate who slept beside me in my new house would stay up all hours of the night to speak with me and help me get through the pain.

A month later, that same roommate drank herself to death.

I couldn't take it. I felt that I was living alone in some sick universe. I didn't want to do it anymore. I went to the beach on a hazy afternoon to calm my nerves. No one was in sight. I looked out into the ocean and started to scream. I screamed until my voice had no voice, letting out my sadness. I begged God for a sign, I told him I needed it. I told him I wanted to give up. I slouched down to hold myself together, because I felt I was falling apart.

Within a minute, a large figure knocked me down with such power, right out of my position and onto the ground. After a moment, I realized a large golden retriever was licking my face. It actually made me laugh for a second, and while the dog ran full force back to its owners, it hit me. I realized it was the sign that I had begged for only a moment ago. The golden retriever from Adam's book!

The sign was so forceful it knocked me right off my feet. I couldn't deny it. I took note that angels were with me and I promised in that moment that I was not going to give up.

As tough as it was, I stood up, took one last look at the ocean with as much appreciation as I could muster up, and made my way back home to begin the process of healing.

Nothing about it was easy, but I was determined to become better and reaffirmed to myself that one day it'll be worth it. I enjoyed seeing the life come back into my eyes when I looked in the mirror, and I promised myself that I will truly love myself one day. I worked dead end jobs because of my record and told myself that it's only temporary. I faced all of my court hearings, went to a meeting or two a day, spoke at high schools, helped suffering addicts and completed all of my steps as vigorously as possible. After three years, I toyed with the idea of leaving the meetings. I was aware of how dangerous it could be. I spoke honestly about it for over a year before deciding to step away to fulfill what I felt was best for me.

At twenty-six, I bought my first home. I felt that I had completed another milestone, and I couldn't wait to achieve more.

At one point I was convinced I met someone I thought shared the same perspective and goals as my own. I wanted to grow and conquer the world with him, only to realize that as time went on, I started noticing the changes and forms of abuse that I could no longer ignore. As if it were a facade. My energy began deflating. But because of my own self growth, I had faith that anyone could get better. They just had to want to. I did anything I could to help, but it only got worse and I began feeling like a cancer patient, stuck in a constant grip of anguish and forever despair. I knew that my life was bigger than the script I was allowing myself to play in, so I walked away.

I went through many years not appreciating the ability to choose that other path. I promised myself in the beginning of this new journey that I would learn from mistakes and grow from them. Most importantly, I'd always choose to love myself enough to do it, no matter how difficult.

Warm weather called out to me, so I sold that home with the help of my family, packed up my car with as much as I could, and made my way down to warmer weather without even having a job lined up. Everyone said I was crazy, but it made me feel alive. I felt that I had no other choice in the matter. I had faith. My family ended up moving here too.

Zooming forward into my life today, I am overwhelmed with gratitude for all of what life has shown me and allowed me to be. I continue to take leaps of faith, and I continue to trust myself. I understand that following my heart will never lead me wrong, and if anything, I will walk away with a lesson that will propel me forward. I have worked my way up the ladder and have started new business ventures, things I once never thought possible. I'm surrounded by beautiful people who love me and want the best for both me and themselves. Today I love the person who I've become and know that there is still so much work to be done. If I'm not stretching, I'm not growing. I still use a formula and daily practices to expand.

I am still to this day astonished that I was able to overcome such challenges. It shows me that no one is incapable. I owe a lot of it to my family for pushing me to be better. I pray that no one will ever have to go down that path.

My eyes tear up as I look back on these moments. I believe that my struggles were gifts to me to force myself to live to my highest potential and to overcome. To believe in myself and so very much more. And yours are too, no matter what kind.

ABOUT JENNIFER SOMERS

Jennifer Somers was born in Philadelphia, Pennsylvania. She then relocated to South Jersey with her family before moving to Florida. After struggling for seven years with addiction, she is now living in freedom. She is working toward launching an idea for mental illness that she believes is prevalent for our future generations. She believes it is only the beginning of so much more in leaving her imprint on overcoming the impossible and stopping mental illness from forming to begin with. You can catch up with Jennifer by email at jensomersdreams@gmail.com or Instagram at jenashleysomers for any updates.

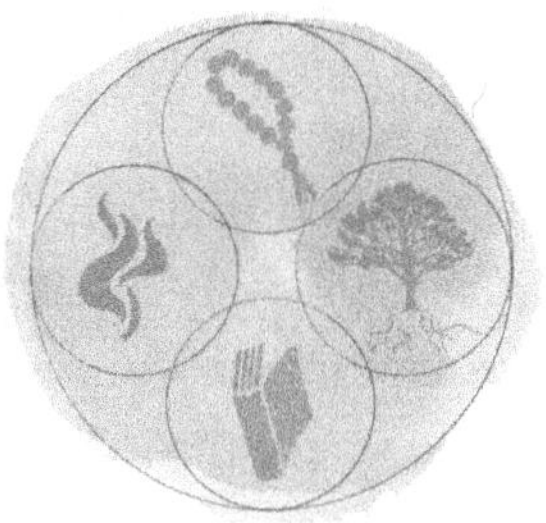

IS THERE REALLY A LADDER TO SUCCESS?

Maggie Sullivan

"Obstacles are the cost of greatness."
-Robin Sharma

All of my adult life I have been a high achiever climbing ladders to success. There has always been a little voice in my head instructing me to go on to reach new heights. Sometimes the voice is afraid to move forward but for the most part it perseveres. This voice has been shaped by all of my childhood experiences–positive and negative.

Growing up was difficult for me. My father died when I was three and my mother experienced severe mental health issues and was an alcoholic. My mom was unable to work, and we had limited funds. She did not drive so we did not go anywhere. I spent a lot of time by myself and had a lot of conversations with my little voice in my head. My siblings were older than me, so I did not have very much interaction with them. I do remember my brother taking me to the circus when it was in town and dancing with my sisters to Diana Ross and The Supremes. But my memories are few and far between and there are definitely more negative ones than positive ones. I do remember my childhood inner voice being adamant that my life would not be the same and I would do whatever it took to be, do, and have the things that I wanted when I was older.

Since I grew up in a dysfunctional family, my development was clouded by a lot of toxic behavior. As a result, I have realized that I have developed characteristics that are common among adult children of dysfunctional families. These common characteristics have become known as the "Laundry List" that was first developed by Tony V. in 1978 and followed by Janet Woititz in her 1983 book *Adult Children of Alcoholics*. Everyone's experience with dysfunctional families is different. However, the following ten characteristics are typically quite common among children who grew up in dysfunctional homes. They include:

1. Having to guess at what normal behavior is
2. Having difficulty following a project from beginning to end
3. Fear of authority figures and angry people
4. Judging themselves very harshly and having very low self-esteem
5. Difficulty having fun and taking themselves very seriously
6. Difficulty with intimate relationships
7. Constantly seeking approval, and are afraid of abandonment
8. They are either super responsible or super irresponsible
9. Being extremely loyal, even when the loyalty is undeserved
10. Loving those who need rescuing

I was first introduced to the concept of Adult Children of Alcoholics when I was a research assistant in my early twenties when I was studying the effects of overuse of alcohol. I was surprised to realize that I was an adult child of an alcoholic and decided to enroll in some group counselling sessions. After a few years of counselling, I thought that I had put these characteristics to rest, but they resurfaced when I experienced a tremendous blow to my career. After working at the same school for twenty-one years, I was involuntarily transferred to a different school in a different region and my fear of abandonment re-surfaced. I was devastated and my self-esteem plummeted and kept me paralyzed for over two years. It felt like I was a pawn in a game of Snakes and Ladders and slid all the way to the bottom of the board. I was crushed and it took a tremendous amount of courage to pick myself up and start over.

Thankfully, I had my strong inner voice in my head that told me to continue. The one that was there when I was a child. It said, "Keep going, Maggie. Yes, you fell off the ladder but take a step over and start climbing another one." And that is exactly what I did.

I am grateful for that strong inner voice that is part of me because of the dysfunction I grew up in as a child. And, I am grateful that I had started back to counselling and had in place a morning routine where I would start my day reflecting in my journal, meditating, and reading great personal development authors.

My meditations helped me identify where I was stuck. I realized that negative thought patterns from childhood were preventing me from moving forward. I still had some of the lingering characteristics from the above-mentioned list that needed to be addressed. I returned to the work of adult children of dysfunctional families and after deep reflection, realized that I was blocking my emotions by not addressing them. One thing that showed up for me was the fact that I had a number of messes and incompletes that I needed to tidy up.

Not long after my transfer I decided to retire from teaching and focus on my side business. Yet, I lacked clarity and had too many projects on the go. I had clutter everywhere—clothes, books, journals, magazines, photos, files, projects, programs, knick-knacks, jewelry, recipes, toys, stuffed animals; basically lots of stuff. I never knew where to get started to eliminate the abundance of stuff. This clutter was preventing me from addressing my emotional needs and moving forward. The more I purchased, the less time I had to think about addressing these needs. The clutter was keeping me stuck and I realized that I needed to eliminate it in order to free space in my head to address my needs.

I made a very detailed list of my messes and incompletes and devised a plan of eliminating something every day. I made numerous trips to Goodwill, sold things that I didn't need, and let go of a number of projects.

Then I started taking action on one project. My goal has always been to become a motivational speaker, yet my low self-esteem prevented me from believing that this was possible. I enrolled in a training that encouraged me to go beyond my comfort zone and this helped me shift my mindset. I started to believe in myself again. Since that training, I have gained greater clarity about my life purpose and I now welcome the endless possibilities that the universe presents to me and my mind is clear without all of the clutter.

I am now on the other side of fear and I am a motivational speaker. I speak to groups about the importance of becoming the most awakened person that you can be and the importance of eliminating self-doubt. Through my stories, I speak to groups about how to wake up, the benefits of waking up and co-creating a life that you deserve to live. It starts with listening to the voice in your head and turning your inner critic into an inner coach.

I often hear from people that they fear they will wake up one day and realize that they have been climbing the wrong ladder. But I reassure them that there are no wrong ladders. Each ladder is a lesson that has brought you to exactly where you need to be right now. I think that we get so far on one ladder and the universe provides us with an opportunity to move to another ladder. Everything you learned on the first ladder is part of the journey. If you do not move to another ladder sometimes the universe helps you along and knocks you off, like it did me. I now consider my transfer as a gift. At first my inner voice wanted to quit and stay at the bottom where I felt safe, but it was overwritten by the childhood voice that learned to be super responsible. She told me to get up and keep going. My inner voice told me that I have a mission and that it is to help people wake up and stay awake. Falling off that ladder was the best thing that ever happened to me because it has brought me to where I am today.

I believe it is important for anyone who has lived through situations such as abuse, trauma, or any type of dysfunction to be aware of possible negative characteristics that may be lingering in the subconscious mind and robbing them of living life to the fullest potential. I recommend continuing to develop self-awareness by daily self-reflection, meditation, and finding a tribe of like-minded people. Following this practice on a daily basis can lead to greater inner peace, joy, happiness, and taming the inner critic so that you can reach your highest potential.

I persevered and found another ladder to climb and I am so grateful that I did. For additional information on how to reach your highest potential, visit my website – maggiesullivan.ca.

ABOUT MAGGIE SULLIVAN

Maggie Sullivan is committed to making it her mission to help awaken people to reach their highest potential. She was born and raised in Ottawa, Ontario, Canada and attended Carleton University to complete her Bachelor and Master of Arts in Sociology. She then went on to receive her Bachelor of Education at Nipissing University in North Bay, Ontario, Canada and worked as an elementary teacher for over twenty years. Maggie took an early retirement to fulfill her true passion of sharing her purpose of helping others deepen their self-awareness and inner peace. She does this through sharing her stories of adversity and perseverance. Maggie has inspired many people through her stories, keynote speeches, and live events. Her online programs focus on topics of everyday life and how to create and enjoy a beautiful life.

Maggie Sullivan is a #1 Best Selling Author, Certified Canfield Methodology Trainer, Speaker and soon-to-be author of her first children's book, *The Story of Max.*

Maggie is married and has two sons: Alex and Andrew. She currently resides in Northern Ontario, Canada, and loves to travel to warmer climates.

To book Maggie for speaking or training:

Email: msullivan@persona.ca
Website: maggiesullivan.ca
Facebook personal page:
https://www.facebook.com/maggie.sullivan.180
Facebook business page:
https://www.facebook.com/fromtheheartwithmaggiesullivan/
https://www.instagram@maggiesullivanfromtheheart
https:/www.twitter@maggiefromheart

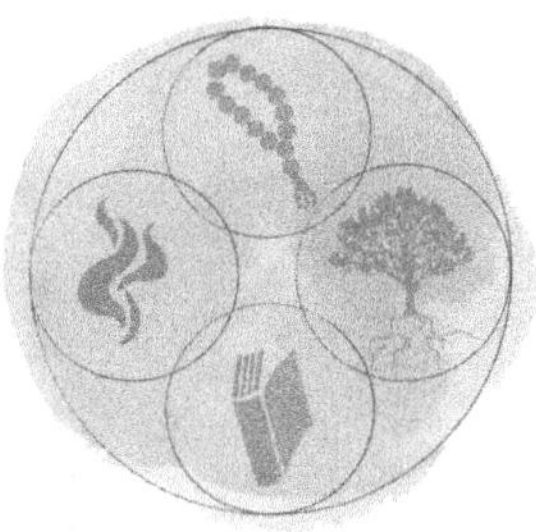

May your spirit be brightened and the words in the pages inspire you to continue to RISE in your own life,

the women who rise

REPRINTED WITH PERMISSIONS

Cathleen Elle
Ann Marie Smith
Jennifer Amabile
Eva Asrun Albertsdottir
Donna Brown
Sally Dunbar
Claudia Fernandez-Niedzielski
Holly Fitch Stevens
Angela Germano
Jeanie Griffin
Dr. Donna Hunter
Tara LePera
Laura Summers
Amanda Autry
Jenn Baus
Carol Dechen
Jillian Blosser
Rebecca Chalson
Nastassia Cornett
Solina Feliciano-Gonnion
Pamela Harris
Cindy Kelly
Mona Meland
Adrianne Murchison
Tatjana Obradovic
Jeanette Paxia
Ashley Richards
Kristen Riddell
Jaimee Roncone
Jennifer Somers
Maggie Sullivan

Have you ever dreamed of
becoming a published author?
Do you have a story to share?
Would the world benefit
from hearing your message?

Then we want to connect with you!

The Inspired Impact Book Series is looking to connect with women who desire to share their stories with the goal of inspiring others.

We want to hear your story!

Visit www.katebutlerbooks.com to learn more
about becoming a Featured Author in the #1 International
Best-selling *Inspired Impact Book Series.*

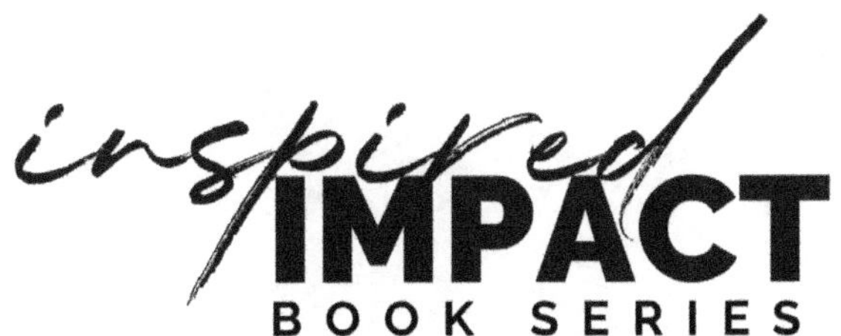

www.ingramcontent.com/pod-product-compliance
Lightning Source LLC
LaVergne TN
LVHW010053110826
845155LV00028B/321

* 9 7 8 1 9 4 8 9 2 7 1 3 0 *